WEATHERING THE STORMS

Dealing With Grief Through Faith

JERI M HART

WestBow Press books may be ordered through booksellers or by contacting:

WestBow Press
A Division of Thomas Nelson
1663 Liberty Drive
Bloomington, IN 47403
www.westbowpress.com
1-(866) 928-1240

ISBN: 978-1-4497-3637-8 (sc)

Library of Congress Control Number: 2011963690

Printed in the United States of America

WestBow Press rev. date: 1/19/2012

Preface

I am angry Lord, I am angry at you, you said you would never leave me or forsake me. You said you wanted me to be happy and prosper. Are you really there? Do you really exist? Why won't you answer my prayers?

As the warm tears flowed uncontrollably from my swollen eyes, I screamed these words to the heavens above, and before they finished leaving my lips, my heart was heavy with sorrow and remorse. I was ashamed that I had let Satan cause me to doubt and to weaken my faith.

I had recently lost my husband of 25 years, he had been my soul mate for over 29 years. We were best friends and had been through so much these past six years. But together, with trust in God we weathered the storms, until March of 2010.

We had been struggling with our business for five years, but we still had hopes of saving it. We had been trying to get a non profit going and every time we got close, something would happen to set us back. We were going further in debt, everything was spinning out of control. Then my nightmare really began, my husband was diagnosed with cancer. We had no medical insurance because it was cancelled when we got behind on the $ 2250.00 a month premiums and we still owed medical bills from his previous hospital stays. We decided there was no other way but to file bankruptcy.

When my husband started chemo and radiation, he became so ill, he needed me at home, I have never in my life seen anyone so ill, and I couldn't leave him at home alone the first few days after treatments. I held out the business as long as I could, my good friend Katie and my Mom had worked it alone as best they could, while I took care of him, but it was too much. I closed it on November 6th. He passed away on the 28th of November 2010.

At that time I was scared out of my mind, I had just lost my husband, I had no job, they had stopped my husbands social security when he passed away and my son could only draw it until he graduated a few months later.

And then the life insurance we had on my husband was ordered turned over to the bankruptcy trustee, they wouldn't even let me pay my husbands funeral or keep any of it to live on until I could get through this crisis and find a job that will support my family. The bank, where we have two mortgages financed, agreed to modify my loans but wouldn't do it until the trustee settles the bankruptcy and he had just gotten a court order to move the bar date back five more months. I don't understand how our judicial system can do this to a family.

Through all of this I had people telling me all of the time how much my strength and faith inspired them . . . . If they only knew. They were not there during my moments of weakness, when I was hysterically crying, or yelling at God, or curled up like a baby, not wanting to face life without him. But, at the end of the day, I knew where my strength came from, God was in control and he would see us through. I believe we are only as strong as our faith, even then satan can get to us. That's when we pray more, trust more, and walk even closer to him.

This is why I have chosen to type up my prayer journal. This is my conversations and prayers with my Lord. I want people to know that even though we strive to be the very best Christians we can be, that Satan can still sway us. He will especially attack us when we are vulnerable and overwhelmed. It is my desire to share my testimony with any who need it. If what I have been through and am still going through right now will lead even one person to the Lord, then everything we have been through will have been worth it. And to those who are saved and know that they are, I hope to show that even we can have moments of weakness and lash out at God. But isn't it wonderful to know that even when we disappoint him, he is always ready to forgive us?

CHAPTER 1

Storm Warnings

It begins in April 2010, the week of Easter. I love Easter, its spring and life is renewing itself. Jerry always loved it because it was time to plow the garden and work in the yard. He could spend hours after work in his building working on a project. The last one he was working on was a little country church for me. He had a lot of it done including the pulpit.

Easter is also special to me because it is the time we observe the crucifixion of my Lord and Savior, Jesus Christ. When I think of what he endured for me, even now, just writing about it brings tears to my eyes. I usually start a 3 day fast on Thursday afternoon and don't have anything but fluids until dinner Easter Sunday. This purges my body and clears my mind and since I spend a lot of time during this period in prayer, I can focus on God and what he wants for me.

Journal Entry April 1, 2010

Thank you Lord for my life, my salvation and all of my blessings. This is the first day of my Easter fast. Cleanse my body and my mind Lord. Sunday I pray that my body and my mind be cleared of all worldly thoughts so my focus will be on you alone. Fill me Lord with the sweet Holy Spirit. Let us have a full, Spirit filled, Sunday meeting. Easter is such a blessed time for me, it is the celebration that touches me the most.

Lord, use me and my family to do good works for you first of all, for our church, our family and church family, and any whom you send to us. As I sit here talking to you Lord, Vestal Goodman is singing "This is what Heaven means to me" on tv, what a beautiful song.

Let me share this message with the lost, let me plant seeds that you will cultivate into saved souls. I want to help in your desire to make sure as many souls as possible are among those who will be at that Glorious meeting in the sky. I especially pray for my family Lord. My children are precious to me and I want to spend eternity with them in Heaven with you.

Use my children to inspire other young people who are lost. Keep evil from them and protect them. Let only your will be done where any of us are concerned. Use us Lord, its my desire to serve and please you and to do whatever I can to please you.

I pray these things
In Jesus' precious name
Amen

PRAISE GOD ! MY SAVOUR LIVES

This was the first day of my 3 day fast and I was already excited about Easter. I am always thankful for what God does for me, but this was the ultimate blessing. To think that he gave what was most precious to him, his son. This is why I feel so sad and depressed when I have moments of weakness. As much as I think I am suffering, it in no way begins to compare to what my Jesus suffered for me. Because he did this for me, when my time on this earth is done, so will the pain, sadness, and loneliness be done. This alone should make me want to spread his word, and to strive to be the very best witness that I can be, by being the best Christian that I can be.

Journal entry April 2, 2010 Good Friday
HE LIVES

MY SAVIOUR LIVES

My precious Lord, thank you for all that you went through for a sinner such as me. I can never repay the debt that I owe. It fills me with such joy to know my sin debt has been paid.

When I get down and out and let the devil mess with my mind, all I have to do is get alone with you and you always lift me up. It doesn't matter how scared I am or how confused, you always, always comfort me. You are the only one who can calm me. I know sometimes people think I'm stupid and don't know what I am doing. Maybe I don't, but you do and I will wait on you. I have faith that you will place me where you want me.

Lord, I don't know what is going on with the non profit, but I pray it doesn't make things harder for us. I pray for Harold, Bette, Wilma and all of those who I have bore hard feelings for. Forgive me as I forgive them Lord. I pray for a better year and a closer walk with you.

Bless my family Lord with all that we need to do your will. Let us get to the point where we can catch up our debts, pay more then is ask to our church, send our kids to college, help my mom, and most of all be able to help people. You alone know my heart Lord, you know my desire. You know I want to be used for you Glory. I thank you Lord for my life, for my salvation, for my family, and my church. There are just too many blessings to try and name them all, but you know what they are. Lord let me some how have the peace of mind, the time and the money to take my kids camping next week and spend some family time together. I need a miracle Lord, and only you can provide it, if I am in your will. Lead me Lord.

In Jesus name
Amen

We were trying to establish our non profit so that we could solicit again for donations. Nothing seemed to go right, we talked to a man about possibly working with his charity, but nothing ever came of it. I was really torn about whether or not I was doing Gods will, every time I was ready to give it up, something would come up to make me think this is where he wanted us. I had been praying about it for years, but I must not have been listening to the answer he was giving me. We sometimes fail to realize that just because we ask him for what we want, he is not always going to say yes, sometimes he says no, sometimes later. It all depends on how it is going to fit into his plan for us.

Journal entry April 3, 2010

Fill me Lord, let me feel your Holy Spirit. Wrap your loving arms around me and comfort me. Stay my mind and let me see clearly your plan for my life, at least as far as what you want me to do next. I really feel good about the man we spoke to yesterday. I like the idea that it is a church and they have a non profit that works with foster parents and children, and that they are opening a senior center. These are things I have wanted to do. I want to do what is in your will Lord. If you don't want me to be a non profit but rather to work with this one then please show me you will. Its all I want.

I love you so much Lord, and I know because we pray for things that will bring you Glory you will give them to us, if its in your will. I have ask for a way to keep the business and support my family while still having good quality time for them as well as have more time for my church and my Christian duties. I couldn't ask for anything more then doing this while helping others. Its my prayer Lord, I've waited so long and I will wait as long as you want me to. Just guide me Lord, direct my path. As much as I want this, it is more important to me to do what you want me to do. I want only to serve you and please you. I won't lie, I would be excited to serve you in this way, but its not my will, but, yours be done.

Now it's the Saturday before Easter, it's the third day of my fast. I have about eleven more hours. Give me the strength and the stamina to stay busy and get a lot of work done. Lord please let us have an extremely busy sales day. I am so looking forward to church tomorrow. Easter Sunday is my favorite day in church, I feel your Holy Spirit moving so strongly among us when the youth sing and perform for you Glory. These kids are awesome and I love each of them. Touch David Lord, fill him to over flowing, give him the sweetest message he has ever preached. Let tomorrow be special. Let us each and everyone get excited to the point that we break out in revival. I want to experience it and I want my kids to experience it. Fill us with love for not only you but each other. Jesus come join us like your spirit did that October night we prayed for Randy Fletcher. That was such an amazing time. So sweet was your spirit moving among us. I know with out a doubt you were in our midst. I know you are always with us, but I know when the Holy Spirit moves me, its so sweet, and there are no words to describe it. Bless us Lord.

Lord take the pain and discomfort from Mayford, Gene, Kathy, and all who are going through serious health problems. Let them enjoy and experience a beautiful Easter Sunday. I pray Lord that tomorrow every single person in that church will have their eyes opened to the true sacrifice you made and what my Jesus suffered for us. Make us all humble in your presence Lord. Let us set aside our own thoughts, our own desires and just spend the whole service tomorrow worshiping you, praising you, thanking you and loving you. I am excited just thinking about it. It would be so awesome of you came to rapture the church right in the middle of it. What better place to come and get your bride. I pray my family, especially my kids and grand kids will all be ready.

One more request Lord, please let us have a wonderful picnic and afternoon with my mom and our family. Let us enjoy each other and worship and fellowship. Not one complaint or worry please Lord. I love you so much I praise you, thank you, and give you the glory, Amen

At the top of the page that Saturday I wrote, He is alive, death couldn't hold him, the devil doesn't win. He has washed away my sins.

At the bottom I had written, He's alive, He lives in my heart, and on that glorious day, I will join him in Heaven. Thank you, Thank you, Thank you.

I was close to the end of my fast, and I was so full of the Holy Spirit that night. I was ready for church and time with my family. I was busy at church all day and with my family so I didn't post anything that Easter Sunday. I was ready for revival, but it wasn't to be. There were not near as many people there as there usually are. This was so sad. I couldn't understand why? I realize now that satan was at work, he was trying to destroy our little church. He hates us because we are a church of God fearing, Bible preaching children of God and we are not ashamed to share that with the lost. We will stay strong and we will not give up, so leave satan see who else there is to devour.

Journal entry April 5, 2010

Thank you Lord for a beautiful Sunday with my family. I enjoyed service yesterday, but it sure wasn't what it used to be. We have got to get more people in church and stop losing the ones we have. I know that you were there Lord, I felt you move. I felt you watching over the kids, keeping the devil away. I thank you for getting Kaylain through her song. Help me to think of something that I can do with her and Haley that will help people and please you and bring them closer as sisters in Christ.

Lord let this be the week that my working life changes for the good.

Lead me by the heart Lord to pursue that which you want me to do. Whatever we do, let it be pleasing to you and bring you much Glory. Use us Lord you know it is our prayer. I like the gentleman we spoke to the other day if that's the way you want us to go then lay it out for us. If you prefer for us to do our own then let it work out this week. If you want me out of it all together, then lead me that way Lord. I am confused

In Jesus name
Amen

We had two dogs that were a part of our family for 13 years. One was Caseys big hound that he picked out at the shelter and the other was the little Yorkie we bought when our first one died, this one was supposed to be mine but took up with Jerry as soon as we brought him home. When Jerry had his by pass surgeries a few years ago, Scooter (our yorkie) laid beside him on the bed when I was gone and kept him company. These two were a part of our family and died within a week of each other. This was such a sad time, little did I know that it was just the beginning of the saddest time of our lives. My family was fixing to walk through the deepest, darkest valley we have ever known. Satan himself had his hand in this trial. I learned that no matter how strong I thought my faith was, satan can make us weak and destroy what we work so hard to protect if we are not careful.

Journal entry April 8, 2010

Thank you Lord for not letting Scooter suffer and taking him on before we had to take him to the vet to be put down. Jerry buried him and shadow side by side. That for some reason gives me peace. We are going to miss those two. I pray Caseys new pup gives him comfort. He is an eight week old Siberian Huskey and he named him Balto. He is cute and very playful. The first day Casey had him I noticed the markings on his face formed a cross, I hope that doesn't change.

Lord let us please continue to have good sales and to have a good check to send Jerry so he will work with us. I pray it is your will to follow through with the non profit and thrift store until I retire, then I would love to see one of my kids take it over and use it for your Glory. I think new vision churches foster and senior care programs are awesome and I want to help even if I get my own non profit. Besides helping people through family aid, I would like to start a teaching program, taking people who like myself, having limited education, but are willing to work hard and teach them Job skills. I.e. dependability, work ethics, team work, and loyalty. I would like to use my testimony to show them how believing in themselves and more importantly putting their faith in you and waiting on you, that life will be a joy to live and even though there will still be hard times, they will be fulfilled. I love you Lord. Life, though a constant struggle is full of joy and peace.

Thank you Lord
In Jesus name
Amen

Journal entry April 10, 2010

My precious Lord, after sitting here reading the brochure sent to me from choices, I get very excited about wanting to help people.They are doing such wonderful work, in a way I envy them. I pray with a faithful heart Lord that you will use me in a way that will help many people.

Lord, your word says, if a man does not work then he shall not eat. I would love it, if its your will, to build a program that would teach people who are limited in education, guidance, and finances to become ideal employees. I would love to help them line up child care, secure transportation, then teach them, while working at the store earning a wage, good work ethics.What it means to become a valuable employee. How important it is to an employer to have people who are loyal, trustworthy, dependable, hard working, and team players. I really believe that I could do this Lord, if its your will. I believe if there were more honest, work oriented people in the workforce, we wouldn't be in such a mess.

These executives at big banks, corps, etc. that are getting huge bonuses and healthcare and perks while the workers suffer are appalling.

I see now how I was like this at one time. I have learned so much. Politicians should be made to pay for their healthcare then they would have done something about it long ago. They should drive their own cars and with conference calls there is no reason for them to fly all over the place. Except the President and top officials. Men and women in office should be put out of office for having affairs outside of their marriages. This world is evil and we as Christians should not keep quiet about it.

Amen

Journal entry April 11, 2010

My Lord, new day, new beginning. Fill me Lord with your sweet spirit now and let me absorb your word and the message you alone want me to take from it. Lord I ask you to forgive my missing church Sunday and Wednesday nights. You know I am not feeling comfortable with the way its going. If I am wrong then deal with me Lord, if others are wrong then deal with them. I don't agree that we should speculate on who the anti-Christ is. I think that could stir things up and innocent people could suffer the consequences. I believe until you are ready to reveal him, it will be you alone who will know who he is. I believe he will be someone who will be well loved and respected, because satan who will be in control of him is the great deceiver.

Let us, through sweet Jesus be fishers of men, let us witness to many and plant seeds. I know the end days are close or are even now. Use me and my family Lord to win people for you. Put your loving, yet powerful arms around us. Fill us with your Holy Spirit, keep us calm and focused and moving in the direction you want us to go.

Let our church have a good Vacation Bible School, the best ever. Let us open the minds of many children and their families, let us have many to get saved. Lord, guide our footsteps as we walk down the path you would have us to take. Don't let us stray and when we do, bring us back. Don't ever let me or my family get so far away that we don't hear your voice.

I love you Lord, I want only to serve you
I pray these things
in Jesus name
Amen

Journal entry April 13, 2010

Lord I am so sorry I didn't take the time to do my prayers yesterday, or at least my time each morning I try to spend alone with you. It seems hard to do lately. There seems to be constant interruption. When I get my car back from the shop, I am going to stay home after everyone leaves. I am going back to having this time dedicated each day to my alone time with you, spent in prayer and praise to you.

I love you so much Lord and you ask so little from us, and give so much. I don't know why I lay awake thinking about what I'm going to do, when I know you will lead me. I want to be in the center of your will Lord, always. Please, I beg you end this roller coaster of uncertainty once and for all. I don't hesitate to work hard, you know this. I love to help people. Yes it does make me feel good, but that because I know it brings you Glory. I so like for people to know when we help someone only because it lets them (others) know we do use the business to help people in need and their donations are put to good use.

If you allow us to stay Lord, please fix the roof and heat pumps, and show me what I need to do to keep lazy people from dumping their trash at my back door. If the business is in your plan, but the location is not, then show me Lord, please. I have big dreams to maybe someday open a second store in Clinton or Oakridge or both. But, I will give up these dreams if they are not your will. Open my eyes Lord to your plans for me, and keep the devil out of it.

Watch over our church Lord, let it grow, unite us and grow us. Its not what it used to be. We need to get on our knees and pray. Lord I know we don't have the people we used to, but let us have a really good vacation Bible school. My Almighty God, please lay your healing hands on Mayford and Betty and Gene and Charlotte, Ms. Mamie, Kathy and Dewie, lift them up Lord. Touch Jacques' body and let her heal quickly. Lord heal me and Jerry also Lord. Give us strength and stamina to get a lot accomplished.

I asked these things in Jesus' name
Amen

At this time in our lives we had many dear friends who were fighting cancer and many other serious illnesses. We also had a friend who was fighting the system to get help while fighting for her life, little did I know that in a few short weeks, we too would be dealing with these things and more. My heart was so burdened for people we held so dear. There was Charlotte whose husband Gene was battling cancer. She had been through so much these past few years. She had lost her first husband, who was the pastor of our church, to cancer, then she lost her mother, and several other family members and then she lost her son, this was something that I could not even begin to imagine the pain she felt. She always demonstrated such grace and faith in these situations. She truly inspired me through the years to seek a stronger faith in God, to seek a closer relationship with him. I am so thankful for that. And there was Mayford W. Head deacon, strong church leader, incredible family man, this sweet soft spoken man was loved by many. This man never missed church and he raised his family in church and what a good family he has, then there is Betty his wife who is also dealing with her own health problems. These two have been married over 60years, can you imagine. I haven't even been alive that long.

I was really conflicted as to whether God wanted us to keep the business. I wanted so badly to stay, we had put so much time, money, and work into it. I had been praying about it for years, but evidently I wasn't listening or was listening to the wrong one. How do you know? I have since learned to answer this question this way, if its Gods will, it will be easy, he will clear the way and you will feel good and confident in what you are doing. Learn to listen with your heart, you will know its God because that is where he is, so the devil can't go there.

Journal entry April 14, 2010

Thank you Lord for all of my blessings. I am so grateful for everything you do for us. I appreciate how you always come through when my hope begins to fade. We have lost a lot of worldly possessions and given up a lot of pleasures, but I have never been happier. I won't deny that the uncertainty drives me crazy, but I'm not afraid because I am confident that you will guide my way and keep me in the center of your will.

Lord if it is your will for me not to start our own non profit, but to work with the charity that I have spoken to, then, please let me know. Either way use me and my knowledge and experience and most of all my faith to do good works in your name, for your Glory. I want to be your instrument in changing peoples lives for the good. Give me the speech, knowledge, and wisdom to do what is pleasing to you.

In Jesus Precious Name
Amen

Journal entry April 15, 2010

Lord I thank you for my blessings, especially my salvation. Thank you for another day. Use me Lord to do good works according to you plan. Let me and my family be a light for you in this world of darkness. I pray the lost open their hearts to you and to the joys of salvation. Bless me Lord with all that I need. On a selfish note, please let me plan and achieve a good senior trip for Casey.

Lord forgive me for not going to church last night, but I just am not comfortable with this study on Revelation. Its not that the scripture that bothers me, it's the thought of people trying to point out an anti-Christ. I personally don't believe anyone will know who it is until you reveal him Lord. I know we are living in the end times, there are many signs it seems that are coming to pass. I am going to study Revelation on my own, with you, so please open my mind to the lesson. Give me the message that you want me to receive. The correct understanding. Let me read and learn with a Christian heart so I will get the true meaning of your word.

Lord, I am worried about Kathy. I pray they are doing all that's humanly possible for her. It just seems that if you don't have insurance or money they don't try as hard. I know we are living in a wicked time when money is more important then human life.

I wonder how many people of this world will actually go to Heaven. So many proclaim to be a Christian but, how can a true child of God have prejudice in their hearts, or not feed a brother or sister when they are hungry or who won't speak out to protect a child. Lord I pray that you provide me with the time and money to help in the areas that we can. Give me the wisdom and words to battle injustice and sin that some don't see. I know only you can handle sin, what I mean is to speak out against bigotry, ignorance, and stupidity. Let me reach out and be a good example.

Thank you for dealing with my family. I am glad they are rededicating their life and getting back in church. Bless them Lord with the joy I have found in my walk with you. Lord thank you for being there to set me straight and lift me up when I let the devil get in my head with fear, and confusion. Keep me focused on you, that is all that is important.

I want the business and your charity to get started and be a work for you, and bring you much Glory. Let me succeed Lord if its your will. If its not your will, then please show me what to do. I don't know if satan has blocked my vision, I'm sure he is trying, or if I am not looking in the right place. Lead me Lord I ask that you keep us in the center of your will and our feet on the right path.

I love you Lord, I praise you,
I thank you, In Jesus' name
Amen

Journal entry April 18, 2010

Thank you Lord for my many Blessings. Thank you so much for a beautiful day. I am so full of Joy to see Taylor and Jimmy Baptized today. I can't wait for Mom and Candace to get baptized, I thought Candace would today, but she is going to wait until mom goes, when her ears are better. Lord, I thank you for a good service at Grace today. I really enjoyed it. it's a nice church, but my heart belongs at Riverview.

Thank you for an enjoyable time at Miranda Daniels' bridal shower. I pray you will bless their marriage Lord. She is a sweet girl from a good family. Now I can't wait to see them and James and Megan get married.

I also ask a special blessing for Justin and Hannah. May their little girl be healthy and bring them as much joy as mine have brought me. I hope she looks like her moma and has the spirit, faith, and enthusiasm of her father.

I hope it is your will to let me live long enough to see Casey and Kaylains babies. Casey will be eighteen soon, my how time flies. A few more years and he will probably get married. I look forward to that also. I hope to be here to help Kaylain plan her wedding, unless the rapture comes first.

What I pray for most is that my children and grand children all are saved and will live with us in Glory with our precious Lord. Give me strength and health and wisdom to get through another week. Please let us have good sales and get a lot paid.

I pray in Jesus name.
Amen

Because he suffered for me on his cross, I will carry mine.

About this time I started to become very anxious, I couldn't put my finger on it. I know I was over whelmed with worry about so many things, our business, our church, friends who were fighting huge health issues, my kids, And I felt something wasn't quite right with Jerry. He kept having bad head aches, mostly at work. He thought it was the mildew in the carpet where the roof had leaked. I was so uneasy, but wasn't sure why. Now I believe it was God getting me ready for the storm, no the hurricane would better describe it. I have been through many, many hard times, but nothing like what I was fixing to go through. I didn't know that's what it was, but I kept on praying that we would get through whatever was making me uneasy.

I mentioned my concern to Katie at work, after a couple of days she told me something that really alarmed me. She said, Jerry told her that he was working in his building and fell somehow and woke up with the table saw on top of him, and he couldn't remember what happened, looking back now I believe he blacked out. Why he didn't tell me this I don't know.

Journal entry April 19, 2010

Thank you Lord for another day, for we are not promised another day, even another minute, so let me use this day for your Glory. I want to pray for our church. I love this church and everyone in there. Right now, and I don't know why, I feel so disconnected. I don't know if it's the devil trying to cause trouble or what, but I pray that I come to know what's wrong and work on it. Let me do more for our church, and any who might need us.

I pray for all of the requests that have been made. I pray for healing and Grace for Mayford and Betty, Gene and Charlotte, Kathy and Dewey and all who need to feel your spirit Lord. Give them comfort and peace and to be able to feel the Joy that is part of their souls.

Continue to lift up our youth Lord. Help us through VBS, to win more people over and fill our youth classes. Help us to fill our church. I thank you for the couple we heard at Grace Sunday, bless their ministry. Lord I love you so much and I want to please you. Let me be able to do good works. Lord, let me help people not just financially, but spiritually. I don't want to preach, I want to teach. I am going to get into my Bible so I can learn the lessons and get the messages you alone want me to have and let me lovingly share them with others. I love talking to Ms Clara, and Granny (Eva) and those who teach me life lessons and who love you as I do. Lord, I know I beam when I am acknowledged for doing something good, but while it does make my heart swell, it is with love and not pride. And its because I am excited when I feel like I have done something that pleases you and brings you Glory. Lord, I don't know why Robert left church, but I pray he is where you want him to be. If he is not bring him back home to Riverview. I pray for him and Amanda and Jarrod, and also Justin and Bro. Langston and all of those that I know work hard for you. Help us Lord, bless us with what we need this week. Watch over my kids and let them do well on their T-caps. Watch over all of my family In Jesus' precious name

Amen

Journal entry April 20,2010

Bless me Lord with you Holy Spirit, let me feel you so I can face the day without fear and doubt. I know whatever your will is, that you will take care of us, I just would like to know what direction to take.

Lord I pray for Grace and comfort for those involved in the shooting at Parkwest hospital. I pray for peace for the families of the ones who died. I know satan is responsible. I see so much in the way of evil. Some people are so full of evil they actually don't feel anything. When you can't feel love, especially your love, that is the saddest thing I can imagine. I also pray for the family of the 16 year old boy who killed his grandparents. I pray that you will speak to that boys heart and touch him in a way that only you can. Save him Lord, make him see and feel the evil that controls him and to change his ways through salvation. He is but a baby, Lord, don't let him be another lost soul.

Lord, I pray for Kaylain. I don't know whats going on with her breathing and her back, but you healed her once when I ask you,

Lord, I am asking you again for your divine intervention. She is so young and has been through so much, touch her Lord, only you have the power. Watch over all of my children Lord. I pray for peace for Rick and Mike and their families. Heal their hearts Lord, and lift them up as a family. I ask special blessing for our church Lord. Unite us, grow us, lead us in the way you alone want us to go.

Lord I ask that you watch over all the kids this weekend. I know Prom night is a night many kids use to drink and other things they shouldn't. Keep them safe, let them have a night to remember. Kaylains trip is coming up in a couple of weeks and I pray that she has a great time and doesn't have any problems. Wrap your arms around her and protect her Lord.

I pray these things in
Jesus sweet name
Amen

Jerry and I were again hoping to get our non profit going and turn the business around. Jerry B. was once again willing to work out something that would allow us a little more time to get the non profit going. We were so excited. I wanted so badly to keep it going. It always did so well before the devil got his hand in it. I remember the days when Jerry and I and our former partners were so close and worked so well together. We did good and helped the Veterans organization we were contracted with. We looked forward to coming to work, we had many good people who worked with us and the best customers. It was actually fun and we looked forward to being there each day. God what I would give to have that again. What happened is a long story and when I get on my feet again and have the time, I hope to write about it, if people are interested in this book, then I will do it.

Jerry and I wanted to start our own non profit after we lost the contract with the other one. We wanted to help families who had worked all of their lives and fell on hard times, but fell between the cracks when it came to getting help. If you suddenly lose your job, or have a health crisis and because you can't afford the high cost of insurance, you will have astronomical medical bills. Because you don't qualify for tenncare or any other government assistance you are out of luck. Because if you have always worked and have a home and a car, you don't qualify. But they will take the taxes you have paid for years and pay the medical treatment of a person who has never worked a day in their life. Even people who have worked hard all of their lives should be able to get aid during times of crisis without giving up everything they have worked for. And I don't mean toys like boats, campers, pleasure items, I am talking about needs like their home. My Lord in heaven we have veterans living on the streets. We have seniors who have worked hard all of their lives having to choose between food or medicine. Then on the other hand we have young people, some who are still babies themselves, popping out babies right and left, drug addicts and drunks who are filling the emergency rooms to get their knife wounds and gun shot wounds sewn up. And while hard working people are losing their homes, many who wouldn't work in a pie factory are living in low rent or rent free housing, and I might add they have their baby daddies living with them, although they claim they don't know where they are and some even claim they don't know who the daddy is. People are so unconcerned about the condition of the world, and about their souls. God is telling us loud and clear according to his word, time is running out. If you have any doubt about your salvation, you better nail it down.

Journal entry April 21, 2010

Lord, light my fire today. Let me accomplish something good for your Glory. If someone I come in contact with today needs help, even if its just a word, if it allows me the opportunity to plant a seed then let me do so. Let me be a light for you Lord.

Bless us Lord with all that we need to keep going. Its in your hands and I trust in my faith in you.You're the one sure thing in my life, my faith is in you alone. I thank you Lord for my salvation first and foremost, My husband, he is my life partner, for my children and grandchildren. I pray for our sons and their wives. I pray for a strong and loving marriage for both of them. Watch over Casey and Kaylain as they face challenges everyday. Keep them both on the straight and narrow and focused on school and church.

I pray Casey has found his life partner because I don't think he could find anyone more perfect for him then Anna. I pray Kaylain finds someone as good and that both of them will marry their soul mates and raise good, God fearing families.

I pray in Jesus Name
Amen

Journal entry April 22, 2010

Lord thank you for filling my day with hope. Jerry B. is yet again being so good to us. Now I pray with all that I am, all that I have, that you push to get our non profit going. Help us Lord. Make it come to pass if it is your will.

In Jesus name
Amen

As I read this next page from my journal, I am racked with guilt, and shame, and sadness, because I realize now that this was probably the beginning of the end of our life as we knew it. This was probably the start of Jerrys' health declining, and I didn't catch it.

After all of the years we shared, why did I not see sooner that something was so wrong. And if he had any idea something was wrong, why didn't he tell me. Were we that wrapped up with the store and everything else we were struggling with that we couldn't see what was right in front of us. Yes we were, because that's what satan wanted. Nothing would change the out come of the months ahead, because that is Gods plan, but how he chooses to allow satan to move is also a part of his plan, he has a reason that we don't understand. I believe he was strengthening me and the kids through the added trials the devil was throwing at us. He was preparing us for what was to come, if you can be prepared for something like this.

Journal entry April 22, 2010

Thank you Lord for all of the blessings both big and small. I realize some of the most important ones, I don't give a second thought until I am in danger of losing it. My health, my home, my job, most important, my family.

Keep us in your will Lord. Move me in the direction I need to go to be in the center of your will. I am willing to work hard and I know it will be up to me, Jerry just isn't there for me like I need him to be. He is going to do just what he wants to do. When he wants to do it and would rather help some one else then to help me. I know now that I am in this business alone as far as humans, but that's ok because I have my God. No power, strength, or love is greater. Bless me Lord, give me what I need to get the job done. I am grateful for what Jerry does and for the man he is. I guess I am just tired. Don't let me give in to the the ways of the devil. Don't let him put false thoughts in my mind to cause problems. Open my eyes Lord, Bless me, lead me, watch over my family.

In Jesus Name
Amen

Journal entry April 23, 2010

Lord calm me right now. Between the dog and his poop (which I just stepped in) and my kid that won't get up, I'm ready to explode. Don't let satan get to me. My mouth tends to speak things in anger, so like the shirt says "put your arm around my shoulder, and your hand over my mouth.".

Lord it's the kids prom tomorrow night, and I pray that you keep them safe because its supposed to storm. Please let them have a wonderful, memorable evening. Please hold off the storms until they are all home safely or let them come through tomorrow morning and clear up and be beautiful tomorrow night.

Lord please heal Kaylains body. Help us both to lose weight and live better life styles with better eating habits and more exercise. Please let them get through with our non profit and let us get things started with our solicitation program and get sales up and start helping more people. Lord please get all of this settled and moving forward. Lead me Lord through it all. Let me get a computer and learn the program so I can do most of the work myself. I want to do your will Lord, I feel like I am because you have opened so many doors. Its been a long five years Lord, please let these next five be easier. I pray we get the business at least back to where it was and all debts caught up and paid off. Let us retire Jerry and put the kids through college. I ask a lot Lord, but I know its nothing for you. I am tired of living this struggle Lord, But if its your will, I will continue on. I will work hard, pray even harder. I will do my best to do what you want me to do and not what I want to do. I pray for Mayford Lord, he is going through so much as is Gene and Kathy. Lay your hands on all of them and their families. I ask special healing for Granny Lord. Let her be relieved of these shingles that are torturing her so.

I pray in Jesus sweet name
Amen

There was so much going on at this time. So many were afflicted with health problems. Including Kaylain, and so many worries with the business and our finances. It was prom time which is always a busy time. We were all going to meet over at Buds house (Annas' grandfather) before they left to go to prom and take pictures and then the parents were going to have dinner together while the kids were gone. There is one ray of sunshine in our lives, that is the friends that Casey and Kaylain have. These kids are awesome. They are all Christians and are like one big family. They would do anything for each other and I love them all, and so thankful for each and every one. I have made good friends with their parents, these people are so good, its easy to see where their kids get it from.

Journal entry April 26, 2010

Lord, first I want to thank you so much for watching over all of the kids who went to the prom, for letting them have a good time and for getting them home safely. I know it was your hand that split that storm and let them have a wonderful time. You gave me exactly what I ask for. I know it was prayer and faith. There were so many others who were hit by these storms, ten lives were lost. I pray they were saved people. Bless all of the families Lord with the Grace to get through it.

Lord, thank you for all of your blessings. Give me the knowledge and the words to get things moving with my non profit. I feel so tired from this five year struggle, so much has happened. I pray Lord that you would please see fit to allow us a few years of calm. Let us do really good with the business, not to make us rich, but to pay all of our bills and hire and build a good team of people we can trust so that we can take more time for our family, our church and most of all doing works for you. I would not only like to help families but, good organizations that help people also. I would like to get a motor home and trailer to stock up, then take it to disaster areas in the US with in hours and set up a portable kitchen to help feed people who have been displaced, to minister to their souls and just try and comfort them through the shock. I would like to do good works in your name.

Lord, I felt like you wanted me to share Kathys card in church yesterday, it kind of went with the lesson. I hope they took it the way I intended it.

I pray for Mayford today Lord, let his surgery go well and heal him quickly, wrap your loving arms around Gene and Charlotte Lord as they get through the next few months. Bless Kathy and her treatments Lord. Send her a Dr. who will really help her. Touch Kaylains little body Lord, I don't know whats going on with her, but I pray you heal her. Watch over us and guide us as we start a new week.

In Jesus Name
Amen

Journal entry April 29, 2010

My precious Lord, its been a rough 24 hours. I pray that Kaylains health begins to improve. The Dr.s can't find anything, yet she still is in pain. So this morning I prayed with her and now I pray during my own prayer time. Heal her Lord. When no one else seems to know what's wrong, you know all about it. Touch her body Lord, make her well, I would gladly take her afflictions, just don't let her continue in fear and pain. Bless us all Lord with better health. I am worried about Jerry, please help him Lord to quit smoking and help me to eat better and lose weight, I really want to.

Please help us with the business. I'm trying really hard to leave everything to you, but you know its hard for me when things don't happen. I have a hard time waiting on you Lord, please forgive me. I will leave it in your hands and wait on you.

In Jesus Name
Amen

Journal entry April 30, 2010

Dear Lord, please slow down my mind. I am going to wait on you. I am scared and aggravated about the non profit. I gave it to you Lord, your will be done. If there is something I have done or am doing please show me so I can change it. Please let me have enough in my account to pay what I need to pay to get me through this week. Bless me Lord with what I need to survive in the business and to be able to help people. Fill me Lord with your Holy Spirit and let me shine to all that I speak to today. Let me witness to someone in need of salvation. Let me be a tool in your work. Use me Lord, I am willing, you know my heart. It is not my concern to please people, it is to please you and bring you Glory.

Thank you Lord for putting your hand between Casey and that van, I don't know where his mind was but please keep him focused and alert when he is driving. Please continue to keep him and any with him safe. Deal with his conscience Lord, wrap your arms around him. Lord please give the kids what they need to get through this school year and pass. Let them get their GPA up especially Casey. I wish he would take more concern with his studies. I want him to be able to provide for his family and do good works.

Lord I ask if you would, to please let us take a little time and money to spend some time with the kids. Watch over all of my children and grandchildren Lord. I pray they all are saved before you come for your church. Lord I am sorry for all that I have done lately that I know doesn't please you. Like, missing church, and yesterday I said a cuss word. You do so much for me, and bless me in so many ways, I regret anything that displeases you, please forgive me. Let me be a good example to all of those around me. Please give healing and grace to Kaylain, Jerry and those who are gravely ill right now. Mayford, Gene, Kathy, Jeremy, Ruth, Burl. There are so many Lord. Bless Jons new little baby, Kaydence. Lord don't let family on either side cause them problems. Let them grow close and marry.

In Jesus name
Amen

I believe this was the night that we were eating dinner, Alex, a good friend of Caseys' from church was eating with us, and I looked up at Jerry and noticed this huge knot on the side of his neck, just under his ear. I said, "what in the world is that on your neck". He didn't know and hadn't noticed it. I remember thinking this might be what is causing his headaches. I was also thinking about the cancer he had six years before on his tongue. I said I am making a Dr appointment tomorrow, we are not waiting until your next appointment. If I had known what was coming, I probably would have had a nervous break down. I guess that's why God doesn't reveal the future to us. I don't want to know mine. Its probably easier to face in small doses, although mine have all been big doses lately. But one thing I am sure of, big or small I couldn't face any of it without my faith in my almighty God, and I was about to find out just how mighty he is and how strong my faith was.

CHAPTER 2

Big Storm Brewing

The storms that had been predicted for the night of the prom didn't come as early as I had hoped, but, they instead split as they approached our area and went north and south of us. Now how is that for answered prayer. All of the kids had a wonderful time as did the parents, and everyone made it home safely.

I was still worried and uncertain about the business. This had been a nightmare for years and I was getting tired. I really believed that we were where God wanted us, But I should have realized that it wasn't to be. Now I had more important things on my mind to pray about. We had discovered a large knot on Jerrys' neck, and of course it had me scared. I was trying to be brave because I didn't want to scare the kids if it turned out to be nothing to worry about. I don't know how Jerry felt, he was one of those that kept it in when something worried him, and I tried not to let him know that I was afraid because I felt like that would just make things harder for him. Besides it might not be anything. Oh was I ever wrong, but it still wouldn't have helped anyone to panic before we knew what was going on. God would see us through what ever we had to face, it might not feel like it while we are going through it, but he will.

Journal entry May 2, 2010

Thank you Lord for all blessings big and small. Lord keep everyone safe through these storms that will be coming through.

Lord I am worried about that big knot on Jerrys' neck. Please don't let it be his cancer back. Please I am begging you. Please in Jesus' name give us some good times without so much stress and health issues. Let us build our charity to do much in the way of helping people. Lord I don't want to be known, but I want the charity to grow and become well known so that we can both receive a lot of donations and be known to those who need help. I pray that you send the ones whom you want us to help. I also would like to help small non profits that do not have a solicitor to raise money for them.

Lord keep us focused and on the right path. Give us good health and energy and stamina to accomplish a lot. Send me good, faithful, honest people to help us. Let us be able to take the time to go on a much needed family trip.

I ask in Jesus name
Amen

Journal entry May 4, 2010

Thank you Lord for a good sales day. Please continue to bless us so we can get caught up. Please fix our roof Lord, they sure don't seem to be in any hurry to fix it and I need the room. Let us pick up and start to increase in donations so we can increase sales. Give me strength and health to get a lot done. You my precious Lord are the only one who can get us through this. I am so amazed at how you always give us what we need just when we need it.

Lord I ask special blessings for Mayford, Gene, Kathy, Granny, Burl, Jeremy, and their families. I pray good health for my family. Please heal Kaylains little body and let that knot on Jerrys' neck just be a swollen gland. Heal them both Lord. Guide me this day Lord, let me be a weapon in this day of Spiritual warfare.

In Jesus Name
Amen

Journal entry May 5, 2010

Thank you my precious Lord for all of my blessings big and small. Bless us Lord with all that we need to continue our work if its your will.

Lord watch over my children, keep evil from them. Give them knowledge and understanding to do good in their school work. Lord I ask that you guide them through school and help them to establish good careers that not only will support their families but also serve you in some capacity. My mighty Lord, I ask you to work in the lives of my oldest son and his family. I'm worried about Michael and Elizabeth, keep them safe and from evil. Get them involved in church someway please. Put a hedge about them Lord, protect them from the fighting and cursing and whatever else they might be exposed to right now.

I also ask special prayer this morning for my families health. Lord touch Kaylains body and heal her. Please don't let her continue to suffer. I don't know what else to do. The Drs can't seem to find whats wrong, but I know theres something. You are the great physician Lord, heal her body, let her enjoy her youth. I ask also that the knot on Jerrys neck just be a swollen gland or something minor. Please God don't let it be anything serious. I pray also that I get my own health improving by eating healthier and losing weight.

Lord bless all those we know right now going through health crisis'. Bless their families also Lord. I know first hand what its like to care for someone ill and still take care of everyday tasks. Let me help anyone, anyway that would be a blessing to them. Show me what they need that I can help with.

Lord I see so much evil, from people constantly stealing from us right now, to what I believe are drug deals in the parking lot. Show me Lord what I can do. Please surround our area, keep evil out.

In Jesus Name
Amen

Journal entry May 6, 2010

I know my Redeemer lives

Lord watch over us this day. Please let Jerrys' Dr appointment turn out good. Let them be able to cure his neck without surgery. Please let it be minor. Continue to touch Kaylains body and let her be healed from whatever was causing her pain.

Lord I ask for good sales today, let us do well and get some bills paid. Help me Lord to get all of these taxes paid and the rent caught up. Please let us do well this week.

Let us do well enough also to take a camping trip with our kids and really have a wonderful time. I also ask Lord that besides bills and camping that this month we make enough to give all of the kids graduating some money, especially Taylor, Rebecca, and Chucky. Keep them all safe after graduation and on senior trips.

Bless all those who are struggling with major health battles. Bless them with Grace and Peace.

Thank you
In Jesus name
Amen

❧

When Jerry went to the Dr. on the sixth, the Dr said he didn't like the way it looked, so he set up a cat scan for him. Then I was really scared. I have a lot of faith, but when some one this close to you is in trouble and you don't know how bad it is, its scary. I am the type of person that the unknown is what scares me. If I know what I am dealing with, I am still afraid, but I will face it head on because I know God is in control. It also lets me know when its time to call on prayer warriors to help me pray. I really wasn't prepared for just how strong I was going to have to be.

I remember when my oldest son was a baby and he would spend the night with his grandparents, I would be so afraid and nervous when I was home alone. But even though he was a little baby, I was never afraid when he was with me. My grandmother asked me why I wasn't afraid when he was home, he couldn't help me if someone did break in and after I thought about it for a moment, I told her this. "Well I guess I know that when he is with me I have to protect him so I don't get scared."

When someone you love needs you, you just don't have time to think about yourself. You are so afraid of their pain and their fears that you are focused on that, on what you can do to make it better for them. You can't begin to imagine the strength you can find in these situations. You won't believe the things that you will do for those that you love when faced with it. The strength, the stamina to go and go without sleep, to stay calm even when your heart is beating out of your chest, and to stay firmly on the rock when satan is attacking from every direction.

You will learn little tricks to keep your family from knowing just how afraid you are, like crying in the shower or waiting until the kids are at school to go walk in the woods or sit in the gazebo to get hysterical. To lay with your loved one, holding them until they go to sleep before letting the tears gently, quietly roll down your cheek.

Don't keep things from your children, let them know every step of the way what is going on. Its better to give it to them in small doses as you deal with it so that it is not a complete shock to them, but don't let them see your fear. If you talk to them and stay calm, they will too. If you get hysterical, so will they. Pray a lot, pray in your quiet place, pray as a family, Jerry and I prayed when it was just he and I laying there.

Journal entry May 7, 2010 Ephesians 1

Here I am Lord, Leary of what we are about to face. I am not afraid, I know you will see us through anything and you will give us grace to face whatever your will might be, it's the not knowing that is unsettling me. I won't deny the financial part really worries me. Lord please let them help Jerry and work it out so we don't have to use what little we have saved for Caseys' college fund.

God I have ask you many times to save him (physically), I pray that you will heal him yet again. Lord I am not afraid to live without him, I just don't want to. Its so hard now, I hate to face life without him. I know I could drop dead tomorrow. I just pray you give us more time for our kids and more importantly for your work. Whatever we go through this year Lord, let it be a good witness to those who are lost around us and even those who are saved. Let my faith and prayers make people think, and may many seeds be planted. Lord I need you more then ever. This is a lot to deal with. But you have always brought me through the valleys. This is my prayer list Lord, I pray I can check each one off this year. But I already know that it will be done in your time and I will wait and I will accept your will for us.

I know that you will give me grace for the no's, mercy for some, and yes for the ones that are your will. Whatever your answers, I am your child always.

1. Salvation or dedication for my son Michael and all of his family.
2. Healing for Jerry
3. Healing for Kaylain
4. Casey ready for college
5. Non profit started and growing
6. Business increasing, bills paid, lots of donations.
7. Health Insurance acquired
8. Many people helped through difficult times.
9. Better health for me through better eating habits.
10. A nice vacation for my family, just to get away for a while.

As you read this book and these entries from my journals, remember these are my prayers and conversations with God. When I spend these times with God, I usually do it some where alone and quiet with no distractions. The best prayer times I have had with my precious Lord is during my three day fast I do every Easter. It is so amazing how much more I feel the Holy Spirit when I have purged my body.

Its wonderful how when I am at the end of my rope and am nothing more then a heaping pile of sobbing mess, all I have to do is get in a quiet place and write in my prayer journal. And never do I get up from this time with my Lord without feeling comforted and at peace. What I want people to understand is that its not enough to pray. You have to faithfully pray, believing that God has the power to do anything, but you have to still trust in his plan even when its not what you want. His plans are beyond all understanding and we won't know the answers on this side of Heaven. That's what faith is, trusting when we don't know why things happen the way they do.

Remember Job?, God took everything from him, and because he remained faithful God rewarded him with more then what he took. He is not punishing you for anything, he is just closing one chapter of your life and starting another.

Journal entry May 8, 2010

I know it may sound silly to any who might read these journals after I am gone. It may even sound like I am foolishly testing you, but you know that's not the case. I will accept whatever your will is for me, with the grace you have always given me. I just like to look back time to time and remember these valleys and how you brought us through them. I find it amazing to see how it strengthens our faith, I always feel closer to you, so if satan is doing these things to tear me down, he is doing just the opposite.

Lord, yesterday lying in my hammock, thinking and praying about all we are facing, I felt like that hammock wrapped around me, was your arms and you were rocking me and soothing my fears like I used to do my children when they were young and fretful.

I love the feeling of your gentle touch, of your Holy Spirit letting me know I don't have to fear anything for you are with me. I so look forward to the day when we all will be risen to join you in Heaven. I pray the rapture will be soon. I see so much evil Lord.

I pray for all who are lost, that they don't wait any longer, for evil walks the earth and absorbs those who have hardened their hearts against you and then uses them to torment your children. I hate it. But I know one day it will all be wiped away and the time will come when we will rejoice and suffer no more.

Lord I ask also for comfort and peace for not only Jerry, but, Mayford, Gene, Kathy, Burl, Ruth, Granny, Katies sister, and all the families involved. Lord I pray for all those prayer requests that have been made at church and on my own prayer list.

Lord bless our church, fill it with your Holy Spirit Lord, let us grow it again and fill it with the lost that they might be saved. With all the members and their families going through these crisis' I pray we still can pull off a good VBS and that many are saved and many seeds are planted.

I ask all of this in Jesus name
Amen

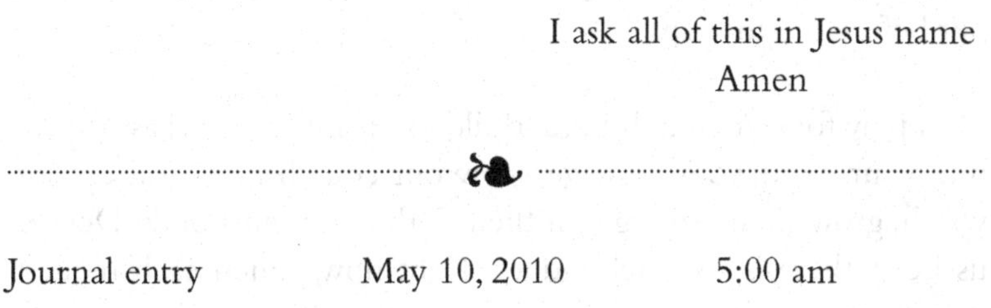

Journal entry May 10, 2010 5:00 am

Lord calm me right now, my mind is spinning out of control and I am afraid of the unknown. I know satan will throw everything at me right now because he thinks I'm vulnerable. But I don't care what I have to go through, what I have to face, I will stay faithful and trust in you Lord. I faithfully ask your healing hand on Jerry Lord. I see his pain, I'm afraid its going to be bad. My mighty God, I know you are the only one who can heal him. I need him Lord. We can do good things with our charity if its your will. My precious Lord, I have so much swirling in my mind. What do I do?

Keep me focused, give me strength, stamina, and guidance Lord. I just want to crawl up in your lap and watch you work, but

I know I have to walk through this valley, and I also know you will walk every step with me.

I ask peace, calm and grace not only for us but for Mayford, and his family, Gene & Charlotte, Kathy & Dewey, Miss Clara, and all who are facing difficult times. Guide me Lord, let me feel the Holy Spirit at all times. I thank you for leaving us our comforter after the death and resurrection of my precious Jesus. I don't know what I would do without him.

I especially pray for Casey right now Lord. He is so much like Jerry and keeps so much inside. Please don't let it pull him down. Put a hedge about him and Kaylain. Don't let them be afraid and don't let satan get a foot in their lives. Protect them Lord as only you can. Lord lift me up, fill me up, use me up. Use me Lord until the day you call me home. Use me to be a good witness to those who are lost, to plant many seeds and be a comfort to those you put before me to help.

I pray for our church Lord. Build us up. Lift up our Pastor, give him your word, your message, grow our church Lord, Lift up our youth, grow them, strengthen their faith and their bonds. Deliver us Lord, there is so much sadness right now, Touch each request that has been made.

In Jesus' name I ask these things
Amen

P.S. Thank you for a nice mothers day with my mom.

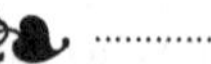

This was the beginning of our storm, our hurricane. We knew Jerry had a large mass and they were going to do a biopsy to see if it was cancer and if it was, what kind and what would have to be done to treat it, if it could be treated. Its overwhelming the things that start running through your mind. You don't want to think about the what ifs. You think about, Are the Drs going to help him even though we don't have insurance? How long will he have to go through treatments? How will we get through this while trying to run a business? Then there are the scariest thoughts that start to creep in, Can he be cured? Is he going to die? What will I do?, I can't live without him. What about the kids? Can I take care of him the way he needs to be cared for? Oh God why? Why do you keep putting us through these trials? I know we have valleys to go through but why so much for so long? You said you would not put more on us then we can bare. I gotta tell you Lord, I'm there I just don't feel like I have the strength to handle anymore. Hold me in your hands Lord, my faith is in you, please keep me strong and show me what to do, what is your will for me?

Then you still have to deal with the problems that are still there from before. We are broke, and now we need to focus on him and getting him well, the business will have to take a back seat. God lead me in every situation, that's all I could think of. Tell me God, I had no idea what to do from one minute to the next. And I was trying to handle it alone because I did not want to put more on Jerry then he was already facing. And the kids, I didn't want to worry them anymore then I had to, but at the same time I didn't want to hide anything from them in case it was bad, I didn't want it to catch them off guard. I just kept praying for God to have his hand in every decision and that he would guide every step we took, and when I was weary from it all, to carry me when I needed to be carried. I knew that he would, he always had.

The storm warnings had been issued, we were bracing to ride it out. God was piloting our ship and what ever was coming, he would give each of us the grace we needed to face it. He was my life preserver. My anchor in the storm, I knew we would all get through this. And even though my faith was strong, I couldn't help but wonder where we would be when the storm had passed and the sky began to clear. Would we be the same people or would this forever change us. Would the change be for the good or the bad. Its scary to think about, but these trials can be for Gods glory or they can be a means for satan to get control. Ultimately the choice is yours, that's why God gives us freewill.

You have to lean on God because the devil is powerful and we are no match for him, but our father is.

Journal entry May 10, 2010

Lord please let me get a good nights sleep tonight. I don't know why I let the devil keep me awake all hours of the night, running through all of the negative scenarios' that could happen. I know Lord that you are in control and that no matter what your will is, that you will give us Grace to get through.

I pray Lord you especially protect my kids. Casey is so much like Jerry, he keeps everything inside. But, it comes out because my sweet, loving child gets snappy and hateful. He always feels bad after, you can tell. Don't let him be afraid, let him feel the Holy Spirit and know that we are going to be ok no matter what.

I ask with the most faithful of hearts Lord that you please get Jerry through this and let us have added years to do your work. Let us get through this valley quickly and have some quiet family time together to gather our wits and strengthen our resolve to serve you. Use my whole family in whatever capacity you see fit. I know Jerry must have some fear, he's not afraid of death, like me though I'm sure he fears the act of dying. I know you give us dying grace Lord, but I guess until we personally experience it when that time comes, we will fear it, we just don't realize how much you love us and will comfort us as we do our own children. You are after all our Father.

Lord you know my heart and that you are my rock. But you gave me Jerry as my soul mate and next to you, he is my rock here in this world. He is the only human who can calm me in any situation. Let me be strong now and see him through this without showing fear. I want to be an assurance to him and the kids. Don't let satan use our fear to get into our lives. Put a hedge about us Lord. Keep us calm, comfort us, lift us up.

Lord I ask this same prayer for Mayford, Gene, Kathy, Clara, and all of those going through the same kind of burdens. Strengthen their families, their faiths, and their backs. Just keep reminding us all that you are in control and we pray your will be done and you will give us Grace.

God I thank you for my life and if mine should end tomorrow the only regret I have is not living for you earlier in my life. I regret not getting in church when our older boys were younger. I hope they can one day forgive us for the stressful environment they were raised in. I am so sorry and so ashamed.

I pray that they find their way to where you want them to be Lord. I pray you keep Casey and Kaylain in church and serving you always. Bless them with Christian spouses who love you as much as they do. (I believe Casey has found his in Anna) I hope. And if Jerry and /or I don't live to see them married with their own children, I just hope they know God is always going to be there for them as he will for Michael and Rick and their families. Lord I know its selfish, but, I don't want to let Jerry go right now. Please let us get the kids grown together.

I humbly ask these things
in my sweet Jesus name
Amen

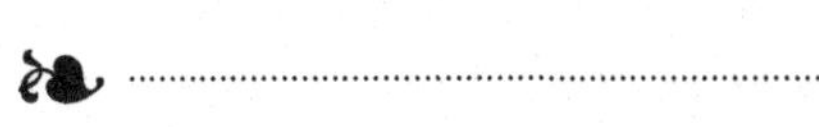

Journal entry May 14, 2010

Lord its been a trying couple of days and I am tired. I have no doubt that you are with me, sometimes when I feel so hopeless, you fill me with your Holy Spirit and remind me that you are here. I am not afraid of my future, I just don't want to lose my best friend right now. I don't care what we lose in material things, I just pray you give us a few more years. Lord you know my heart, you know my faith and my trust are in you alone. I don't even care if I have to give up the business. I do pray if that's your will that you will give me something that will help many people while supporting my family. Show me your will Lord so I know that I am making the right choices.

Lord please, please heal Jerry. Let this mass be removed and him be cancer free. I pray also for Mayford, Gene, and Kathy, Burl, and all my prayer requests. Strengthen me Lord and give me stamina, and wisdom to do all that I need to do, and let what I do be of your will and not mine. Give me the wisdom to know the difference.

I love you Lord, you know you are first and foremost in my life and Jerry is next and my kids and grandkids. Forgive me Lord for spasing out and being ill to Jerry over something so trivial, when he may be fighting for his life. I am so ashamed that I let the demons of satan take over my emotions and fill me with hurt and anger. I know Jerrys heart, and I am so sorry I acted so stupid. Wrap your loving arms around my family Lord let me feel your presence. I have peace and comfort and know with out a doubt that no matter what we are fixing to go through, you will give us Grace.

I see a change in my mom and sister and my brother in law. I pray you use me as a witness, as a light, to be a good example of strong faith. I pray you touch our boys Lord, get them all on the right paths. I thank you Lord for every single blessing.

In Jesus Name
Amen

Journal entry May 15, 2010

Thank you Lord so much for all that you are and all that you do for me. Touch my soul Lord, keep me calm and focused no matter what I have to face. Comfort me and my family as only you can. I know you are my strength and only through you is anything possible, my faith is in you.

I pray you touch Jerrys' soul. I'm sure he is more afraid then I am. Wrap your loving arms around him, let him feel your peace and comfort. Give him strength Lord. Give him Grace. I also pray for all those we know going through health crisis' right now. Bless them all Lord, and their families. Bless my children and comfort them, don't let satan bombard them with fear and doubts. I will pray more with them to strengthen us all. I know this is short, this is whats on my heart this morning. So touch us Lord with all that we need to face another day.

In Jesus name
Amen

Journal entry May 16, 2010

Lord, thank you for another day and all of your blessings big and small. Thank you for the comforter who makes these times bearable. I pray my precious Lord that Jerry's' test tomorrow reveal something easy to cure. I pray for strength to face any situation that comes.

Help us Lord with the business, Please bring us many, many donations. I don't mind hard work and I will do what it takes if its your will.

Lord bless our church, our pastor, and our youth. Bless those graduating today, guide their paths Lord and keep them in the center of your will. I love you Lord, more then anything or anyone. I will do my very best to serve and witness. Use me Lord, there is nothing that would give me more Joy. Keep satan from my children. These scary times can go both ways, they can weaken or they can strengthen us. I pray for the others we love who are going through it also.

Lift us up my precious Lord
In my sweet Jesus name
Amen

❧

Journal entry May 17, 2010

Lord Bless us this day with a good report from Jerry's Dr. I don't care if it takes every dime I have put up for college fund, I know you will take care of that when the time gets here. I pray also that we get more donations then I can keep up with this week. Please let us have good sales so that I can pay bills. Please let things go well with the business so I can take care of Jerry. I pray that you take care of all of us. I don't know why I ask that. I know that you will, you always do. Lord be with us as we dive into this day, this week, please let us get good news.

In Jesus Name
Amen

2nd Journal entry May 17, 2010

Its me again Lord, I got ready faster then I thought so I thought I would spend a little more time with you. It doesn't seem like Daddy has been gone 21 years and Grandma 19. I sure miss them. I pray I will see them again as the rest of my family.

What a time of rejoicing, when we all meet in the sky. What a reunion, I look forward to that day. Imagine, to be with you and all of my loved ones. To live without pain, without fear, without anger, without hate. To know only Love and peace, no sickness, no worry, a permanent vacation.

Be with our church Lord, strengthen it. Unite us, grow us, bless us. Keep satan out. Please let this be a wonderful summer for my family. Casey only has one more year of school then its college. Kaylains growing up faster then I can keep up with. Let us have some time with Rick and his family and Mike and his family. Please God make this a good year.

In Jesus name
Amen

My journal entries may get a little boring to someone reading them because they are so repetitive. When I am afraid, and unsure of what I am facing, I pray constantly about it. I know that God heard my prayer the first time, its more for my benefit then anything else. The same is true when I don't know what to do in situations like the business for example. I think where I fell short on things that I prayed about was not taking the time to sit quietly and wait for Gods answer. Instead looking back, I can see how I would pray about something, then try to handle it myself. If we pray and turn our burdens over to God, then we have to keep our hands out of it and let him deal with it.

Then we have to be willing to accept the answer that he gives us. It is not always going to be what we want. Sometimes it may not be when we want it, he may wait on his answer, God does things in his own time. This is so hard for me, I panic when things don't go the way that I want them to or when I want them to. That is why I like keeping my prayer journals, not only so that my kids can read them and learn things about me that maybe they don't know, but also so when I go back and read them, I can see how you handled every situation that I prayed about. My faith will always be in God as well as my trust. No one but him can do miracles, and even then he will only do them if they fit into his plans for us.

CHAPTER 3

Category 5 Storm Warning

The severity of a hurricane is measured on a scale from one to five with five being the most dangerous.A tropical depression can change to a hurricane in hours, and a hurricane can change from a category one to a five so fast that you hardly have time to prepare for it, if you can prepare. No matter how ready for it that you think you are, when it hits it is devastating. You try to prepare for the worst while praying for the best. It is so much bigger then we are and we are so afraid of what the out come will be.

Cancer . . . . Just the mention of the word will make your heart skip a beat. May 18, Jerry was having a biopsy to find out what kind of cancer we were dealing with and how we were going to deal with it.We had been through so many health crises with Jerry these past 6 years. In January 2005 he had cancer on his tongue that was surgically removed.Then in, I think it was labor day of 2007, he had a triple by-pass heart surgery, followed within a few months of each other, three more artery by-pass surgeries.

Through it all he kept on smoking. I quit when he had cancer on his tongue. He tried and quit for a little while, but it's the one vice he couldn't conquer. He had quit drinking years ago, and since we got back into church in 2004 we had quit cussing, and gambling. We were both doing our very best to be the best Christians possible.We wanted to teach our youngest child and our granddaughter by example. I wish we had made this commitment long ago and been there for our oldest boys.

Sitting in the hospital the day that they were doing the biopsy, I remember thinking about what I was going to do if it was bad. It was too much with everything that was going on with the business and our financial struggles. But now the importance of the business and trying to save it seemed so minimal. All I could think about was Jerry and what was going to happen with him. I prayed so hard that day. I knew the only way I was going to make it through the day was with the peace and comfort that only the Lord could give me. If I had known that day what we were fixing to go through I probably would have had a nervous breakdown.

Journal entry May 18, 2010 11:20 am

Happy Birthday, Grandma

Lord, I thank you for another day. As we sit here waiting for them to take Jerry down, I realize Lord how much he means to me. He is such a good husband and the best father. He is just an all around good person. I don't think I have ever known anyone who didn't like him.

I pray with a faithful heart Lord that you get us through this and heal him completely. I am scared, but you know its not a lack of faith. I fear the worst because I don't want to face life with out him. But I also know that if that should be your will, you will get me through it.

Casey is the one that I worry about the most. He seems to be handling it very well, but I know him, and I know how much he loves his Dad. Protect his heart Lord, don't let satan get so much as a toe hold. I pray he leans on you and doesn't get mad at you. Watch over my little Kaylain while she is out of my sight. Keep her safe and on the right path. Don't let her be afraid through all of this. Bless us Lord with the Grace to face whatever we have to.

In Jesus name
Amen

2nd Journal entry May 18, 2010 5:41 pm

Just want to take a minute and thank you Lord for being with me today, keeping me calm and focused. As bad as it all is or sounds, he has a 70% chance of beating this. But you are the great physician so I know he will beat it, if its your will and I pray that it is. I know that you are taking care of the business, just please let me get medicare going for him to help with all of these expenses. Keep my kids safe tonight Lord since I am not with either one of them right now. Lord please let him beat this, only you can beat it.

I thank you with all of my heart
I love you with all of my heart
I praise you with all of my being
In Jesus precious name
Amen

Journal entry May 19, 2010

Lord thank you again for getting us through yesterday and for giving us hope. I was so scared but at the same time, so calm. I now ask you Lord to please let the chemo and radiation completely kill the cancer cells. Please let us be together a few more years to raise our children and start our non profit and build it into a true Christian Entity that will help many, many people. Guide each step that I take, each decision I make, each choice we have to make.

Lead me the way you want me to go Lord. Show me the path that keeps me in the center of your will.

Bless my children with the wisdom to make good choices and to do well in school and go on to college. Give us the means to send them to college. Please let us get aid to pay all of these hospital and Dr. Bills. I pray for the sales to get out of debt and for the donations to generate more sales.

I pray for healing for Jerry, Mayford, Gene, Kathy, Clara, and those who have great health concerns. I pray for the lost, use me to plant seeds every day Lord.

In Jesus Name
Amen

Journal entry May 20, 2010

Help me Lord, even as I start this prayer it pops in my mind that I have to pay sales tax today on top of everything else. Lord I need to pay bills and Jerrys' medical treatments please, I beg you send me a lot of donations. I will work hard for what I need.

Please God let them make Jerry an appointment and get him started with the treatment that he needs to save his life. Lord I am asking right now if they aren't going to do it that you lay your healing hands on him and heal him completely, only you have the power to do it, and I have the faith to believe it can happen if its your will.

Lord bless my children, keep them on the right path and in the center of your will. I pray they pass their grade. Lord keep them focused on their school work next year so they can move on to the next phase of their education. Use them Lord for your work, your plan. Use all of us. Give me the wisdom and Grace through this valley that I need to be a good example. I pray that our trial will benefit a lost soul and turn them toward you, and to you be all of the Glory. Everything we do, everything we say, let us bless and inspire in some way that is pleasing to you.

Please let Jerry get in touch with Rick today. He needs to know what's going on in the event that your will is different from ours. I pray that is not the case. Lord I pray for any of my children and family who are lost. I pray they seek salvation before it is too late. I look forward to the day I can look on your face and be united with my loved ones. I thank you so much Lord for my precious family. You have given me so many blessings in my life to treasure.

Again I ask blessings on our lives Lord, get us to a happy time. It has been such a struggle the last 5 years. Please let us get our bills caught up, the business going well and Jerry healed and healthy and let us have 2 weeks for a vacation with our kids camping across the country.

I ask all of these things
In Jesus Name
Amen

It had only been a few days since the hospital visit for the biopsy, we knew it was a large mass and that it was Squamish cell carcinoma, same thing that he had on his tongue before. We were waiting to get an appointment with the Dr. to find out what to do next. I know there are many people fighting this dreadful disease and that they would get us in asap, but it sure didn't seem that way at the time.

When you are so scared of what is coming and what you are fixing to go through, your life suddenly seems to be in slow motion. Your mind is constantly racing in every direction with so many what ifs and scenarios and how you are going to handle each one? All of a sudden your life is so very different, its almost as if it really isn't your life at all. I think that's because you don't have any control over what is happening, but what we have to remember is that God is in control and he doesn't make mistakes and everything is according to his plan. And even though we don't understand right now, we will. Satan doesn't want us to believe that, so he will plant doubt and make us nervous and uncomfortable. There is nothing he likes better then for a Christian to squirm. But he can and will be defeated, we as humans can be defeated, there is only one who can never be defeated, so where are you going to put your trust?

When there is so much uncertainty in your life and how things are going to go, it is so unsettling. You feel so weak and hopeless. This is satan using the situation to pull you down. Everything happens good or bad according to Gods plan. God allows these valleys to teach us, to strengthen us, but he will not make us walk them alone, he is always with us. For me this uncertainty is the worst feeling there is, I would rather know how bad a situation is and then I know how to prepare for it.

Journal entry May 21, 2010

My Lord, hold me please. I am so close to tears right now, the kind you have when you feel helpless and don't know what to do. I am helpless but I do know what to do. I am going to trust in you. I feel your holy spirit Lord, fill me up, leave no room for doubts and fears. Keep my family safe.

Please God let them call with an appointment and get his treatments started. Please lay your healing hands on him. Give us peace of mind Lord please. I also have special prayer for my kids.

Don't let them be swayed. I am very concerned about things I saw written in his yearbook. Casey didn't write it, but a close friend did and its not something I would expect. I am really shocked Lord, remove these thoughts from all of their minds. Keep my kids on the straight and narrow, keep them out of satans hands, don't let him use them for one second. Use them Lord for your Glory.

Bless our church. We really need you right now. Strengthen and unite us. Satan is on the move, there are so many families right now, including mine, facing life and death situations. Let us plant many seeds and grow our church. Lord bless our VBS this year. I pray we have many saved and I pray that we get at the very least 1 new family for our church. Let us help them to grow in their faith as this church has helped mine.

I pray for our charity and business Lord. I gave it to you a long time ago. I pray for a lot of donations to get sales up. You know I am willing to work hard, I just need something to work with. Bless me Lord with all that I need to get through this valley. My faith is in you and you alone.

Lord please heal my sweet husband, please keep him here a while longer. Please let us have at least a few more years. We will use it to work for you God, just lead us. Give me strength, health, and peace of mind Lord to get through all of this. I am going to try and lose weight and get my own health in better shape, please help me.

Thank you Lord
In Jesus name
Amen

If it seems like I was doing a lot of begging at this time, I was. I was constantly pleading with God to heal Jerry completely, I didn't want to lose him. But it didn't matter what I wanted, it was more about what God wanted. I knew this, but I was having a difficult time accepting it. You try so hard to keep on living your life through these times, because life keeps on going. You can't just crawl in a hole and hide. There is work to be done and graduations, weddings, and showers to attend. There are Drs appointments, chemo, and radiation treatments.

But there are also the times we just need to be still, to pray, to meditate, to listen. There are times we need to just sit or lay beside those that we love who are sick and talk and more importantly listen. When you are the care taker, you have to focus on the one who is facing this, its about them and what they want. This is also a good time just to talk about your lives together, your memories, your good times. Talk about your hopes for the future, and pray for them. Also as hard as it is, you need to talk about what ifs in the event God has different plans. This is so hard to do because you feel like if you talk about it that you are giving up hope, but it is definitely something that needs to be done. As hard as it is to do, it gives you both peace in different ways. It gives the person who is sick the peace in knowing that their loved ones are going to be ok. This is so important when they are so sick and they need to focus on getting well and getting through the pain and strife that comes with battling serious illnesses. Then it gives the family peace in knowing that if things do get bad, that you will know what the person who is sick wants done.

Journal entry May 22, 2010

Lord I am so tired, please keep me going. I was so down yesterday afternoon. Jerry went to bed at 6:30 pm, he sleeps a lot, I pray it's the pain medicine and not the disease. But anyway the kids were gone and I was lying in my hammock, I felt so melancholy. I remember so well the first time Jerry looked at me, really looked at me. I fell for him in that moment. He truly is my soul mate, and I thank you for him.

Today is Taylors' graduation, Yeah !!!!!! She has done so well, we are all very proud of her. Let today go well. I wish Jerry were going. I have mixed emotions right now, I am very happy for my sister and her family while being very sad about the uncertainty of mine. Will Jerry be there next year to watch Casey get his diploma? My God, my Lord, please let it be so. Heal him Lord please.

I love you Lord, I trust you, my faith is in you alone, Thy will be done.

In Jesus Name
Amen

Today is March 18, 2011 and you just don't know how hard it was to write this page. Jerry has been gone almost 3 months now and within the next few weeks Casey and Anna will be attending their senior prom and shortly after, their high school graduation along with their friends. I am so thankful for their friends, they are the best group of young people you have ever known in your life. They are all so close, and even when they don't see eye to eye they are always there for one another. I would do anything for any of them.

It seemed that everyday brought a new trial. We received a summons on an old hospital bill from Jerrys last health crisis. Satan was beating us down every time we turned around. He was trying so hard to break us. Not only is he a liar, he must not be too smart either, he just pushes me closer to God and God allowed it to prepare me, to strengthen me for what was and is about to come.

Journal entry May 23, 2010

Lord empower me with your Holy Spirit. Don't let me weaken under satans pressure.You alone can lift me up and get me through this valley. Lord let this lawsuit from the radiologist be resolved without any problem. Let me get all of my bills caught up. Lord please let us get enough donations to make good sales to get them paid. Lord, I don't understand why these huge valleys keep popping up before me, I am tired, but I will never give in to satan. I am your child Lord, and even though I don't understand why you keep allowing these mountains for me to climb, I will never doubt you. My faith is in you alone, I can only do what you allow me to. I trust in your plan for me Lord, lead me, use me, let me be a light to others who are lost. Lord bless other families going through this, it can be just as hard on the family as it is on the person who is sick. Bless my kids, especially Casey, I know he is worried.

I pray in Jesus name
Amen

Journal entry May 24, 2010

Lord touch me, steady my mind and let me think clearly. Lift this fog from my mind and open my ears to hear clearly what it is you want me to do. Guide my footsteps, control my every decision to keep me in the center of your will. Lord I am scared out of my mind, but, I give you Glory for each day. I praise your precious name in spite of the devil. I am your child Lord, do with me as you will, my faith will not falter. I don't know how people go through the valleys without you.

Lord I am suffering so much watching my beloved husband going through this. Its as if the life is draining out of my once strong, hardworking man. I know it hurts him Lord, please cure him, heal his body. Give us Grace, all of us, to get through this. Bless others we know going through this. Bless our church, church family, youth group, pastor, and church leaders. Strengthen us and grow us, use us. Let us have many saved at vacation Bible school.

In Jesus name
Amen

We wanted so much to get our non profit established and get the store turned around. But it seemed that there wasn't anything that would go right, it was taking too long. I began to notice Jerry withdrawing more and more. He was afraid of what he was facing, he was still holding up better then I ever could. I know he was concerned about me and the kids. He knew I was a strong person, but he realized what the devil was doing to us. I didn't want him to worry about anything but getting well and getting strong again. I did my best to assure him that everything would be ok according to Gods plan. I didn't let him see me cry unless it just snuck up on me. I wanted him to feel confident that I would be ok if God chose to take him home. I am so thankful he could not read my mind or see the fear I was trying to hide deep down inside.

I wasn't strong at all, I had to lean on God every minute of every day to keep from having a complete melt down. I couldn't show my fear because I did not want to put any more on the kids then they were all ready dealing with. I didn't want to make Jerry feel helpless or worry anymore then he already was. My sister would fuss at me about telling the kids everything, but I always told them everything. I would rather them be prepared for any possibility then to be completely caught off guard. I believe people handle things so much better when they know what they are dealing with. If you provide a false sense of security in times like these and things do go wrong, I believe it is more detrimental then when they are prepared for it.

I also used these times when I would sit the kids down and talk to them about what was going on as an opportunity to talk about our faith and trust in God. It was a time to reassure them that no matter what was coming, God would give us the grace to get through it, and with Casey I would stress to him that his dad was not afraid and that he was fighting as hard as he possibly could to live and that even if it was not Gods will to heal him, he was saved and knew he would be in heaven.

Journal entry May 25, 2010

Lord I pray that it be your will to let us make real progress in setting up the charity and getting the business turned around. If its not your will for us to do so, then let it end today and guide us where you want us to be, doing what you want us to do. When we go to the accountants office let me see with real clarity, your will for us.

I just pray two things Lord, and I pray them with all the faith a child of God can have. I pray that

1. Jerry make it through this and 2. That whatever you have planned for us that it gives us what we need to support our family and that it helps many people, not just ourselves. Lord I don't care how much of me it takes and I may even cry a lot when I am tired and discouraged, but I will take care of Jerry through all of this, he will be first and foremost and I will work hard for the charity if its your will. Bless our church, Pastor, and members, all of who are going through these trials also. Let VBS be a huge success. Keep evil from my children.

In Jesus name
Amen

At this point I was not only dealing with fear, but now anger was slipping in. I had tried everywhere to get help. Our business was sinking further and further into debt and was not making any money. I was so discouraged, I had been to so many government offices to try and get help with Jerrys growing medical bills.(we had lost our health insurance when it rose to $2250.00 a month) I had used our tax refund that we had put up for Caseys college tuition that he would need in just over a year.You know I am thankful to be a child of God, I can see how people who don't have faith can snap and go postal.When you work all of your life and pay into the system and then when you need them, it is enraging when they won't help you.

Six years ago our household income was over $ 90,000.00 a year.We were not rich, but we paid our bills, drove good cars, and took 3 family vacations a year. If you had told me we could be in this position now, I would have said you were nuts. I don't care what kind of job you have, how much money you make, how much you have saved, this *can* happen to you.And what I want everyone to think about is that the government is not going to look out for you.They do not care about all of the money you have paid in over the years. If you have worked all of your life and have a home and others things that you have worked and paid for, they will not help you. I am not saying you should be able to keep all of your "toys" but your home?

I have filled out many forms for employees over the years who wouldn't work half of the time, yet they got Medicaid and food stamps and low rent.They had full medical coverage to have yet another baby, but we couldn't get help with getting the treatments he needed to save his life.What is going to happen when all of the people who do work and pay the taxes that fund these programs are all gone.The ironic thing is that social security that you pay in will go before the programs that benefit people who haven't worked a day in their lives.

I know for a fact there are people who are "depressed", alcoholic, drug dependent, or bi-polar who draw social security that they haven't paid in, but my husband who was dying couldn't get a dime. Its not right and the laws need to be changed. I thank God everyday for my church, if not for them we would be in the streets by now.

Journal entry May 27, 2010

Forgive me Lord for getting so angry and frustrated yesterday. I am already crazy with worry and no one willing to help us really got to me. Lord I don't understand a system that taxes my money and uses it to help people who won't work and have child after child to get money and don't take care of the children, but when we need help they won't do it. Even though he has paid in social security for years and years and he has had seven by-pass surgeries, and two cancer surgeries, and now a third, he can't get medicare. Its just not right.

I am not going to worry about it anymore, I am laying it at your feet Lord, and I will not pick it up again. I thank you with all my heart for getting us through this. I am learning to take one day at a time and in the mornings when I am done with filling these pages with my prayers and my thoughts, my fears and my joys, I will praise your holy name, you always fill me up, and revive me. When the Holy Spirit moves on me, its like no other feeling, I can't even begin to describe it to a lost person. I just pray that I live my life as a light for Jesus. I pray I plant at least one new seed a day. Lord please bring Jerry through this valley and let him stay with us a while longer.

Let us get donations in, a lot of them so we can get sales up and keep the store open until we get our non profit going. Lord I know what I want to do with it now and I pray its your will and maybe its why we have been through all of this these past five years. Lord I have never been so distraught and felt so helpless and frustrated. No one should have to worry about what's going to happen when going through a health crisis.

Now I know I can't pay the medical bills of everyone who can't afford health insurance (not yet) but if we could raise enough money to pay the initial payments and get them started with treatments asap, it would be a good beginning. The hospital we are dealing with has been good to us. I would like to help their program. Lord use me to do this if it is your will, it should not be a punishment for people to work hard all of their lives to have something and have to be denied help when they are going through hard times and run out of money. Your word says for a man to eat he has to work, and we have worked hard, you know this. You know I would not turn down anyone you send me, but I really feel the working people need a hand through the hard times. I get so angry dealing with these organizations and so called help. I pray you empower me to do something about it. Use me Lord to do good. I will give you all of the Glory and praise for it Lord. I want to do it, I just pray it is your will for me to do it.

Lord if Casey Quit basketball just because of the cost and not because of playtime and coming in late, then work it out for him. Not at the expense of someone else, but for him. Watch over my children Lord, keep them safe and keep satan and his demons from them.

God I pray for Gene and Mayford and all those who we had requests for.

I pray in Jesus sweet name
Amen

Journal entry May 28, 2010

My precious Lord, thank you for holding me up through all of this. I know its not my strength but yours. It amazes me when people think I am strong, I do have a strong faith, but it is you who gives me the hope and strength to get through. Lord I ask your healing hand for Jerry, heal his cancer completely, restore his strength so that he can do what ever he wants to do.

I am thankful you sent Bro. Charles our way yesterday, after talking to him again, I really felt like this is the way your will is. If not then guide all of us. He has visions of good things, similar to ours. He wants to help people and to do your will Lord, please let this be your plan. Let this be what we have waited 5 years for. We are so tired and to have some help to get it back on track would be awesome. I especially look forward to some quality time with my husband and my kids. I thank you, I love you, I praise you

In Jesus name
Amen

As we got closer to the day Jerry would begin his chemo (June 3) he started talking about seeing Don and Ruth and Bob. These were his brothers and sister in law. We had planned to hopefully make a trip out west to see Rick and then come back down and see Mike and his family. Its like he wanted to make sure he had gotten to see everyone in case this got really bad. I was praying constantly that God would allow him to stay strong enough to make these trips, and provide us the money to make them. They seem to be so important to him and I was going to do whatever it took, Lord willing, to make it happen . . . .

The full force of this storm was baring down on us and the closer it got the scarier it looked. I don't care how much you prepare, you still have a fear of the unknown. It reminds me of when Paul was on the ship in the storm. God had told him the ship would be lost but no lives would be lost. He had peace because God had told him to stay on the ship. This is what faith will do, while the storms still come, we can have calm and peace if we just trust in him.

CHAPTER 4

Raging Storm

Memorial weekend, Jerry was so weak and still was determined to go camping at the state park where Don and Ruth were working. So Casey and I packed up our camping equipment and we took off. We had never been to this one before so we were trying to go the fastest way so Jerry wouldn't get sore from riding. It poured rain and stormed on the way there but Casey did good when he was driving. In fact I think he drove the whole trip.

When we got there we set up the tent and made the beds, Jerry didn't stay up long he was exhausted and his head hurt him so bad. I guess it was the mass pressing on his artery. He spent a lot of time in the bed, the pain pills made him sleepy, but boy did he enjoy his visit when he was awake. Don called Bob and he made plans to come spend some time with him.

It was hard for them to see him this way. He has always been so strong, and now to see him so frail was heart wrenching. Little did we know it would get worse. He wanted so badly to do more, but he just couldn't. I am so thankful we made that trip, it would be our last trip away from home together.

Journal entry May 31, 2010 Memorial Day

Lord I don't know where to begin. First thank you for a nice and safe trip to see Don and Ruth, and Bob. Jerry felt so bad and slept most of the time but he was glad to get to see his brothers. So much is coming up, it all makes my head spin. First and most important right now is Jerrys chemo. Please Lord, let us get through this. Let these first two treatments get it all so he won't have to do anything else. Heal him Lord, please.

Then Casey is going with Candace and Taylor to Florida for a week and Kaylain is going to spend a week or two with her Daddy. Let them all have a wonderful time and get there and back home safely. Keep me focused, keep me strong, keep me in the center of your will. Let our meeting with Pastor Charles be productive and good. Let us come up with a plan that will help us both and help many people. I pray your hand is in it. I love you Lord, I trust in you.

In Jesus name
Amen

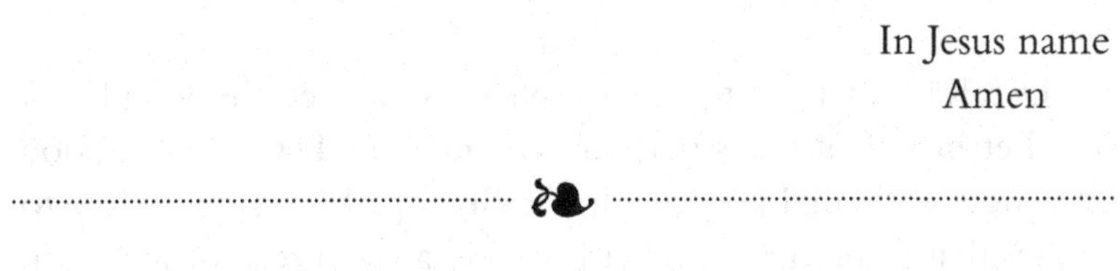

Journal entry June 2, 2010

Lord please bless me today with strength, and stamina. Let me get much accomplished at work and here at home. Let me get everything up stairs where Jerry will be, cleaned and disinfected. I pray your loving, healing hands on him these next few days. Please Lord let his side effects be minimal and let the chemo wipe out all of the cancer cells. Please I beg of you Lord, you are the only one who can.

Put a protective hedge about us Lord, don't let satan in during this vulnerable time when we are weak and worried, keep him away. I pray the same for Gene, Mayford, Kathy, and any who are going through tough times right now. Heal Miss Clara, I pray they got all of the cancer off of her nose. Let her heal quickly. Lord be with Ambers family, death is such a sad time when we don't know if that person was saved. I hope that she was.

I pray you help me through this financial crisis and that you send me donations to put out and get our sales up. Let me start to make real progress with my bills Lord, please. I thank you Lord for sending people my way each day with words of encouragement, they are such a blessing to me.

Lord I ask you watch over my kids while they are out of town, especially Kaylain. Protect her heart Lord, don't let anything spoil her time with them. Let her have a wonderful time. Satan will use this time to test me, don't let him. I want my family to heal. Keep me always in the center of your will.

I pray that my grand babies will get involved in church even if their parents don't.

Use Kaylain Lord to open their eyes and see the wonder of you. Let her plant seeds that you can nurture. Let her be a good influence on them. I pray that if her Grandpa Dale comes there to see her that things go well. Let her have a good relationship with him and Star, she needs to know her family. Let her have a really good time and enjoy it.

Bless our church Lord, I can see such a difference, help us to grow and become stronger. Let us get more families involved and let them join and grow with us. Use me Lord any way you see fit. I am here to serve you.

Please let us work with Bro. Charles in his ministry, in his vision, if it is not your will to pursue mine then let me be a successful part of his. Just let me pay off my debts and take care of my family and help many people. Let me be a light in a world of darkness and a witness to the lost.

In Jesus Name
Amen

Journal entry June 3, 2010 Happy Birthday mom

Here we go Lord, hold my hand through these next couple of months. I am so tired and my back hurts and I didn't finish cleaning yet. Please keep germs away from Jerry and let him do well with this chemo. Protect him, please heal him. We will honor you no matter what your will and I will give you praise and glory for almost 30 years with my precious husband, but I am pleading for a few more years at least.

Watch over my children, I am worried about their trips, especially Kaylain, but I know no one but you can fully protect her from evil, so my faith is in you. I trust you Lord. Please let her have a wonderful time and want to go back next year. I'm leaving it in your hands. I pray this will be a turning point and maybe next summer the twins can come up here and spend time with us. I will be so glad when they are old enough to come on their own, some day they will, I hope I live to see it.

Bless our business Lord. Multiply our donations and our sales. Please let me work out something with Bro. Charles and his church to do good things. I feel he has the same heart that we do, to help people. Let us work together to do good things. Let us build a business that will put lots of people to work, and teach them how to be good employees, and good work ethics that will help them establish good jobs and support their families.

Let us be a bridge from hopeless to hopeful. Most important let us be good witnesses and plant seeds so that many, many souls are saved. God bless our church, our Pastor, church family and leaders, our youth and bless vacation Bible school next week, let it go well and many souls get saved.

In Jesus Name
Amen

Things were going from bad to worse. Jerry was starting to react to chemo, he was so sick. Some people go through it with no problems, but he didn't do well at all. I didn't know what to do about the business. We were running out of time, our landlord had been so patient. Then there were other problems that just added to the stress. Since Jerry had been sick, the dock had become over run with people dumping their trash and junk. He had always kept it clean, but I just was not physically or financially able to do it. We had posted signs and everything to get people to stop dumping. I wish people knew the cost of getting rid of their trash. The sad thing was, there was a dump two miles down the road.

The store smelled terrible where the roof had been leaking for years and the carpet was mildewed. They wanted the bails of clothing removed from the back room, but no one would buy them because they were wet from the leaking roof and I didn't have $1500.00 to have them hauled off. I was tired and beaten down. I still prayed to get the non profit going and fix things up and turn the business around.

We had so much money and hard work tied up in it, and it was just hard to give that up. I really felt I was where God wanted me, I guess I was wanting it so badly myself that I made myself believe that's what he wanted.

I so longed for the old days. We had really good years in the business, it flourished, until tension between ourselves and our partners began to develop. We had worked together (Harold and I) for 20 years. I thought our friendship was solid. He was like a big brother to me. It was hard to accept that he would deceive me and hurt me. I trusted this man. I even had him as an emergency contact at my sons school, and I didn't trust just anyone with my son. I have always blamed him and some others who were in this together, but now after much prayer, and soul searching I can see where my choices and decisions contributed to our down fall too. I take full responsibility for where I am now. I can say with out a doubt that I have learned many life lessons through all of this.

Now the business, which had been in the forefront of our minds for years, would have to take a back seat to Jerry. At this time I was slowly coming to realize that this would not be an easy road to travel and while I had always leaned on him, now he needed me to be there for him. I can't even begin to tell you how overwhelmed I was. Not only did I have the everyday stresses of being a wife and mother, I had to deal with a failing business, a bankruptcy, and now the uncertainty of a husband with a life threatening illness.

My sweet husband was always a strong man. I remember how fast he bounced back after open heart surgery. He was out in the cold with my son and brother-in-law repairing a broken water line six weeks after surgery. If it was nice outside, he was working on a project of some kind. This was kicking his butt, and he hated it and I hated it for him.

Journal entry June 4, 2010

HELP ME LORD !, please. Please get satan off my back, set me straight in what your will is for me. Every time I think things will get better more burdens unload on me. I am tired Lord and I will keep going if its your will. I just ask that you let me know that its your will and make the way a little easier. Please God, I am your child, and I want only to please you, so show me how to do that.

Bless us Lord with what we need to get out of debt and allow us more time with our family and more time for our church. Lord give us happy times, its been five years of stress and worry. Last night for example: just got Jerry home from first chemo and I find out the landlord is not happy about the trash and junk on the dock again. I don't have the money to hire that mess cleaned up every other day and I have posted signs and done all that I know to do.

Then Casey woke me up at midnight sick on his stomach and with a headache. Then the chemo kicked in at 5:30 am and Jerry started throwing up, which made me queasy. He is not drinking enough fluid either. Give me grace Lord to continue on, to get through this.

I love you so much Lord and I know only you can ease my mind and make things better, I pray for your guidance Lord, because I don't know if I am where you want me to be. If I am not, then put me there. I only want to do what you want me to. I don't care what I have to give up in material things, just please let us keep our home and a way around so we can earn a living. Help me Jesus, help me please.

I know in the future I will read these pages and will be filled with joy to see how you moved in my life at this time. If it were not for your grace I would not have made it these past ten years. Bless me Lord, I need you always, but especially right now. Bless all those on my prayer list.

In Jesus Name
Amen

2nd Journal entry June 4, 2010

Lord, I'm back. I'm tired and my head hurts. I fixed Jerry a cheese omelet an oatmeal, he ate one bite. I know how important it is for him to eat so please give him an appetite. Don't let me get stressed out and not be helpful to him, he needs me right now.

Give me strength, let this be a good day.

In Jesus name
Amen

Journal entry June 5, 2010

My precious Lord, fill me with your Holy Spirit, I need my comforter right now. I am weary but I am not down. I know that you surround me with your precious love. Hold me, Lord. I need you more then ever. Let my joy that I get from my salvation bust through this veil of darkness that Satan has put about me. Let me be a light for you in this dark world that is controlled by him. Even in this valley Lord, fill me with happiness so that others will see how you work in a faithful Christians life.

Job was such an example of a man of faith and I certainly don't want to go through what he did, but I know that my faith is strong enough to carry me through whatever your will is for me and I know satan can only do what you allow him to, so I trust in you for the grace I need to over come what may.

I thank you with all of my heart Lord for all of my blessings, right down to the very smallest that we take for granted. Even if it were your will for this cancer to take my sweet husband I would still thank you for all of these years you have given us together.

I am thankful for the child you gave us together to bind our love even more if that is possible, what a blessing he has been to us, and the joy of Jerrys' heart. If it weren't for Casey I don't think Jerry would fight as hard.

I am grateful for our older boys, Rick and Mike and the grand babies they gave us, even though we don't get to see them as much as we would like to. I am grateful for my little Kaylain although I am glad she is with me, I hate the reasons that she is. She is my little companion now that Casey is grown and has a wonderful girlfriend, and his life is starting to go in a whole new direction. He is almost through high school and these next ten years will bring many changes in their lives, college, marriage, probably children, careers. I just pray that through it all they will continue to keep you first in their lives, keep their feet planted firmly on the path of righteousness and they share their love of you with everyone they meet.

I love you Lord, I praise you
In Jesus Holy name
Amen

I was getting worn down by the stress and worry. My mind raced all through the night, every night, making it impossible to get enough rest. I was not managing my time well. I began to slip in my prayer time and Bible study was lacking too. I still prayed a lot, it just isn't quite the same as that one on one quiet time, when no one else is around that I was missing. Those to me are the most important prayers, because when you block out the world and concentrate on your prayer and meditation, you open your heart and mind to God and then you will be able to hear him when he wants to talk to you.

I was also so afraid, Jerry was so sick. I have never in my life seen anyone throw up as much as he did. He literally filled one of those small trash cans ¾ of the way full. I knew he had to be getting dehydrated because he wasn't drinking hardly any fluids. I didn't know it at the time, but I should have taken him right then to the hospital, made him go. So anyone who might be reading this and just beginning to deal with chemo, if they go more then 24 hours throwing up and not drinking enough fluids to re-hydrate, get them to the hospital. He was getting weaker and weaker. I was praying so hard and it didn't seem like God was listening. Why would he let him suffer so much.

Jerry never complained. He was one of those people that did not want to be a burden to anyone and he didn't like to be coddled. I remember laying my hand on his head or chest to make sure he was breathing. Try sleeping through the night when you are so afraid that the person you love may take his last breath while you are asleep.

Its terrifying, you jump at every little noise. Then when you do wake up you can't go back to sleep, this is when your mind wanders, all of the what ifs take control. I think the mass had to have partially blocked his airway because sometimes he would sit straight up and gasp for air. This would scare the devil out of both of us and I would be awake the rest of the night, Finally he started to get better a little each day. He finally got strong enough that he assured me he would be fine for a few hours while I went and tried to work some at the store.

Journal entry June 7, 2010

Lord my body is tired, but my soul is willing. Lead, guide, and direct me. I truly don't know if Bro. Charles is the way you want us to go, if his non profit is who you want me to work for, I am ready, make it happen. I am so tired Lord, Jerry was sick all night. This is really scaring me, I have never seen him so sick, so down, lay your healing hands on him Lord as only you can. Strengthen his body, and his mind. Send your Angels to fight for him Lord, he can't do it, only you can.

Thank you so much for getting us through this day. Bless Vacation Bible School. Let everything go well tonight and all week. Let us have souls saved, even one precious soul is worth it. Bless Gene and Charlotte, Mayford, Kathy, and Jerry. Thank you Lord for your grace.

In Jesus name
Amen

Journal entry June 10,2010

Lord thank you so much for watching over us. I truly thought Jerry was going to die these past few days. He was so weak when I took him to the Dr. yesterday (which was his birthday). Its so hard to watch him go down hill so fast, he lost another 15 pounds these last ten days. He looks so frail. They gave him intravenous treatment for dehydration and gave him some medicines for nausea and vitamins. He finally slept all night and looks so much better this morning. They gave him some new medicine for nausea so I pray that it works. As soon as he is able I'm going to fix him a big pot of beans, fried potatoes, and cornbread and slaw, his favorite meal.

I am thankful that Rick and his family are coming up in a few weeks, its been so long since we have got to see the kids. Rick said he and Robin are back together and things are good. Thank you Lord for that. I ask you also touch Michael and his family, make it strong and get them in church. Let Kaylain plant seeds while she is there, especially with Michael and Elizabeth. Let this week with her family be the best she has ever had with them, let them heal and enjoy it so she will want to spend more time with them.

Lord bless us with good sales and donations and please let us get something worked out soon with the church we have been talking to. I still want to help people in our situation Lord. Its ridiculous that we can't get help (because we have worked hard to have something) we are in a financial crisis right now. Let all of this be for a good purpose that will make the devil stomp his feet in anger while you bathe in the glory. Use me Lord, I pray.

Bless our church, our Pastor, and our youth. Move among those who are lost at VBS, and let many people get saved, even one is a triumph. Bless us Lord with all that we need.

I pray in Jesus name
Amen

This was the day after Jerrys birthday and we had something special for him.

About a month before Jerry got sick, our little yorkie died. His name was Scooter and we had him for about eleven to twelve years. When Jerry had his by-pass surgery and other surgeries over the past few years, Scooter would always lay with him after I went back to work. This kept him company.

That morning I mentioned it to him, because I was going to work, that it was too bad we didn't still have Scooter to keep him company, he joked and said for us to ask Lecia at church if we could borrow her new yorkie puppy. This got me to thinking, I wish we could get another one, but with our financial situation we just couldn't afford five or six hundred dollars for one. I prayed that morning for God to make a way for us to get another one. I bought a paper on the way to work and when I finished with getting the store open, I started looking under pets. Oh My Gosh, there it was, a yorkie for three hundred dollars. I called the lady and she said she had several. I told Casey, he had over a hundred dollars he said he would put in and I added the rest.

Casey and Taylor took the money and went to pick one out. They came back with the tiniest little girl puppy I have ever seen. She was adorable and so sweet. She was a hit at the store all day. Casey didn't want me to give her to Jerry until they got home from church, so I took her down stairs when I got home and put a gift bag on the counter. When they got home I told Casey to bring her up stairs in the gift bag. Jerry was so tired and was almost asleep. I told him to stay awake for a minute because the kids were home and they had a birthday present for him.

They walked in singing happy birthday. Jerry was so tired he didn't even want to open it, he told Casey, "take it out and let me see what ya'll got me" he barely had his eyes open. But when Casey pulled her out of the bag, his eyes popped open and he raised his head and reached for her saying "Lecia let me borrow her? ",

I said "no baby, this one is yours". He was more excited then I had ever seen him about a gift. He named her Missy and she was his baby from then on. She was such a blessing to him until the day he died.

Journal entry June 15, 2010

As I write this Lord, it is 7:30 a.m. and I am so tired, I feel like I could sleep 24 hours straight. But as long as you give me the strength, I will keep going.

I thank you Lord for Sundays service, I felt you moving on me, I knew I needed to kneel on that alter and pray, I am so weak, but you are so strong. As I told the church, I am thankful for their support and prayers and for these two kids who have been such a help and blessing. I also told them how thankful I am for a mighty God who reaches down and cradles me like a little baby when I am scared. I don't know how anyone makes it through these times without you Lord, you are my rock.

Thank you for making Jerry feel better, I was so afraid you were going to take him a week ago, and though it still may be your plan, right now I am just so glad he is not still throwing up and in pain. I see him getting stronger. I pray with a faithful heart Lord that you lay your healing hands on him and erase every cancerous cell in his body. Heal our lives Lord, its been a long 5 years, actually since 2001. Please let us have as many good years. I pray for Gene, Lord. I am broken hearted that he and Charlotte and Doyle and their families have to go through this. Bless them Lord, strengthen Charlotte, she has been through so many heart breaks these last 5 years. Bless also Mayford and the Watson family. Heal him Lord and let him come home. If its your will that this is his time, then let him come home and be comfortable. Give Deb and all of the family the strength to do all that they need to do, I know how hard it is.

Lord bless our little church, our Pastor, church family and especially our youth.

What a a blessing it was to see them all behind me praying when I lifted my head up from the altar, with all the love a person could handle, they are so special. And Curtis, God love his heart, he worked his tail off with Casey yesterday and wouldn't even take a dime for it. Lord, before summer is over, the end of July, let us have our campout, let Jerry be strong enough and able and let us make this a really special time for all of them. I hope Rick and the kids can stay at least one of those nights

In Jesus name
Amen

I am your humble servant Lord, use me

Journal entry June 21, 2010

Lord I feel so far away from you right now and I know I am the one who has drifted, for you are always there. My faith is in you alone, that hasn't changed, but I am tired, stressed, uncertain, and emotionally drained. I just don't take the time for you in my prayer journal, my bible, and church. Please forgive me Lord I am so unworthy. My burden is nothing compared to what yours was. I can't imagine the pain, fatigue, and hurt that you felt when you carried that cross to your own crucifixion. God you gave your only child to die for me, I am sorry for being so whiney. Please watch over my baby boy today and all week. Give them a safe and uneventful trip. Let Casey have a good time Lord, he needs a break. He works so hard to help me. I hope he takes a lot of pictures. I wish we were all going, I would love to see everyone.

I am tired of that business, I am not making enough to pay the bills much less help anyone. I haven't heard from that church that I was hoping to work with, so I guess he changed his mind. I just want to rest. I don't want to go any farther in debt, please do something one way or the other.

Lord bless our church, its in trouble, there are so many who have left, so many who are sick, and like myself, many who are out of your will. Pull us all together, get us all back in church and strengthen us. Lord lay your healing hands on Jerry, Mayford, Gene, Bud, Suzette, Billie Powers mom, Kathy, and all of those on my prayer list, I can't remember them all, but you know who they are and what they need.

Help me Lord as only you can. I love you, I trust you, I thank you, I praise you

I ask these things
in Jesus precious name
Amen

Journal entry June 22, 2010

Thank you Lord for letting me get the lights at work fixed without letting it cost me a fortune. You always take a crisis and minimize it for me, it amazes me. Bless us please Lord with really good sales the rest of the week and let us get some bills paid. Let us get out of debt and please let us send the kids to college.

Please God, lay your healing hands on Jerry, let this next round of chemo cleanse his body of all cancer cells. Watch over Casey and keep him safe. I love you

Lord, watch over and keep us.

In Jesus name
Amen

At this time, I felt so far away from God. I kept praying, but I couldn't feel him like I usually could. This frightened me and made me feel like a little child lost in a store who couldn't find their father. It's as if I was looking everywhere and yelling out to him, but I couldn't find him. This also began to anger me, I didn't feel like God was keeping his promises to me.

This is why I keep telling my kids and those that I know going through the same thing to be careful, these stressful times are when satan likes to strike. He will attack from every angle. He will plant these thoughts of doubt and fear. Ever had thoughts like : God can't exist or he would do something, I have been faithful. Or, He said he would never leave me nor forsake me, but I don't feel him or hear him. Or, the times when after going years without cussing you let out a string of them, or you think after not smoking for years you should smoke again to calm yourself, or maybe you should buy a bottle of wine and have a glass to calm your nerves instead of turning to God to calm you.

These times are when we have to be even closer to God, this is when we really have to be faithful. What seems like forever to us is but a blink of the eye to him, he does things in his own time. This is what I have the biggest problem with, this is when I get angry. I felt like, I have been praying for so many years and he hasn't given me what I want, and he hasn't answered my prayers. These times are when he speaks to my heart and whispers gently, I have answered you my child, just not the answers that you wanted. It is then that he will show me what he has done for me and what I should be thankful for. We take so much for granted, we don't realize what amazing things he does for us because we are so focused on the bad things that are happening.

Don't let the devil win, when you have these feelings, go to your quiet place and pray. Really, faithfully pray. God will speak to you, I promise. So many times he has pulled me up and gave me what I needed to go a little further. He never promised us tomorrow, he never promised it would be a life without trials and heartbreaks. What he did say is that when we go through these times, he will be right there with us. He doesn't move away from us, we are the ones who move from him.

Journal entry June 29, 2010

Lord why do I feel so far away from you? I know that you haven't moved. I know I love you with all of my heart, and my faith is in you alone. I think I am angry at you because you won't help me the way I want you to. Forgive me Lord, I beg for your guidance in the plan you have for my life. I don't feel like I'm where I am supposed to be or things would be going well.

I guess I just feel sorry for myself. I am so sorry. Lord put me where you want me, that's where I want to be. Take my dream away of a non profit and making the store successful again if its not where you want me.

I would rather have that time with Jerry right now, taking care of him while he struggles to get through this battle with cancer. Please touch his fragile body and heal him Lord. Restore his body. Help me also Lord, I am so tired. Let Casey have a really good week for his birthday and don't let him worry so much, he is still so young. Watch over all of my babies, watch over us Lord.

In Jesus name
Amen

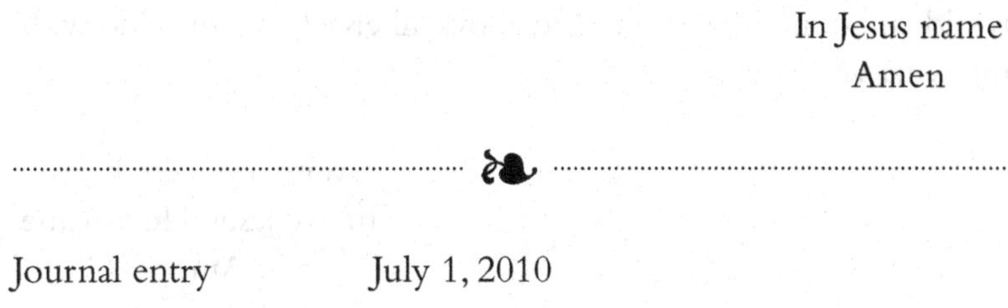

Journal entry July 1, 2010

Lord thank you for getting Mike and his family here safely, thank you for a nice day. Let him and Kaylain have quality time since they don't have a lot of it.

Lord you evidently don't want us in that store, so please get us out of it. I called the city to see if they could help me stop people from dumping and instead they come out and write me a citation and give me seven days to clean up a mess that Casey just cleaned up a week ago or they are going to fine me. On top of this the roof has been leaking for over a year or more, which has mildewed the carpet, the lights are shorting out catching on fire, and then there's the bats that keep invading us. Add to that poor sales which have us one hundred thousand dollars behind on rent. Twenty five thousand behind on taxes, and all of this while dealing with my husbands cancer which in turn produces huge medical bills because we have no health Insurance, that was canceled when we got behind on the $ 2250.00 per month premiums.

Forgive my anger and frustration Lord, you know I am repenting with a faithful heart. Its just I am so tired and for the life of me I don't understand why you allow this.

I am angry Lord, I do trust in your plan but, when can I relax, its been 5 years.

My mighty God, I am asking in your son Jesus' name to please give us what we need to get out of this mess. I believe your word Lord and you said you wouldn't put more on us then we could bare. You said you would never leave us or forsake us. My faith is in your word so forgive me when I get angry and tired. When all is said and done I love you Lord above all else. I am yours, do with me what you will.

With a sincere heart
In my Jesus' Holy name
Amen

❧

Journal entry July 8, 2010

Lord I am going forward with this bankruptcy. Please let us raise enough money to pay off all of our debt and still be able to keep our home and vehicles and personal belongings. I am not listing anything that belongs to the kids. That wouldn't be right.

Lord please let me come up with the money for another cheaper car I can pay cash for and get out from under that debt. I pray Lord to sell out the business and pay off all taxes and as much if not all that we owe white realty. I don't feel anyone else has been fair and helpful. You know who they are Lord, if I am wrong about them then show me.

I pray that this process doesn't take long and that I am free from it all soon and that I can do something that I will enjoy and that will please you. I would love a little antique store or a little mom and pop restaurant. Mon—Fri. breakfast and lunch only.

Something not so stressful. I continue to pray for all of the prayer request I have. Bless us all Lord with what we need.

In Jesus name
Amen

Journal entry July 16, 2010

Thank you Lord for being right here with me through all of this. I don't know what it is that you want me to do or where you are leading me, but I pray that you clear my mind and my heart so I will be focused on your plan and to know that I am in your will. Please let us get through this and be able to pay our bills and send the kids to college.

God you are the all powerful, all mighty and nothing is too big for you. Please calm these stormy waters that are my life right now. I just want you to cradle me in you arms and comfort me, calm me. I want to feel your Holy Spirit Lord. Since it is your will to move me instead of this mountain that has been before me for so many years, please let the journey be calm and stress free. Let us have peace. Lift us up Lord, use us for your glory.

Please lay your healing hands on Jerry as well as Gene, Mayford, Bud and Kathy as well as all of those we have requested prayer for at church. Please let Jerry tolerate this chemo and radiation treatments that he is starting next week. Let him be able to eat and keep up his strength and his weight. Get us through this Lord as only you can. Thank you for good news and progress for Gene, I know this is answered prayers. I can't wait to see Mayford at the wedding tomorrow I pray he will be home soon.

Lord please hold back the rain and storms tomorrow for James and Megans wedding. I pray for the marriage of these two wonderful young people Lord, they both have been through a lot in their young lives, yet they are wonderful people who love you.

Bless their marriage and their lives.

I ask all of these things
In Jesus name
Amen

I was trying so hard to focus on the good things of life that were going on at the time. Weddings, showers, graduations, any and everything that brought a few minutes of happiness to our nightmare. Then something else would come along to ruin it. To ruin what precious few moments of fun we could find.

I knew most of my fear and sadness would go away if I would just focus more on God. I was letting the devil sneak his way in and I had to stop him. God is the only way to do that. But ole satan just kept throwing stuff at me right and left.

Journal entry July 25, 2010

First it's a water leak we can't find and our water bill is up $20.00 a month, then as soon as I got to work the other morning, Jerry calls to tell me CUB is there to turn the power off. All this and trying to keep up with the store, Dr. appointments, and getting stuff together for the lawyer is just too much.

Its Sunday morning Lord, Rick and the kids are here, my back is killing me and Jerry is sick. I really want to go to church and take our family to meet everyone, so please make it possible. I need to be there, I need to be filled up. Help me, I need you. Jerry needs you, we are your loyal servants.

In Jesus name
Amen

Oh how tired I was. The devil was all over me, I was resisting as hard as I could, but there were moments that I caved in. Usually it was a cuss word, crying hysterically, or just withdrawing from God. I didn't study my Bible, I would turn to it once in a while for comfort, but not study. I didn't dedicate my time each day to God that I had done for years, I would go days at a time without sitting down with my journal. Most of the time it was just sheer exhaustion, but there were times when I thought, what's the point, it doesn't do any good. I have begged him but he doesn't answer. When the body is this tired, the mind is weak, and that's when satan pounces.

When I would go through these periods of weakness and lack of faith it would make me feel so guilty. After a few days of these attitudes, it would hit me, I am such a disappointment to God right now and I would then have some of the best prayer times I have had in my life with him. You can tell these times in my journal because I would write pages and pages. I would be so deep in prayer that I could feel the Holy Spirit in every fiber of my being.

You don't have to be in church or on the alter for God to move on you in a way that you know its him. I have had some of my best conversations and prayer with him when I'm alone in my car. I know people have been beside me or behind me and wondered what in the world is that woman doing? There have been times that I am so filled with the Spirit that I will have my hand raised to Jesus, and tears just rolling, I will be having revival, just me and Jesus. But, if you feel the Holy Spirit moving you to go to that alter, you best put one foot in front of the other and get there. If you have to drag your body up there, just go, because I promise you, you will float back to your seat if you have been obedient.

We tried to get to church as much as possible. There were times that I know Jerry would be so sick, or so weak, but he would go. You need your church, the fellowship is important. You need the messages the pastor is giving you, and you need the words and prayers of your brothers and sisters in Christ. I know of many times that I would make myself go and the message would be exactly what I needed to hear. So if I had given in and not went, I would have missed it. The times we couldn't go we would watch one on t.v.

Journal entry July 29, 2010

My kind and loving Lord, I have wandered so far from you. I mean, I pray everyday, many times, but I feel they are hollow prayers, just words. I feel lonely and I know that I am not alone. I feel numb and lost. I don't even want to get out of bed because I feel so tired all of the time. I am in pain a lot and I don't know what it is. I cry so easily these days. I never thought I could feel so down, because I have so much faith in you, but I do.

These past few weeks have been so much to deal with at one time. Jerry is not tolerating the chemo very well and I am so scared of losing him. Please don't let that be your will Lord. Give us a few more years together to enjoy each other, we have been so busy raising kids and running a business that we have had little time just to do things together, just the two of us.

Kaylain found her mom (or rather I found her). They have been talking every since. Now she wants to go out there to live. I just want her to be happy. I know she wants to be with her mom, she has always wanted to live with one of her parents, to be a part of their family.

She can't stay with her Dad, she won't even go for a visit unless I go with her and even then it stresses her out. I am afraid that she is expecting to much. She has this perfect life imagined in her mind. I want her to go spend the summer and then make up her mind. I have talked to her, I have explained that her step dad would not love her and Kierra like he does his own. Its easy for a person with no children to accept another persons child and love them as their own, or so they think. The truth is we as humans can not love anothers child like we love our own and anyone who says they can is lying. If they don't have children then they can't compare the love they are feeling. We can give a step child a lot of love, but, its different from the love we have for the child God created for us. The key to being a good step parent is not to show the difference, never treat them differently. I hope Gina and her husband have considered the way their lives will be turned upside down. Two teenagers on top of he two little ones they already have. The cost of living for their family will increase greatly, and they can't expect financial help from anyone because we can't, not now anyway. They will have to share the time they spend with Madison and Haley with Kaylain and Kierra. I'm afraid there may be some jealousy, which would only be normal. Kaylain is used to having a lot because until the past couple of years we have always provided well for she and Casey. They have been places and seen things that most people don't see in a life time. I am just afraid she is expecting to much. I am afraid after the newness has worn off she won't be happy. I pray for your guidance Lord, I pray your will be done in this and all matters in my life right now.

Lord please this week, let me get everything together for the lawyer, let me get a lot of stuff sold, I wish I could just sell the whole thing as a business. Please let the kids have a wonderful time on their campout, I wish Jerry and I were going. We have always enjoyed the campouts with the kids and their friends.

Its been such a long week. Jerry has been so very sick from his treatments. He has lost 36 pounds. Today is the first day in a week he has been able to keep food on his stomach. On top of that I haven't been feeling well and the kids are here from Oklahoma and we haven't been able to do much with them. I think its been a little much for Jerry, but at least he has gotten to see them.

We lost a very good friend and brother in Christ this past Sunday. He was the head Deacon at our church and a man of good character. He was a soft spoken man, but

Everyone knew he ment what he said and he was a just man. He was the patriarch of a good family and his legacy will live through his family. I know where he is and we will see him again. I pray that you comfort and bless his family Lord, especially Ms. Betty, she is not well herself.

I pray you also be with Bud and his family. I pray for Molly and the girls and Will, this is hard for them. If we can do anything for them please show me what and how. They too are a wonderful family and he has raised them to be good Christians. Casey dates his granddaughter Anna, and has for almost three years. We love her a lot, she precious. I know they are young but, I hope someday they will get married because I really do believe they are meant to be together. But that is up to you Lord.

I pray for your guidance, I pray for your direction, for your will. I don't feel like I am doing what you want me to because things are so bad. I am just going to sit here and wait on you, Lord. Please get me back to the center of your will. Fill me to the top with your Holy Spirit. Get me back spiritually to where I was. Satan is on me so bad, please put your loving arms around me and let me feel peace and joy. I won't give in ever, and I know that's why he is after me, so I beg you Lord, put him in his place.

I pray these things
in Jesus name
Amen

Journal entry July 31, 2010

Wow what an afternoon. Lord the devil is trying hard right now to ruin our kids, he is on them so bad. Lord, give all of us adults wisdom to guide and direct them. Don't let satan evoke anger in us so that we become a bad example to our children. You know we are weak when it comes to our families and satan can use this when it comes to our witness.

Lord, I was so angry to think someone would question my kids witness, but when I got up to where the man was and he and CG were screaming at each other, I came to the realization that anger was not the Christian way. When I saw the looks on the faces of the kids, not only ours, but others who were around us, I felt so ashamed and wanted it to end right there.

God I want to take this moment to ask you to wrap your arms around me, when I let satan get to me, and stop the anger. There really is something to be said for the phrase

"What would Jesus do?" I think this is something that not only myself, but, CG, Vickie, the man from the campground and anyone who has trouble keeping their anger under control should keep in mind. I am going to do my best to take that literally when I find myself in these situations. I love you so much Lord, as do these kids and I want them to continue to grow in their faith. Please let them learn from this, let them learn only good not bad.

In Jesus Precious Name
Amen

Journal entry August 20, 2010

Lord, what is it that you want from me, I just don't know. These five and a half years I feel like I'm walking through hell. Why Lord? I don't understand. I live right, and obey your commandments. You know my heart. You know I don't only talk the talk, but also walk the walk.

I know that just because I'm a Christian doesn't mean that I won't go through difficult times, but does it have to be one after the other, two or three at a time. Take today for example. Had to spend another five hours at the hospital with Jerry. He is so sick from chemo, I had to write a letter to our landlord begging for a few extra weeks so I can get the bankruptcy filed and get a trustee, and on top of that we have a water leak which is running my water bill up to $90.00 that's double what it usually is. The bad thing is I don't have a clue how to find it. Then my sister called to tell me that the finance company is looking for my car and I haven't yet been able to find any with what little money I have. On top of all this I am sick.

Lord what is it you want from me, you have my soul, you have my heart, my faith is in you alone, I have not faltered. Set me right in the middle of your will right now Lord. I'm not asking for worldly riches, only what I need to take care of my family and send Casey to college. I guess Regina will send Kaylain.

I know Michael is mad, but, what does he expect from her. She can't stay with him, and he knows why if he is using his brain. She can't have any quality time with him, and there is always drama, it gets on my nerves. The only way he is ever going to have a relationship with her is to plan time with just her. It really did something to her (even though she didn't want to go) when he didn't take her back to visit. All the stuff that was said to her before they came, Mike would not be happy if he knew. If he says anything to me I am going to tell him. I hope one day they can have a close relationship, I just hope its not too late.

Now the most important things, I love you, I praise you and I thank you, because in spite of it all, I am blessed and I am your child.

In Jesus Name
Amen

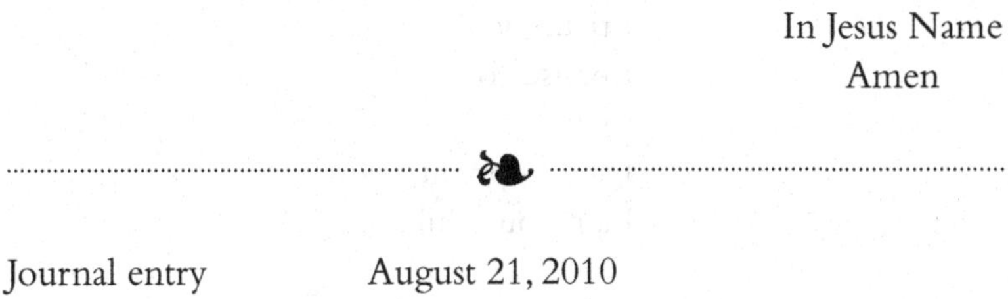

Journal entry August 21, 2010

New day, new mercies. Thank you Lord for being so patient with me. I know I disappoint you more often then not. But, we will slip, that's why you give us choices. The devil is more powerful then us. I will say in my defense, he may provoke me to anger, beat me to some of the lowest points of my life, take every worldly thing we have (besides what we need) attack our health, put fear in my children, and bring me to tears quite often, but, he has never, ever caused me to falter in my faith and he never will. If this should be the last day I live, I pray someone was touched by my life in a way that gives you glory and that my children know I don't just talk the talk, I do my very best to walk the walk.

I love you Lord, and when I feel alone and can't see an end to all of this strife, forgive me. I don't want to do anything to give satan a smile, I want only to do what will bring you glory, only what pleases you. I want to inspire people to want what I have. Without my salvation and the knowledge that this life is just temporary, I would be so depressed. Lord I don't know where you are leading me, but I trust in you with all of my heart. I know you are in control, my trust and my faith are in you alone.

Lord when the door is closed on this part of my life, I pray you lead me where you want me to be. Use me Lord to do your work in whatever job you provide for me.

Give us all that we need and please let me afford college for my children and please use them, they love you as much as I do.

I love you Lord
I thank you
I praise you
I trust you
I worship you
I am your child

In Jesus precious name
Amen

Journal entry August 31, 2010

Lord, this is the last day in our business, we have given up a lot and suffered a lot and I have trusted you through it all. Now my glass door shattered, we have a water leak that can't find I need money for graduation stuff, we just found out Jerry has fourteen more treatments instead of five, and yet I still trust in you. I am tired and sitting here crying my eyes out, I am in pain from some kind of female problem that I don't have money to get checked, but I still trust in you.

The most hurtful thing of all right now is fighting with my first born. He all but called me a liar and in fact he lied to me. He said he heard me say things that are not so.

The things he said defending that woman is the final straw. I can't believe he is stupid enough to believe the things he said to me. Lord it shreds my heart to pieces, but I am done with it. I will not have a relationship with him if it means dealing with her. If I should ever cross their path, keep me calm and keep me away, keep my mouth shut and my hands to myself, because right now I would finish what I started ten years ago. I would go right through him to do it. That is the most evil, conniving drama queen I have ever seen. She is dangerous. I pray now Lord because I know the day is coming, if she ever does anything to hurt my child or my grandchildren it will be so hard to wait on you to exact your revenge.

Lord you know I have prayed for her and Mike both and I still hope that you deal with their hearts. For now, keep me away because if I see them satan will surely use it.

Please surround me with your love and with your power, and your comfort. I don't want to give in to the devil. I am trusting in you, let me be a good witness and not let me destroy my testimony. Please God, don't let this continue to hurt Kaylain. I would rather take the pain myself. Please Lord, I will lay spread eagle face down on the floor if that's what you want. I have been taught to wait on you, and I have been for years now. I will continue to do so, but, it is so hard. I know the devil is mad because we are back in church and living by your word, but please put him away from us. All I ask is for good health for my family, a roof over our heads, and all that we need to get through this world.

Please Lord, let Jerrys illness and losing the business and the bankruptcy all be handled by October. Please let us go into the holidays with peace in our hearts. I love you so much Lord, and

I praise your Holy name. To you alone be the glory. I pray our burdens are someone else's lesson, or leads them to you Lord, then its all worth it.

I thank you for the sweet Holy Spirit I felt in church Sunday morning as the youth led the service, and I thank you for the joy I felt when my baby boy got up to sing, he sang Hold my heart by Tenth Avenue North. I know he is worried Lord, calm him and comfort him, keep him in the center of your will.

I love you Lord,
thy will be done
In Jesus name
Amen

❧

Going through all of this, I struggled to keep my sanity, and for the most part I did ok.

But, when satan started on my child I was petrified. I didn't care what he did to me, he could take my life right then, but I prayed so hard that God protect the kids. I hate more then anything to see my children hurt and know there is nothing I can do myself, but I can give it to God, who better to protect them.

CHAPTER 5

Eye of the storm

People who live in the south or anywhere that is prone to hurricanes know what the eye of the storm is. When a hurricane hits, it is forceful, the winds are furious, the trees bend over to the ground, often snapping under the pressure. Roofs fly off buildings and homes, windows shatter, debris is flying everywhere. Power lines begin to break, many areas begin to flood. Its terrifying to go through. Then the howling winds slowly fade and there is a calm, a false sense of safely making it through the storm. This is called the eye. People who are not familiar with hurricanes think its over, this is how many lose their lives.

It is a small blessing in that it gives you a short time to catch your breath and assess any injuries and get to a safer place if yours has been too badly damaged to stay there. It gives you a moment to strengthen your resolve and get ready for what's coming.

The bad thing about this time is the false sense of security that everything is going to be ok. As you read this chapter, you can see how we were lulled into a place of calm. Things seemed to be getting better. We were very excited and for the first time in months were making plans for our future. Things were looking good. I was confident that God was finally answering our prayers.

Journal entry September 2, 2010

Lord, thank you for all of my blessings and for Michaels phone call after my big fight with him. I don't like to be at odds with my children. Its about 3:45 am and I have been awake since 1:20 am. There is so much on my mind about getting the business closed, getting stuff finished up for bankruptcy while taking care of Jerry. The trips to the hospital everyday and Drs appointments. I am not afraid, I am just tired. Help me to stay calm and not let satans little demons get to me.

Lord lift me up, not only for my sake but for my little family as well. Use me Lord I pray that wherever I end up after all of this, that it will be helping people, witnessing to them, I want to do good things in your name and I will make sure to give you all of the glory. Lord guide my kids through this school year in their studies and activities. Use them Lord, they love you and want to serve you.

I ask these things
in Jesus name
Amen

Journal entry September 5, 2010

Thank you Lord for the good report from the Drs, Jerrys' cancer is almost gone. I pray that by the time his treatments are done that it will be completely cured. I pray we will sell as much as we are going sell this week and can get out of the business. I give it to you Lord, its too much for me. I am tired. I would love to get it all done and spend fall break in the mountains, just being together, picnicking, relaxing, having fun. Help me to achieve this Lord, please. I love you Lord and I am grateful for all that you do for me.

In Jesus name
Amen

Journal entry September 7, 2010

My precious Lord, lift me up, give me Grace to face the problems these next few weeks. I pray with a faithful heart that by October 1, 2010, Jerry will be cancer free. Your will for the business be done and the bankruptcy settled and finalized and that we have a good start on getting Casey financially ready for college.

I would like to make a special request for Janeens dad, that they remove all of the cancer and he is fine. Give Janeen the grace to get through it. Bless Gene and Charlotte may he get better and Bud also. Bless the families Lord, we know how hard it is.

Thank you for the wonderful labor day celebration at David and Diannas, it was so much fun and nice to get Jerry out in the fresh air for a change. He had such a wonderful time.

I trust in you Lord,
In Jesus name
Amen

Journal entry September 11, 2010

Lord be with the families who lost loved ones on this tragic date nine years ago. I pray for healing. I also pray for grace and strength for Janeen Pointer and her family.

Lord I pray for the meeting that I have with a lady named Becky, if its your will that I be a part of it and can earn a living for a while doing it, then make it happen. But if it is your will that I only assist her in getting started, then use me to do so, I am gladly willing. Whatever your plan is for me in this situation I give you the glory and thank you for the opportunity to help either way bless her with what she needs. Lord I ask for a speedy recovery for Jerry, please let him build his strength back up.

In Jesus name
Amen

Journal entry September 20, 2010

Lord, as I sit here and try and focus on my quiet time with you, I ask that you please touch my body. My back hurts so bad and I keep having sharp pains in my lower left side. I am so tired Lord, my mind doesn't function right now and there is so much to do. Lord I don't understand why everything has to be so hard, you evidently don't want me at this job, so please, I ask for a miracle either way because that is what it is going to take. I ask either something happen to keep the business going or give us the means to clear it out and sell everything for enough to pay off our debts and let things go smoothly and be done with our bankruptcy.

Lord I keep having this strange feeling that I may be the one you are getting ready to call home. Its odd, but I feel like you are getting rid of this business and debts now because there is no way Jerry could handle this. And that we found Gina so Kaylain would have a place to go and that you sent our precious Anna and her family to take care of Casey and be there for him. The only one I worry about is Mike. Take care of him Lord if this is your will. I don't want to go right now, but I am ready if it is your plan. I pray the rapture come so that we will all meet in the sky. You know Lord, I get down and think I have really suffered, then I think of my precious Jesus and what he endured for me and I am so ashamed to even think that I have suffered. I love you with all of my heart. I have great love here in this world for my husband and my children, but there is none can compare to the love I have for you. I want to walk the path that pleases you Lord, and brings you glory.

Saturday morning we had a gentlemen come in and he noticed my Addicted to Jesus shirt that I was wearing. We started talking and then this other lady joined in the conversation and the three of us were getting more and more excited and Katie was standing there listening, I think it may have touched her in a good way. I believe a seed was planted, I pray it was.

Lord I want to ask special prayer for the family friends we have who are going through a really bad time. Their son reminds me of Mike at that age, he is an angry young man, but you know he has a caring heart. He needs you Jesus. Take hold of him and show him how to keep satan from using his anger to hurt others and to destroy his own life. Use his pain for good, just as you did with Billy S. (God bless him). Make Billy realize what he is doing to his kids. There are five lives here Lord, touch them, help them as only you can. The power of addiction is one of satans tools that is so powerful, only you can stop it. Make them see that. If I can help in some way Lord, show me what to do, use me for your glory. This family has been through so much also. Heal them Lord, don't let satan hurt them anymore.

Please wrap your arms around Janeen and her family, I know this is a very scary time for them. Touch her fathers body Lord, and if its not your will to heal him, then give him grace as well as the rest of the family. I love you so much and I know what you have done for my family. I ask also grace for Molly and her family and Gene and Charlotte and their family. I ask you to watch over my kids, give them knowledge to understand their school work and get through college. Use them, their lives, they are your willing children Lord. Well I am going to start my day, take each step with me Lord.

In Jesus name
Amen

Journal entry September 21, 2010

Thank you Lord for another day. Put me where you want me today. Open my heart, mind, and ears to what you want me to do. Praise be to you Lord, today is Jerrys last radiation. This has been a long five months, but knowing he is getting better makes the rest of it bearable.

Lord some one from Community Chest came by and might be interested in buying the business. Please let it be so and let me sell it for enough to pay off my debts. I would appreciate it for three reasons. 1. I will be out from under the devils thumb and 2. It will give white someone to lease the store to, and 3. There would still be a thrift store for the people in this area. If this is your will for me to leave the business then let it go smoothly. If its not then provide a miracle for me to keep it, because I truly don't know anymore.

Touch each person on my prayer request list and those who aren't.

In Jesus name
Amen

This time of my life was so . . . . I can't even think of a description for it. I was so relieved that Jerry was doing better. The Dr. told us that the cancer in Jerrys neck was almost gone. I was so thankful for that. Now I just wanted to get through the bankruptcy and get the business situated one way or another. Every time I thought ok, we are going to close the business, something would happen to make me think God wanted us here. I was packing up, trying to sell stuff, when my landlord responded to a letter that I had written. I can't even remember when I wrote it. Any way he agreed to give us three more months to get our non profit up and going. We were excited. Jerry and I talked about it. I was really tired. My energy was spent. But I was so happy that he was getting better, I was willing to tackle anything. Its hard to give up something that has been your life for so long. We had put so much money, time, sweat, and hard work into the store, it was just so hard to walk away. We thought this is a new beginning, Jerry was almost healed and we were going to move forward with trying to turn the store around. We both enjoyed what we did and we loved all the people who we had come to know and love over the years.

Journal entry September 27, 2010

Lord guide me this week. My mind is like mush right now. I plan to close the business this week and start packing it up. I need to get out. If this is not your will then send me what I need to save it. I won't go looking. I haven't made good decisions it seems. I trust in you Lord, so bring to me what it is you want me to do. I don't feel hopeless at all. I feel overwhelmed and uncertain of what you want me to do so put me where you want me.

I want to thank you Lord for a good weekend. I did get a little rest and I enjoyed Sunday with homecoming and fellowship at brother Davids' and sister Dianas. They are sweet people who love you very much. They love our youth and that is a blessing.

Lord I ask for revival in our church. So much has happened these past couple of years. Almost every family has been touched by satans works this year. We have lost sweet Mayford and so much illness, including Jerrys' cancer. Gene H. and Bud J, so very many. My family has certainly been under attack. But praise your Holy name we have made it through with our faith in tact. We know where our hope lies.

Watch over my children Lord, keep satans hands off of them. Keep them focused on school and let them do well. I ask you to deal with my oldest childs heart. He is going through a lot too. He just hasn't learned who he needs to count on. He seems so dark sometimes. Bring him into the light Lord, show him the way. Please don't harden your heart against him. Deal with him and his wife, Lord bring him happiness and true joy that only comes from salvation.

We are gong into a busy time of year Lord and it peaks with my 2nd favorite time of year, second to Easter. I love Christmas because it is such a festive time of year. But, I feel like its getting too commercial. I think the focus should be put back on its true meaning. The spring time and Easter are my favorite time of year because life is renewing and because of what my Jesus did, my life is renewed and I will live forever with you in Heaven.

I am so blessed to be a child of yours. Because I belong to you, satan will try to beat me down, to steal my joy. He will torment me because I gave my heart to you. Because I gave it to you, it is full of joy and that's something satan can't touch. Oh yes he can take my happiness, but he can never touch my joy.

I face a lot of things right now. Jerrys cancer, my own health problems, the loss of our business, and our financial stability, the pending loss of my baby girl to go live with her mom, the uncertainty of how to get my baby boy through college, the estrangement of my oldest baby and his children. But the one constant in my life is you and for that I am thankful. I give you alone the glory for my life.

In Jesus name
Amen

Journal entry September 30, 2010

Lord I am to that point again. My heart is literally fluttering. The stress has my blood pounding through my head, I am really afraid I will have a heart attack. I felt such relief when we left the attorneys office, one step closer to getting things under control. Then I get home and there is a letter from the mortgage company saying our modification has expired and the payments will be going back up $1100.00 to $1600.00.They took an application to extend the modification, now I have yet another long list of documents to find and fax to them. I pray they will approve it or we will lose the house. I am so tired Lord. Take all of my stress and burdens Lord, I lay them at your feet. I am no match for satan, but you are. Hear me Lord, help me, I need you. No matter what happens, I am your child and my faith will always remain strong, even when the flesh won't.

In Jesus name
Amen

I was so tired, I was beaten down so badly. I just wanted Jerry to get well and to start a new chapter in our lives. The business had been good to us once, but now it was putting us further and further in debt. I wanted a fresh start, a better life for my kids. I just wanted to be able to lay down at night and go to sleep. I wanted normal again.

One night I was laying there thinking, why is God putting me through this? What did I do to deserve this? What lesson was he trying to teach me that I was not learning?

I was overwhelmed with fear, sadness, and uncertainty. I was so thankful that Jerry was getting better and I wanted things to be easy for a while, we needed it.

Journal entry October 1, 2010

Lord let me get out of the store and get everything situated for the bankruptcy. I am so tired and just ready to move on. Please let me be able to extend the modification on our mortgages so I can have time to get back on my feet. I promise not to ever get in this situation again. Except for college or real estate, if I can't pay cash, I won't buy it.

Things will be very tight until I can get a job, so please give us what we need Lord to get through. Lord, I am not sure what other lessons you want me to learn, but I know these past ten years have taught me more then the forty three before them.

LESSONS THAT I HAVE LEARNED

1. That you will do things you never thought you could handle when someone you love is hurting.
2. I have learned that satan can put killing in my heart when someone hurts my family. (but prayer and faith conquer all).
3. I have learned that all though your children are Gods gift, they are also the satans biggest tool. (but no matter what, you don't love them any less.)
4. I have learned that I don't have to make a lot of money to be happy. Trips, things, Luxuries, don't put joy in your heart, God does.
5. I have learned to appreciate the blessings that most take for granted, such as a Good husband that puts up with me, and good kids who love God, and live for Him.
6. I have learned that even people who you know and trust can turn on you, and that You have to really forgive and move on or it will make you bitter.

7. I have learned that belonging to a church with a good church family can help you Through difficult times with prayer and compassion.
8. I have learned that helping others brings more joy then any gift there is. (except Salvation)
9. I have learned the importance in teaching my children good morals and living by Example.
10. Most of all, I have learned the importance of my relationship with God, and that Keeping strong in his word, in my faith, in his love, I can get through anything And everything.

Thank You Lord
Amen

When you are going through so many things at one time and it gets to be so hard to face each day, you tend to push everything deep down inside. Its like you are hiding from it all. You just stand there and do nothing watching your life go by because you just don't know what to do.

You pray and pray and beg God to show you what to do. And you get so mad because you think he doesn't listen, that he hasn't answered you at all. Is this really the way it is?, Has God just turned his back on you?, or are you just not listening to him?

Journal entry October 3, 2010

Long day, loved church. Lord, I hate facing each new day because I don't know what to do, I leave it in your hands. I am tired and my house is a mess, I feel like I am standing here watching my life go by. Please, please I am begging you, get me out of this mess.

Put me in a job that I can really be of help to someone and a job that will please you.

Watch over the kids on their camping trip, keep them warm, keep them safe.

Lord please heal Jerrys throat so that he can eat. I want him to get stronger and put some weight back on. Please let Saturday go well and let us make lots of money to pay on taxes. Let things go well with Katies mom, heal her of this awful infection. Bless me Lord with all that I need to take care of my family, use me Lord for your will.

In Jesus name
Amen

Journal entry October 4, 2010

Lord this morning I pray that you watch over and protect Casey, Anna, and all of those on the camping trip in the mountains (school trip). Be with us today as we continue to try and work out what to do. I am so worried. I know we will get through it, but I am tired of the stress and not knowing. Now we may lose our house. Please Lord at least let us keep that. But if its not your will, I will accept that. I don't know why things won't get better, I know it will be ok. I just wish we could start up the mountain instead of continuing in the valley. Show me Lord what you want me to do. Keep me in the center of your will. Please God don't let satan completely destroy me. Even if this does destroy me, protect my kids.

Lord let my trials be a testimony for your glory and not a win for the devil. I want people to see your grace when they look at my situation and not satans control. I can't fight the devil he is much to powerful for me, but he is nothing for you. Sometimes I feel like going to bed and pulling the shades and just laying there until all of this is settled. But I can't do that. I feel like David facing Goliath. My giant is the IRS, the bank, the landlord, the insurance company, bill collectors, and lawyers. Every day its something.

I couldn't face the day if it weren't for you Lord. I just pray for my normal life with the means to support my family. Give me what I need Lord, that is all I am asking for.

I ask for your grace, your protection, you guidance. I want only to please you Lord, to bring you glory in all that I do. Lead me on the path that you would have me to follow.

In Jesus name
Amen

Journal entry October 7, 2010

Lord tomorrow I will be fifty three years old. I had planned to be retired by now and have Caseys college paid for and planning to travel with Jerry. But you have different plans. I accept that Lord, I want only to be in your will. I do beg of you Lord to get us out of this valley, I don't know which way to turn. There are so many vultures trying to pick my bones and I just want to walk away without owing anyone and start over.

I am closing down after Saturday and everyone (debt collectors, IRS, lawyers) can do what they want, I am tired and I don't care what I lose as far as material things, I just pray you protect my family, especially my kids. Please let Casey get into college, its always been his dream to be an architect. I pray it be your will. I don't care if me and Jerry end up in a camper, just please bless my kids. They are your kids Lord and they love you as I do, use us all for your glory.

In Jesus name
Amen

2nd Journal entry October 7, 2010

Lord, I beg you please do something before I lose my mind. Calm my mind, give me peace any way you see fit. If you take me home, take care of my Casey, he is the one who cares. I pray this stress will leave him soon so he can calm down and enjoy his senior year. He loves you Lord and lives for you. Keep him and protect him. Watch over Kaylain, don't let her stray when she goes to her moms, keep her in church.

I don't know why my burdens are so many at once but please, please I am begging you help me, you are the only one who can.

I love you
In Jesus name
Amen

Journal entry October 16, 2010

Lord thank you so much for the last three days camping with the kids. I needed that. It made me realize that besides you, my family is all I really need. I know that because I am your child, our needs will be met. I want to make a special request Lord, I pray with a faithful heart that you will let things go well today when Casey goes to UT. If this is your will for him then let things go smoothly. Let him get the funding he will need and give him the knowledge to do well. I don't care what we have to give up, just let him be successful and use him for your glory.

My Father in heaven let me get through these next 7 months and handle all that comes my way. Don't let me fall to pieces when Kaylain leaves me and keep me strong and don't let me collapse under the pressure. Put me where you want me Lord, I am your child and I want only to serve you.

In Jesus name
Amen

Journal entry October 19, 2010

Lord thank you so much for your blessings. When I saw Jerry B. walk in yesterday I thought, this is it. I got so excited when he said he was still willing to work with us. I could have shouted, I was ready for church.

Revival was great last night, I needed it. I pray there are more tonight and that if any are lost when they walked in, they walk out saved. Lord watch over bro. Langston and his wife, keep them safe as they travel back and forth.

Lord it was such a joy to hear Jerry giggle last night, what a blessing it was. He was in the bedroom playing with his puppy and I don't know what she was doing, but she had him laughing harder then I had heard him laugh in a long time.

I am struggling with my back right now. I pray its just muscle not my kidney. I want to get my eating under control so I can in turn get my diabetes under control. Watch over my children, give them guidance, keep them on the path that is your will for them, use them Lord, use all of us for your glory. More tonight Lord, fill our church with you Holy Spirit and bless each and every person who walks in the door

Lord please watch over my mom when she has her next eye surgery. Continue to heal Jerry and Gene. I have a burden for Molly and her family, they have had such a hard time and lost so much these last couple of years, the Jenkins and Watson family need the comfort that only comes from you. Bless this day Lord with what I need, thank you

In Jesus name
Amen

Journal entry October 20, 2010

Lord thank you for your many blessings. Thank you for a spiritual filled service at revival last night. I pray the spirit grows each night so that by the end of this week there will be shouting, praising, and worshiping that will be heard all over the hill. I pray this will lift us up, each and everyone and put us back on the right path. I pray that you will touch Bro. David with your word. Give him the lessons you would have him to speak.

Guide and direct him Lord, fill our church with the lost so that we might welcome them and love them and nurture them when they accept you as their savior. Lord touch and bless those who can not be there. Lay your hands on Gene and Charlotte and Bud J. and their families.

In Jesus name
Amen

Journal entry October 26, 2010

Lord I love you so much and all I want to do is serve you, please you, bring you glory. Put me where you want me and use me I am your child. Watch over my family today through the predicted bad weather. Keep them safe on their way home from school.

Thank you for your word and your messages from revival and both services Sunday. I pray for the youth as they get ready for Sunday, I hope everything goes well and David and Diana really enjoy it.

I look forward to the celebration of the birth of my Lord, I am going to make it my mission this year to make sure the little ones understand what it is all about.

Lord I ask you this day that you let me get everything started with the charity and let things move forward. Keep my back strong so that I can get a lot done today. I love you Lord.

In Jesus name
Amen

Journal entry October 27, 2010

Lord thank you for your many blessings, I am so grateful for all that you do for me. You always give me what I need, and if I wait and trust in you, usually what I want.

The most important thing to me right now is Michaels salvation and living his life for you. I feel like you might be moving in his life, I pray this is the case. Use his friend to teach him Lord. I believe this young man has faith. I want him to get on the right path and not waste any more of his life like I did. I wish I could make him see the joy that is in my heart, even in the bad times.

I know he has a hard time, he has had a hard life and had his heart broken so often. I pray he will just trust his heart to you and see that you are the only one who will handle it with care. Lord I ask your guidance today, lead me where you want me I am your child and I want to live my life to please you.

In Jesus name
Amen

❧

We were finally starting to relax a little. Jerry was getting better, stronger. Our landlord was going to give us more time to get our non profit going. We had contacted our corporate attorney and got the name of an attorney who would set up the non profit for us. We were going to turn the business around and I would run it with a manager and we were going to retire Jerry, he joked he would be the house husband. He could clean better then me and cook just as well.

He had an appointment on November first for a check up to see how the eye, ear, and throat Dr. thought he was progressing. We also had made an appointment with the attorney about the non profit for later that afternoon. Things were looking better for our future. We were so excited about having a future together.

Remember what I told you about the eye of a hurricane.

CHAPTER 6

Back side of the storm

As I explained at the beginning of the last chapter, the eye of a hurricane is so calm that anyone who hasn't been through one can be fooled into a false sense of being safe. They are so ecstatic that they made it through such a dangerous storm that they don't notice the ominous clouds that are starting to move in. This is the back side of the storm, and it can often times be much worse then the front part of the storm. This is how many people get killed. They are caught off guard. They are so sure its over they come out from their place of shelter and before they can get back, it hits.

That's how it was with Jerrys' cancer. When the Dr.s told us that his cancer was almost gone, we thought that was it, that by the time the last radiation treatment was done he would be cured. We hadn't even thought that much about it the last few weeks. We went to radiation and went right on planning our new beginning.

We had our appointment set up to see the lawyer about setting up our non profit. Once that was accomplished we could get our professional solicitation registration filed and get registered with the state and finally begin soliciting for donations again. We were confidant we were going to get the business built back up and we were going to be able to help a lot of people. I was like a kid at Christmas.

We had started planning a vacation for next summer with the kids, we wanted to go across to the east coast and drive up the coast line to Maine and come back down through Pennsylvania in a motor home. No plans just go and when we see something that looked interesting we would stop and check it out.

This was the eye of the storm that had been our life for a short time. The back side of the storm was about to hit us, full force, without any warning. We were not prepared for it, it overtook us and what happened next was shocking. I have never in my life been so afraid, so defeated, and so very angry all at one time. And the questions that ran through my mind, Why? What have I done that you are so mad at me God? I have been forgiven and I have done my very best to be the best Christian that I am humanly capable of, why is satan being allowed to do this to me, to Jerry and to my family.

I knew God was the only one who had the power to stop it. He alone could stop this storm, but it had to be his will. I have never prayed so hard or so much. So many nights I cried myself to sleep, while praying at the same time. And it wasn't just us, many people we loved and cared about were going through it too.

On November 1, we went to Jerrys Dr appointment that morning. We had a full day ahead of us. Jerry was driving to this appointment, he was feeling stronger and eager to get out again. I noticed on the way there he began to drift a little toward the other lane. I told him to keep his eyes on the road, I thought he was just taking in the scenery, this happened a couple of times, I thought it was just because he hadn't driven much lately.

We parked the car and walked hand in hand to the office building where his Dr. was located. We didn't have to wait too long before they called us back. He was sitting in one chair and I was in the other across from him. We had been waiting for a while and I was sitting there with my eyes closed. All of a sudden something made me open my eyes, I can't recall if it was a noise or what, but when I did, Jerry was weaving in his chair, he was looking at me with this look of fear that I had never seen before. I thought he was having a stroke. I started toward him and then thought that I better get help, I ran out of the room yelling for help. Nurses and the Dr came running, three went in to help him and one stayed with me trying to calm me down, I was hysterical. They checked him and could not get him to respond. I went in and stood beside him, his eyes were fixed on me and it was as if he were begging me with his eyes to help him.

I was helpless, but I knew what I had to do. I held his hand with one hand and grabbed my phone with the other and called a friend from church. I left a message that something bad had just happened to Jerry at the Drs office and to please put him on the prayer chain. Then I hung up and began to pray and I kept telling Jerry over and over, while we waited on the ambulance, that Jesus was there, and that he would take care of us, I believed this with all of my heart. I know he was with me, because my legs were shaking so bad if he hadn't been there I would have hit the floor. The ambulance finally got there and they took him through the connecting corridor to the hospital. They sent me on over to meet him there. When I got to the emergency room, he wasn't there yet and they had left before me.

After about ten minutes of anxiously waiting someone finally came and told me he was there and they would take me back in just a minute. When I finally got back to where he was they told me he had another seizure on the way over there. These were grand moll seizures. After a little while the ER Dr was concerned that Jerry wasn't coming around like he should. She ask if he hit his head, I told her not that I knew of. She decided to take him down for a cat scan to see if he had a brain bleed. I told her that he also had been sick on his stomach that morning and about him drifting while driving.

I thought she would come back and tell me that he had a stroke or that he had an aneurism and they could do surgery and he would eventually be fine. I was not prepared for what she came back to tell me. It was the cancer, it had spread to his brain. I thought the lights got dim and for a second I really thought I was fixing to pass out. I screamed in my mind, no God. please, why are you letting this happen?, I can't do this any more. I felt a surge of energy, I guess you would say, where just a moment before I was weak as a kitten. I remember saying ok God, give me grace because now I have to tell the kids this and even worse I was going to have to tell Jerry. I didn't have time to be afraid.

I don't remember who I called when, or how they got there but they all got there. I dreaded telling them. In the mean time they had taken Jerry down for a scan of the lungs to make sure he hadn't aspirated. This is when they found it was in his lungs and further testing showed up cancer in the liver and lymph nodes. It was in the blood stream. He was terminal.

Journal entry November 1, 2010

Lord I need you more right now then I think I ever have before. Jerrys seizure this morning scared the life out of me. I can't believe the cancer has spread to his brain and is in his blood stream. I was praying that it was something else. I am sitting here in his hospital room looking at the shell of the man I fell in love with almost 30 years ago. So fragile, where once so strong. I am afraid for the months to come, not for me Lord, but for him. I do not want him to suffer any more then he already has.

Lord I ask a few things, if it is your will that these be our last fleeting moments together. First and foremost I ask for grace for us all, mercy for pain and suffering, strength to get done what needs to be done. I ask for a wonderful holiday season to celebrate not only the birth of our precious Jesus, but I ask strength and good days until after Caseys graduation. Please allow us this Lord. Please God, I beg you for these blessings. I also want to ask that you use this difficult time to touch some ones heart through our sufferings and fears. I pray that all we have been through will be for your glory. Use us Lord, even in our darkest hour.

Lift us up dear Lord, put your loving arms around us, let us feel your power, your strength, your love, your comfort. I am your child and I need you God. Please reach down and cradle me in your loving arms as only you can. Guide me Lord, I know there are hard decisions to be made, but I know what he wants, thank you for the discussions we have had. Lord more then ever I pray the rapture come because I don't want to be here without him, but I don't want to leave my kids, I will be glad when the day comes, when we will all meet at that gathering in the sky. Help me now Lord, keep me strong.

I pray these things
in my Jesus name
Amen

Journal entry November 2, 2010 4:00 am

Thank you Lord for an uneventful night, Jerry had as restful a night as possible with a tube down his throat. He hates it, and hates being tied down. So please keep him relaxed and calm so he won't fight it. I thank you for the comfort and peace, I feel such a calm, I know its your grace. Give me strength Lord to get through this. Let me have the ability and stamina to take care of him Lord. Give us good quality in the time that we have left together on this earth.

I am not afraid Lord, I know when the time comes I can let go because he will be with you the second he leaves me and I will see him again when my days on this earth are done. I just pray Lord that he doesn't suffer anymore. I love him so much, and I can't stand to see him in pain. Give him grace Lord when I have to tell him that instead of his cancer being gone, it has spread to his brain and is in his bloodstream.

God I have such a peace because I know he is saved and that he is faithful. I ask that you instill this peace in the kids, don't let them be afraid. I also pray that you give Jerry peace in knowing that I will be fine and the kids will be fine. I know he worries about me, but I know where my strength lies, and I know you will lift me up and see me through. Help me Lord, I need you right now. I know you will not leave me nor forsake me because you told me so. Its written in your word so I know it is true. Lead me Lord, use me for your glory.

In Jesus name
Amen

2nd Journal entry November 2, 2010 8:22 am

Lord thank you for making Casey more like Jerry then me. He is so calm in a crisis. I know he draws his strength from you, but if he needs me, or wants to talk, let him know I am strong enough for him too. I don't want him to suppress his emotions for my sake. Don't let either one of them be afraid. Speak to their hearts Lord and comfort them. Lord I pray things settle down and Jerry can rest. Please let him have a good quality of life, he has already been through so much. If it is your will that we are living the sunset of his life, then please give us peace and comfort. Give us joy beyond all understanding and use this time to reach someone, to touch their heart and plant some seeds. If I have to give him up now, I can at least have comfort in knowing another soul is saved. I pray its one of our kids if they are not saved.

I love you Lord
In Jesus name
Amen

3rd Journal entry November 2, 2010 10:25 am

Lord every time a Dr walks in here, its more bad news. Now its showing growths in his lungs, liver, and lymph nodes. Now they are talking about hospice. Lord my world is spinning out of control, I need you, more importantly Casey needs you. He is so hurt Lord, I can see it in his eyes. Wrap your loving arms around him Lord, keep him and guide him.

4th Journal entry November 2, 2010 12:20 pm

Jerry is awake, I've told him what's going on. He's scared and I think even a little angry. He's quiet, not talking. I hope he understands what I have told him.

He was on the ventilator and drugged so I don't know how much had sank in. He tried for thirty minutes to ask me if he had a stroke before I could get what he was asking. That is when I told him what was going on. That he had a seizure caused by cancer on his brain. He went back to sleep and because of the medicine they had him on while on the ventilator he slept most of the time until they took him off.

I wouldn't leave the hospital and I don't remember where the kids were, I think they were staying at Candy's. Casey was getting Kaylain to school and picking her up in the afternoon. He was trying to help me as much as possible and he was watching out for her. He is very protective and worries about her. I was numb, I couldn't let myself feel at that time, it was too much to process. I was just living moment to moment. I did have a sense of peace and I knew that was God. I also knew there were many who were praying for us as I was praying for many of them.

❧

Journal entry November 3, 2010 8:30 am

Had company since I last spent time in this journal. Jacque Moneymaker came by and we talked for a good while, Don and Ruth came in. We went to get dinner with Casey, Kaylain, Candace and Jimmy. Then last night Zach and Alex, Vickie, CG, and Bethany came by. Jerry was in the best mood, he was laughing so hard and cracking jokes. I don't know?

❧

2nd Journal entry November 3, 2010 9:30 am

Jerry ate a good breakfast and is even eating some pumpkin pie. Mike and Rick both called last night to get an update. We didn't get a lot of sleep, Jerry wrestled with wires, IV tubes, and sheets all night. He has his arms bloody from pulling on them.

Candace called to check on us and let me know how the kids are doing? Thank you God for making them the kids that they are. Keep your protecting arms around us all.

God I ask grace for Jerry and I both and the kids. I know Jerry is worried about us, but he doesn't have to. He has to much to deal with, let him know we will be ok. I am afraid, not of death, but what leads up to it. With everything else that we are going through, I need you now more then ever. I don't want to live without my soul mate, but I know that I can get through as long as I stay strong in my faith.

I thank you Lord for keeping me strong, I pray that you guide me and direct me. Help me to see your plan for us Lord. I love you so much.

In Jesus name Amen
Scriptures of comfort
Psalms 50:15, 52:8, 46:1

3rd Journal entry November 3, 2010 8:01 pm

Rough day Lord. I think it hit Jerry hard today that this is for real. His disease is incurable and now we have to plan. My heart is breaking Lord, I can't even begin to imagine my life without him. I have to lean on you. I certainly can't handle this on my own.

I pray for grace for my baby boy, this will be the hardest for him. I've never known two people closer then him and Jerry. I pray grace for Kaylain, this is scary for her, its not anything she has experienced before. I pray grace for me Lord, I am afraid of a future without my beloved soul mate. He is the only one next to you that I can talk to about anything. Please help me Lord.

In Jesus name
Amen

I had been at the hospital for what seemed like forever, I hadn't slept much at all and I wanted to get some more clothes because I didn't know when they would let him go home. So I got up before sunrise and drove home, big mistake, it was raining and dark and I couldn't see a thing. I must have been out of my mind. God had to have his hand in my trip home that morning because I literally could not see. There were no street lights for most of the way home and when a car was coming toward me I was blind as a bat. I had to stop and wait until they got by. I made it home finally and couldn't believe I had done that, I know I can't see when its dark and raining so I don't know what possessed me to do it.

I remember getting in the shower as soon as I went into that empty house. I ran the water as hot as I could stand it, turned the light off, except my night light in the bathroom, and got in and just stood there letting the hot water relax my muscles. After about one minute something engulfed me all at once. The fear, the anger, the grief, the uncertainty, the knowledge that my life was changing faster then I could handle, To know that my life would never be the same. I started sobbing uncontrollably. I was pleading with God, asking him why? I was screaming to the top of my lungs, I was letting out all of the fear and rage that I had been holding in.

Why God?, why are you allowing this. Please heal Jerry, give us a miracle. I can deal with any of this with him, but I can't do it alone. That's when he put his hand on my heart and spoke to me. He reminded me that he was all that I needed to get through anything. He would not change his plans for us, but he would be right there for us and through his grace, we would face what we had to.

Journal entry November 4, 2010 1:40 pm
Happy Birthday Anna

Thank you for getting me home this morning Lord. I don't know what possessed me to drive home before day light and it raining too.

2nd Journal entry November 4, 2010 8:45 pm

I have tried all day to get my prayer journal time. But I am thankful for the love of family and friends. Lord if I am making Jerry sad and uncomfortable, cover my mouth. I am praying for a miracle Lord, I want him healed. Give us five more years, and I promise we will use it serving you in any way you want. Please at least let us have time with our kids and let us all be there for Caseys graduation.

Lord touch all of our family as we go through this. This includes Anita, she is the mother of his oldest child and they will always have that bond. Jerry even got emotional when he talked to her. We all need you to get through this, he is so special to so many,

I need you Lord, more then I ever have. My faith is in you, and I pray for your glory even in our darkest hour. I am thankful, so thankful for the possibility for a few more months then first thought. I pray we make it to his 65th birthday at least. That would be such a blessing. Then he would be here for one more of each holiday and for Caseys graduation.

I pray that in time I can get everything situated and settled so that he will have peace in knowing that we will be ok. I know you will give us what we need, just please give Jerry all that he needs and then some. I truly look forward to the day Lord when we will all be together with you. Oh what a glorious day that will be.

Its so hard to think of life without him, but its even harder to watch him suffer. I pray for complete healing. I know you are the same today as you were yesterday. I pray Lord for a healing miracle.

He is a good man and will serve you well, as will I. I need him Lord, the only person I need more is you.

In Jesus name
Amen

❧

When you are told that the person God gave you to love and spend your life with in this world is dying and there is nothing else that can be done, you really lose your whole sense of being. Its hard to lose anyone that is close to you, but your spouse? This is the one who you joined your life to. When God puts two people together, its no longer two separate people, it becomes two people joined together as one. You are intertwined, meshed together. When one of you dies, it leaves the other with a part of them missing, a void.

That part of you will never be replaced. That doesn't mean you will never meet anyone else to share your life with, God moves in mysterious ways. I have seen people married for years who lose their spouse and after a time, God brings someone else into their life. I couldn't even stand the thought of Jerry leaving me, I was terrified, we were best friends, we shared everything. I have never loved anyone but God more then him.

❧

Journal entry November 5, 2010 5:30 am

Lord I am tired, lift me up and keep me calm and focused on my precious husband. Let me be all that he needs me to be these next months. I pray he is well enough to go home today. We both want to go home and rest in our own bed.

I also pray you help me through this bankruptcy, let me get together the papers I need to cover the taxes and please let my loan modification go through so that we can at least stay in our home, if that's your will. I have no problem moving into a smaller more manageable place.

Lord please let things go smoothly through this year. Let me be able to take care of Jerry and you keep him comfortable, out of pain and at peace. Please give him peace Lord, I know he is scared and he is worried. Please speak to his heart, let him know that you are in control and that you have us in your hands and everything will be ok, according to your will. Give Casey the same peace, keep satan away from him. I would like to also pray for peace and comfort for Molly and their family they are going through the same thing with her Dad. Lord I pray for good holidays and graduation for all of us. Speak to me this morning as I read your holy word. Let me receive the message you want me to have from it. Send me a blessing through it Lord, I need to feel your holy spirit right now. Help me Lord, these are the times when there are only one set of footprints in the sand. I need your powerful arms around me.

In my precious Saviors name
Amen

Psalms 63:3&4 Psalms 63

This one spoke to my heart

Jerry was finally going to get to come home. His younger brother and his wife got to come up and visit him. We had a surprise party for Anna, we were going to postpone it but Jerry wouldn't hear of it. I think we all needed the distraction, something special for everyone to enjoy. Jerry thought the world of Anna and he knew this would be good for Casey. That's the way that he was, he always put us first, that was his nature.

They had given us months and I was determined to make them the very best that I could for all of us. I closed the store that week for good. I was not going to spend one minute away from the love of my life. He needed me to be there for him, and I needed to be there for me too. The attorneys set a date for our 341 meeting, I told them there was no way that Jerry could make it and I wouldn't leave him to go so they postponed it. The Drs had told me early on that another seizure could be it, and I intended to be by his side until God decided it was time.

I had calmed myself and resolved to stay focused on him, to watch for signs that might tell me if things were beginning to change. I had to stay brave for him and for the kids. But when the kids were at school and he was asleep I would go into the other room and let loose. I would pray and cry and beg, I was afraid of losing him but I tried hard not to be sad around him. We didn't tip toe around the subject, we talked quite a bit about it.

We talked about what he wanted me to do with certain things of his, we went and made our funeral plans, we discussed what songs he wanted played. We spent a lot of time when he was awake just laying in bed, snuggled up watching tv or taking a nap together.

We didn't have to talk, we both knew what the other was thinking, we just tried to assure each other as best we could.

Journal entry November 7, 2010

Lord thank you for letting things go good this weekend. Jerry got to come home from the hospital, his younger brother got to come up and see him. The surprise party Casey had for Anna last night went really well. I think she really enjoyed it. Jerry even made it out for Happy Birthday and a few pictures. All of their friends and Candace and Jimmy all chipped in and helped get everything ready. Molly and Melissa brought stuff also. Candace cleaned, we couldn't have done it without them.

Had a wonderful church service, the Holy Spirit was moving. I could feel Gods arms slip around me as I felt like I would lose it. I was so close to becoming hysterical right there in church, but you calmed me Lord as only you can. I am so scared and dread what's coming so much, I need you Lord, more then I ever have. My family needs you, especially Jerry, give us grace Lord.

In Jesus name
Amen

Journal entry November 8, 2010 5:30am

My Lord Jesus protect us from satan right now. I am so tired and Jerry is so sick and we are all so scared. I beg you Lord let him stay and be well enough to attend Caseys graduation. I hate Kaylain is missing her first Christmas with her mom, but I am so thankful she will be here, I pray this Cristmas be a special celebration of your sons precious life and the best Christmas we have ever had. I want to get our kids together and really enjoy it. I love you so much Lord, my trust and faith are in you, please help me, I know that you are in control, but I don't like the thought of whats coming. Please forgive my weakness.

God please let things go well at the meeting this morning and make it so that we don't have to be there. God please allow us to keep what we have here. Also please let us get whatever aid we can to get us through this. I had nothing when I came in this world and I will leave it with only two things that matter, my salvation, and love in my heart.

Jerry I am sure is afraid of what is to come and I know he doesn't want to leave us, but he is not afraid to die and I know when he gets to heaven he won't worry anymore, no one could be happy in heaven if they worried about the ones who they leave behind. We on the other hand will suffer and grieve here until our time comes. I look forward to the day that we are all together at that wonderful meeting in the sky.

Lord give us, as well as Bud and his family, Gene and Charlotte and their family, the grace that we all need right now. Lay your healing hands on Charles Stoneciphers body and heal him. I pray you heal them all.

And last but not least, I pray you watch over David, who goes through it all with each one of us. Also for Diana who is there for him.

In Jesus name
Amen

2nd Journal entry November 8, 2010 7:15 pm

Lord its more then I can bare, this was my day today :

1. Forgot and gave Jerry his medicine (dilantin) that he wasn't supposed to take before labs, so now have to start over tomorrow.
2. Got seven days, four times a days worth of pills put into organizer and when I started closing the little doors, I flipped it over and pills went everywhere.
3. Tried three times to file unemployment, kept hitting backspace and for some reason it erases the whole application.

4. Working on road leading up to house, had to wait an hour to get up to the house.
5. Got two hundred sixteen dollars, have to give Dr. about one hundred fifty and get gas.
6. Mortgage Company messing around with loan, big mess.
7. Hospice came out today, oh joy. (they really were nice, its just not something you look forward too.).
8. Head is throbbing so bad.
9. Then find out that Kaylain may have head lice, that's all I need.

God I am faithful, you know that I am. Why? I don't understand!

Journal entry November 10, 2010

Thank you Lord for a better day yesterday. I have made some to do lists for each day and hopefully will get done what we need to. I haven't heard anything from the attorneys about the bankruptcy. Please let everything be ok there. Let us get it all settled and start over financially. Please God I ask that you provide an affordable solution for our mortgage, one that will allow us to stay in our home. The changes we are going through are hard enough, just please protect us lord, let Caseys grades be good enough for college and lead us to grants and scholarships that get him through college. I ask that you please keep Jerry well enough to get through graduation.

Let us get done all that we need to this day. Give us wisdom to make good decisions. Thank you Lord for another day, each moment is so precious Let us get everything done and just be able to enjoy our time we have left together. Also do the same for Molly and her family, Gene and Charlotte and their family.

In Jesus name
Amen

This was such a hard time in our lives. It was so surreal. We knew what was coming, but we didn't want to face it. I remember so many times thinking of the people who had betrayed us and hurt us. I couldn't understand how such evil doers could do so much and yet, never suffer the great trials that we were. They seemed to always get by, never suffering. Then I realized its because Satan is not going to torment those he already has. it's the ones who are saved he will torture, he uses this technique to make lost souls question God. He will even use it to make we who are Gods children to question his existence.

If there are any Christians reading this and thinking that I am suffering because my faith is weak and you would never question God because your faith is too strong, you couldn't be more wrong. If you are doubting my faith, then I know that you have never been through real trials. The most faithful of humans can be weak for a moment. Real Christians when having these moments will realize it, and go to their knees and pray, and God will reassure them, he will comfort them, and cover them with his grace.

I am not yet through all of this, but God has already strengthened me, and my faith is stronger then ever. So be careful what you say or think, because if you are not where God wants you to be and you don't listen to him, he will bring you to your knees. Not because he wants to hurt you, but when your on your knees, you are in prayer position.

We can get too complacent and think we are in Gods will because we don't have any worries. We think we have job security, we have a nice home, nice things. We travel all we want, we buy what we want, when we want it. We have healthy, happy kids, our spouse is healthy. We have the world by the tail. Do we thank God every day for these blessings? Or do we take them for granted?

I don't care how grand and wonderful you life is, if God is not the most important thing in your life, you have nothing. I don't care if you are in church every time the door opens, if you are not saved by the sweet blood of Jesus, you are going to hell.

How do you think the $ 1000.00 you gave some one in need (when you have a million) compares to the $ 100.00 (that the couple on social security gave), in Gods eyes.Yes the bigger amount will do more for the family in need, but who gets more out of it spiritually? If you have fifty dollars to buy food and you know a family that is hungry, are you willing to give half and trust God to take care of the rest?

My life is a mess right now by worldly standards, some of my own doing and some because of others. I used to say to people when they ask ; how are you today?

I reply "Oh, I've been better, but then again, I've been worse". Now I can only say, I've been better. But I can honestly say that I have never been better spiritually, I have never been closer to God. And I admit there are times when I don't feel that way, and there are times when I give in to satans pressure, and say words I shouldn't, but when I am where God wants me, like typing this book right now, I know that I am.

My prayer is that this book is Gods will for me and that it spreads like wild fire, and will inspire many people who need it right now. But if it is not to be, it has been a blessing for me. It makes me think about my relationship with God. It is helping me to heal and my prayer that it will help others who might be going through a period of hopelessness. I know of one friend for sure that my trial has helped, she is going through it right now and she told me that watching me go through it with Jerry has helped to prepare her.Just talking to her makes me believe it has also helped her spiritually.

Journal entry November 11, 2010 8:05 am

Lord please keep me strong through this day. We have a hard day to face. We are going to see about funeral arrangements for Jerry and I. I hope we won't need it for at least a year. I am afraid Lord, I need to feel your Holy Spirit move about me, calm me, strengthen me. I thought we would grow old together, I guess I will grow old alone. I am already feeling alone. Kaylain is going to her moms and Casey starts college. Please don't let Casey feel he has to take care of me, let me do for him until he starts his career and his family.

Lord I don't know how or where I am going to make a living, but I know you will provide what I need when I need it. Right now I just pray you get our finances so that they allow me to stay with my precious husband.

I pray in Jesus name
Amen

2nd Journal entry November 11, 2010 9:08 pm

Lord I am having a melt down. I was fine all day until now. I just walked by and saw a picture of me, Jerry, and Casey at the stampede. Its breaking my heart to know that my sweet husband is dying. This is killing me.

God I made it through the funeral arrangements today, I am glad that's over with. I am scared, its not lack of faith, you know that. It's being here without him. He is my heart second only to you. I hate this. When will it stop Lord? I could have dealt with anything, but not this on top of everything else. I would gladly give up all of our worldly possessions to have him with me a few more years. I pray he is here for Caseys graduation. It already kills me that he won't get to see him get married, or spoil Caseys children, he won't be here to watch Kaylain get married or give here away. This is more then I can bare. Please give us a miracle Lord, please.

I pray for the rapture. This world is mean and cold and evil. I want to take my family and go home, please come soon. I don't care what I have to go through Lord, just please keep evil from my kids. I pray love and happiness for all of my children. I pray they have the kind of love that Jerry and I have. We are best friends, literally. We can talk about anything. I need him Lord, a lot more then he needs me. The only comfort I have is that we will be together again with you in Heaven. He will get to see his mom and dad and his sister. He will get to see our babies that we lost before Casey was born. Most of all he won't have to go through anymore pain, and suffering. I love him so much and I feel like part of me is disappearing. God please let him know how much I love him, and how much I will miss him. Let him know that you have everything under control and that we will be ok, give him peace.

In Jesus name
Amen

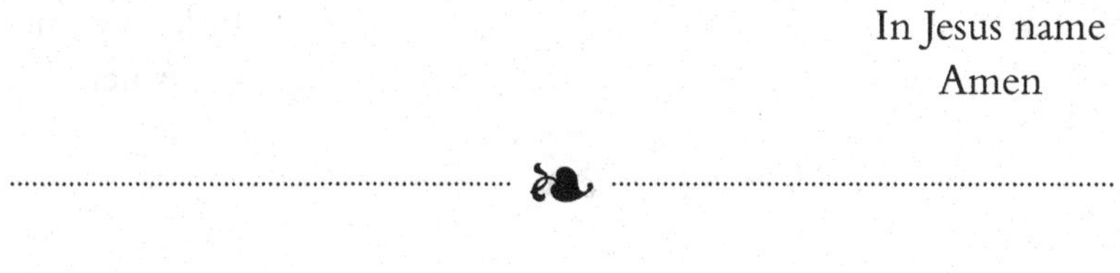

Journal entry November 12, 2010 5:15 am

Lord help me. My mortal heart is breaking and I don't want what time we have to be spent in sadness. Lift us up Lord, let us be happy. Protect my babies Lord. Open up a way for us to spend some special times together as a family. Last night was nice, we all sat in the living room together as a family and watched Karate Kid. Lord this time next year it may just be me and Casey here, be with us. I need your help Lord, because my baby boy is at a point in his life where he will start his life as an adult, so he won' be a constant in mine (not every day). Kaylain will be going to live with her mom, then it will just be you and I at home. This is the time that I thought Jerry and I would grow old together, enjoy some alone time and maybe travel a little. I hate this Lord. I don't mean to be disrespectful, but this stinks.

Please not only let him be here, but let him feel good for Caseys graduation. Please keep satan from us Lord, this is hard enough. We accept your will for us and our lives, just give us peace. Lord I ask you to be with Gene and Charlotte. I respect her faith. She has been through so much, and right now she needs you Lord, and so does Molly and her family. That's the wonderful thing about you Lord, you can take care of all of us at one time. Be with all of us and comfort each and everyone of us.

Lord lay your healing hands on the Buffalos little grandbabys body and heal her. Bless her. Also touch Charles Stonecipher and heal him. Help us Lord, we need you so much right now. You alone can bring us strength and comfort. Use our suffering for you glory Lord, we wouldn't want to be any other way.

In Jesus name
Amen

Journal entry November 14, 2010 Sunday

This is the Sabbath, the Lords day. Thank you for it Lord. Yesterday was quiet, Jerry doesn't feel like doing much, especially after running around all week. This is all draining on a healthy person, much less the one who is sick. We did go to menchies after dinner, he likes that.

He has been telling me who he wants to have what, of his belongings, its so sad. This is killing me Lord, give me strength for his sake. Wrap your loving arms around us and let us feel the peace and comfort of your Holy Spirit. We need your Mercy more then ever. Be with my kids Lord, protect them. Help me God, I am begging !

In Jesus name
Amen

❧

I can't begin to tell you how hard it is writing these pages and reliving these emotions. This was so hard, even with Gods grace, it hurts so bad. My poor child, he is so brave, he gets that from his Dad, and his heavenly Father.

❧

Journal entry November 15, 2010

Lord, tonight I witnessed the most heart breaking moment of my life. I watched as my sweet husband gave our baby boy his dog tags. The dog tags he has carried since he left the Army all those years ago. He is saying goodbye and it is killing me. I have had enough Lord. It is bad enough to lose everything we have worked for, but to take my sweet husband in the middle of it and to watch him and my baby hurt IS MORE THEN I CAN BARE !

I know that I have to accept your will, but WHY so much pain. Enough is enough, satan take your hands off of my family NOW.

IN MY JESUS NAME AMEN

God I need a miracle. Please, with all the faith I have, I am begging.

Journal entry November 16, 2010

Thank you Lord for a little calmer day. I pray things pan out and I find a way to support my family that is pleasing to you. I am still begging for a miracle Lord, at least let us have him here until age sixty five so he will be here for Caseys graduation. Even better leave him and I both for another fifteen years. During that time use us for your glory.

Whatever your will Lord, we will abide, with faith in knowing you make no mistakes. I pray for grace for each one of my family and that we show the power of faith during these horrific times. Lift us up and strengthen us. Show me Lord, make me see where I am failing you and lead me down the path you have laid out for me. I need you Lord, more then I ever have. I want to do your will, just show me.

I love you with all that I am
In Jesus name
Amen

The next few weeks were the hardest I have lived thus far in my life. I have been through some really hard trials, but none compared to what I was going through at this time.

What made it worse was the devil just kept throwing things at us right and left. Everyday brought some new challenge, and for reasons that I have yet to understand, God was allowing it.

Journal entry November 17, 2010

Lord I beg your mercy. I am so tired, so weak, I am overwhelmed by it all. Each day is harder then the day before, and it shows no sign of letting up. This morning not only do I live with the dread of losing my precious husband, which in its self is the worst nightmare I have ever had to live, we are losing everything. We may even lose our home. Today Casey is sick for the second day. On top of my usual health problems, I now have a yeast infection which is enough, but add to that the fall I took two nights ago has my hip, side, arm, and shoulder on my right side hurting.

Lord I begged for years to save my business, you didn't, I ask healing for Jerry and so far you haven't, you have taken our luxuries we worked so hard for, and as of today I don't have enough for the water bill, internet, and groceries. I do not know if I will get to draw unemployment, or if Jerry can draw disability. I don't know how I am going to get Casey through college. My faith is still anchored in you Lord, you know this, you know that I will not waiver, so why?

Why do you continue to let satan have his way with my family? I don't understand, but I know that I will one day, so I will continue to trust in you. I know that what I have suffered is nothing compared to what Jesus suffered for me. I love you Lord, and I know that one day soon we will all be together and these times will be forever erased from our minds.

I look forward to the day that I can look upon your face and be forever reunited with Jerry, and all of the people I love. Replace my fear and sorrow Lord with strength and gladness. I lift up my heart to you sweet Jesus, I draw on the joy given me at the time of my salvation.

In Jesus name
Amen

Journal entry November 18, 2010 9:15 am

Lord thank you for your special blessing this morning. If its approved I will get $254.00 dollars a week in unemployment, I pray it gets approved. Also we are so grateful for the blessing of our brothers and sisters in Christ who are everywhere we go. Our family Dr and his nurse and all of the people who work at their office, gave us a huge basket and large box of food for Thanksgiving.

What was most special was the prayer they shared with me in my hour of need. These moments of kindness remind us of what we have to look forward to. I pray Lord, that you will please keep Jerry strong enough to see Casey graduate on May 15, please give us that Lord, it would mean so much. You are my foundation and even when I begin to falter, I know I can't fall any farther then your loving arms will let me. I know when I'm to the point I feel I will lose it, you will reach down and lift me up. I thank you Lord, with a faithful heart. Amen

Journal entry November 20. 2010

Lord thank you for this beautiful fall morning. As I sit out in our gazebo, spending this time with you, the birds are singing still and there is a crispness in the air. I don't know why, but I feel a calmness this morning that I haven't felt in a long time. I know it is the Holy Spirit, my comforter. I felt a peace this morning when I saw Jerry reading his Bible, I pray that he draws strength from your words and grace from you. Surround him Lord with your love, let him be at peace with the knowledge that everything will be ok. Don't let him worry about us, especially Casey. We have raised a good son. Give him comfort as you have me, that we will all be together one day, never to be separated again.

Lord I wish I could have all of my kids and grandkids together for Christmas just this one time, but I know its not possible unless its your will. I just want it to be a joyous Christmas for my family, it will most likely be our last one together in this world with my sweet Jerry. I hope we get at least two more. But not if he has to suffer. For my Christmas present Lord, I won't ask for a thing of this world, but I would be so grateful for Jerry to stay well enough to see Casey walk across that stage and get his diploma. Now if I can be just a little selfish, please work out a plan for us to keep this house. I would love to see Casey raise his children where there will be so many happy memories for him. I thank you for him and Kaylain Lord, they keep me focused and strong.

I love you Lord
I praise your holy name
I thank you for all blessings
I thank you for my salvation

In Jesus name
Amen

Journal entry November 21, 2010 Sunday morning 10:30 am

Lord forgive us for missing church yet again. Casey is really sick and Jerry is tired from yesterday. Please wrap your loving arms around my family and let us make some wonderful, stress free memories this holiday season.

In Jesus name
Amen

As we began to approach Thanksgiving, things were still going down hill. I was so tired, so defeated. The devil was not only stomping me in the ground, he was even using my children every way he could to try and break me. One day while I was really low and thinking about the upcoming holiday, I thought what have I got to be thankful for.

That's when it hit me to make a list of what I did have to be thankful for. I also challenged everyone on face book to do the same. I think that everyone even in the hardest times of their lives should sit and make a list of the blessings God gives us every day. This is what I did and I can't tell you how uplifting it was for me. It was a ray of sunshine on a dark and gloomy day. Thank you God for reminding me of this.

Journal entry November 22, 2010 7:50 am

Lord help me this morning, I am losing my mind. Casey has been sick since last week, now I am feeling a little queasy. Please don't let me get this mess, and keep it from Jerry Please. I also think Kaylain may have head lice again. That is going to cost me a fortune that I don't have, and now she says she needs a councilor, I think she is trying to get attention from her mom, but if I am wrong only you can protect her Lord.

I have to much to deal with Lord, you have to take it, I feel so fragile, so helpless, so tired. You said cast all of my burdens on you, so here they are :

1. Jerry > cancer, peace of mind
2. Casey > illness, school, college
3. Kaylain > mental stability, family issues
4. Me > all of the above plus health, strength, wisdom, get Jerry through radiation, get bills paid.

Lord help me, I need you now more then ever. Give me the strength to do what I need to do today and still keep my sanity. I don't know which way to turn. Today I have to register for unemployment, Jerrys radiation, find out about bankruptcy 341 meeting, figure out how to pay $ 1600.00 mortgages, $ 200.00 water bill, and $ 100.00 home owners insurance. Find out how to find a water leak and how much it costs. God please stop the madness, keep my spirit strong, my mind strong, my heart strong. Only you can get me through this

I pray for all of this with a faithful heart
In my sweet Jesus name
Amen

Journal entry November 24, 2010 4:34 pm

Thank you Janeen
For this verse
I Peter 1:6,7

Lord help me, I am sitting on the phone on hold with the mortgage company where I have been waiting since 3:47 pm. I am sick of this. It has been a hard day, Jerry had some kind of spell this morning, he dropped his cup four times and when he stood up and walked around the chair, he fell. I am afraid, I hope things aren't fixing to get bad.

Please make these people answer and help us with our mortgage. I am so tired. I finally got a battery for our meter to check our sugar. Mine was 501. I knew it was up because I have been so sleepy, but I didn't know that it was that high. No more sugar, tomorrow is Thanksgiving keep my mouth closed to high sugar and high carbs, you know that I am weak and can't control my eating. The kids took off to moms when they got home, I don't blame them, this is so hard. I couldn't face all of this if I didn't have you. Bless us Lord.

In Jesus name
Amen

This is the list of things that I wrote in the back of my journal that I was thankful for.

1. Thirty years with my sweet husband.
2. My children and grandchildren
3. My baby boy, who gives me no trouble and helps me so much.
4. A home to protect us.
5. Food to sustain us
6. Our church, Pastor, and church family who are a blessing in so many ways.
7. My little grand daughter whom I know God sent to make me laugh.
8. For the memories that I have made, that will bless me until its my time to go home.
9. For my family and relatives.
10. For 18 years in a business that not only carried us, but allowed us to help others and Allowed us to share our faith.
11. For my mom who tries to support me where she can, and help me when she can.
12. For the strength and grace to get through this valley (valleys)
13. For what I need, when I need it.
14. For my salvation, and my precious Jesus who made it possible.

Journal entry November 25, 2010 7:00 am Thanksgiving

Lord thanks for a nice thanksgiving. Jerry made it through the afternoon before getting tired. He ate a good dinner, but he is so weak. I am scared too Lord, I'm afraid this is it so soon. Please give me a miracle. This is too hard. Everyone thinks that I am strong, you know better.

When I feel like I'm losing it I know I can cry out and you will reach down and lift me up into your arms and comfort me. I just ask you to keep Casey and Kaylain strong. I pray they rely on you to get through this. God my main concern at this time is Jerry. I pray that if its not your will to leave him a while longer, that you will not let him suffer. He is so weak and he tries so hard not to be a burden on me, what he doesn't understand is that its not a burden. Its what I want to do for him, because I took a vow when I married him, this is Gods way. I won't have it any other way. Next to you I love no one more. Comfort us, give us what we need, give us peace.

In Jesus name
Amen

❧

These next few days were hell on earth. God had his plan and nothing would change that, but satan sure did use it to make it so hard. But in the end, God won out. The last few weeks had been hard, but I have heard of people who went through much more in the end.

I was tired and Jerry was getting weaker by the day. But Gods grace was sustaining us. I don't know who was more afraid. Everything from the 26th—the 28th is a blur. Friday night the kids decided to go black Friday shopping. Jerry and I went to bed he was asleep pretty quick. Sometime around one or two in the morning, he started getting sick. Then he started shaking. It got worse and worse, I thought at first he was having a seizure, but he was coherent, he spoke, and kept his eyes on me. He had that pleading look in his eyes again, like he had at the Dr.s office. He kept telling me he was sorry, this broke my heart. I kept telling him to please quit saying that.

The kids came in and Casey came in the bedroom just as Jerry got really bad. I had him sit with him on the side of the bed while I called hospice. Rick said to give him another seizure pill and a morphine pill. I did and Casey and I sat on each side of him and just held him as tight as we could. After a while it finally started to calm down. Casey went down to bed and I went around and laid beside him as close as I could get. Then he said the words I didn't want to hear. He said, "I wish God would just go on and take me "

Before I thought, I blurted out, "no, I'm not ready" I felt so bad. I just cried hysterically for a minute and then thought, don't do this to him, don't make dying hard for him, that's what the devil wants. So I gathered myself and snuggled close and told him this. "If you are tired, and can't go on and you see Jesus, you go. I will be ok and the kids will be ok."

He drifted off to sleep, finally resting.

I eased out of the bed and went around to his side and sat in the chair that I had sitting there. I got my prayer journal and my Bible and began to talk to God. To look for comfort in the scriptures. The next morning he was lethargic. I called hospice and talked to a lady and told her that I knew it was a holiday weekend, but I was afraid that Jerry was taking a turn for the worst and I was afraid, I just wanted to know what I was facing at that moment so she said she would come out. When she got here, I took her in to Jerry and woke him up and introduced her. As always he had a big smile and when she ask how he was doing, he told her fine. She began to assess him and when she finished, she motioned for me to go into the dining room. She ask what the drs had told me about how long they thought he had. I told her they had said months, maybe a year.

She said no, we are looking at weeks, possibly even days. My heart dropped through my stomach. It shattered into a million pieces.

She ask me if I was ok and I told her yes, I just needed to know so that I could prepare our children and call friends and family. I didn't tell him what she said. I made the phone calls to let everyone know. I went in to sit with him, I told him that I loved him, he said he loved me too. A little while later our pastor came by. Jerry woke up and said hello, he told David that he loved him and when David ask if he was going to be in church, Jerry said he was going to try. Then he went to sleep again. After David left I went in and laid with him for a while. I told him how much I love him and what he meant to me. Some of my family came over that evening, Jerry had not woken up all afternoon, his breathing was labored, so we all picked him up and moved him to his recliner where he breathed a little easier.

I knew that he was slipping away, my sister and I slept on the couches in there with him. We slept off and on, Candace said he sounded like he stopped breathing or had long pauses between breaths all through the night. I woke up about 5:30 am. I got his seizure medicine and placed it in his mouth and put a few drops of water in with a straw. He didn't wake up. At about 8:45 I woke the kids up for church. They showered and went on. My sister went home to take a shower and change and was going to come right back. My two brothers and nephew came over and sat with me.

It was somewhere around 11:24 give or take a minute, we were sitting around talking. I was sitting next to Jerry holding his hand, when for some strange reason I just stopped and looked at Jerry, I think it was the change in his breathing that got my attention even though it was a very subtle change. I jumped up and ran around the chair to where I could hold him. I knew this was it, he was taking his last breaths. I was softly crying, trying to stay calm for him. I just kept telling him its ok, Jesus is here, if you see him go to him, don't worry, I am ok. This was hard to do because inside I was screaming, oh God help me, I can't do this. I kept kissing him, talking to him, telling him we loved him. And then there it was that awful last bit of air leaving his lungs, you couldn't even call it a breath, just air. I had been with several family members when they passed and I knew that sound. That's when I lost it, I didn't have to be brave anymore, at least not until my children got home. I sent Casey a text, it was the middle of church, but I knew he needed to say goodbye before they came to get him. He text back and said now? I think he knew and was afraid. I said yes now. He got Kaylain and came home. Kaylain was hysterical as soon as she got out of the car and they told them. Casey came in and got a chair and just sat beside his Daddy, just looking at him, my heart stopped. My baby was hurting so bad and I knew nothing that I could do would help. I hugged him and told him I loved him and just let him have his time with his dad. I went to call hospice.

When she got there she ask everyone to step out while she examined him and pronounced him dead. As soon as Casey went out side, he jumped on his four wheeler and headed to the top of the hill where he and his friends had camped many times and his Daddy would come up and sit by the camp fire with them. This was and still is his special place he goes too. He stayed until the hearse came to get Jerry then he had to come move his car so that they could get in.

By now church was over and the word was out, the preacher and everyone was coming in. Casey went up to the Gazebo, his friends were up there with him and Kaylain. My kids are so blessed with the friends they have, there are none better. I ask brother David if he would go speak to the kids and keep them up there until they got Jerry into the car, I didn't want them to watch that. I was so numb, so dizzy with grief, so afraid. It was over, my baby was gone. I prayed that God never let me feel that kind of hurt again.

Journal entry November 26, 2010

Lord I am tired. Went to bed at 4:34 am got up at 6:30 am. Jerry has fever of 104.4 degrees. Can't get him awake enough to swallow pills, trying ice pack, please let that work. He was up for hours jerking and shaking all over. It wasn't seizures, because he was coherent, it was more like convulsions only he knew what was going on. I put his seizure pill in his mouth at 6:40 am I hope he got it down, I can't get him to swallow anything. Oh God, I pray if this is the hour you have chosen, that you not let him suffer. But I pray to keep him a little while longer and a little stronger. Put a hedge about us Lord, protect us, comfort us, give us grace, give us peace.

In Jesus name
Amen

The scripture at the bottom of the page this day read, May God Almighty grant you mercy. Genesis 43:1 I wrote beside of it, for Jerry Amen

---

Journal entry November 28, 2010 9:30 am

Lord, thank you for a quiet night for Jerry. For not letting him suffer through this.

Give me grace Lord, I need it more then I ever have. Watch over Rick as he travels out here, I remember how it was for me when Daddy got killed and I had to drive to Florida and when Kaylain got hurt and I drove to Mississippi. Keep his mind focused on his driving. Lord let us get through this, watch over our kids.

In Jesus name
Amen

2nd Journal entry November 28, 2010

My precious Jerry passed away today at 11:27 am. Lord, you have the sweetest man ever created, tell him everyday how much I love him.

Amen

Scripture at the bottom of this page in my journal read:

For it is commendable if a man bears up under the pain of unjust suffering because he is conscious of God. I Peter 2:19

How amazing is that

Amen

Lost my soul mate and best friend
My husband, at 11:27 am today.

3rd Journal entry November 28, 2010

What an emotional roller coaster I am on. Lord my baby is gone and my heart is broken. Please heal my heart and my body. I don't know how to move forward without him. If I have dreams like I did with Daddy, please let them be sweet and real.

Thank you for you grace. I have a lot more on my mind, but it will have to wait until tomorrow, I am exhausted.

I love you Lord
In Jesus name
Amen

This time was like a dream. I felt as though I was watching someone elses' life. I watched as people came and went. They brought food, and drinks, And some stayed a few minutes to see if we needed anything and to give their sympathy. My family was here, they had called Rick and Mike and Don and Bob and the rest of the family. I wish I had called the boys wives first and made sure the boys were not alone when they found out, because Rick was at work and by himself, I hate that, I am so sorry. I was so hysterical all I could say was call the boys, their numbers are on the phone. All I wanted to do was go to my room and shut the world out, crawl up in the bed, snuggle with Jerrys pillow and go to sleep. But I couldn't go to sleep and leave Casey and Kaylain to deal on their own. I needed to be there for them if they needed me.

CHAPTER 7

Devastation and Destruction

After any major storm, there is destruction everywhere. There is devastation with the loss of life. Lives are forever changed. When you go through a major storm and you lose everything that you have, sometimes someone that you love, you wake up to a new beginning. You didn't ask for it, you didn't want it, but you are faced with it just the same. Even though you had warnings, you can never prepare for the actual grief of the situation, because as much as you think you are ready, it hurts far more then you could have imagined.

As you climb out from under the mountain of debris, your world doesn't look the same as it did before the storm hit. Everything has changed. So many things are gone, nothing feels like it did before. The place you have lived in for years suddenly doesn't feel like home anymore. Now you are no longer a family of four, but a family of three. You listen for that one voice you so desperately want to hear, but nothing. You know they are gone, but you just can't make your heart believe it. You are so tired and so depressed that you feel like your life is over and that you will never be happy again.

But there is hope, there is Gods grace. As long as you trust in him, believe in him, have faith in him alone, he will carry you. He is your father and you are his child. He does not want us to be unhappy. He wants us to be happy and prosper, he said so in his word.

So even though I have lost so much, I know I will be ok. I just don't know how long it will take. I still have so much to go through before I can breathe again. But I know that I have a lot to look forward to with my kids. I know that I can get past the pain, the grief that seems never ending and attacks of grief and loneliness, and hopelessness that hit at the least expected times. But I can only do it with Gods help. These are the times satan likes to attack, and he will. Put your faith in God, he wants to help you, if you will let him.

Journal entry November 29, 2010 7:30am

Thank you Lord for your grace. I have this amazing peace right now. I have so many things to take care of today and I am unusually calm. I am going to have a life celebration for him, not a funeral. I have a couple of ideas that I know Jerry would love, use this sad time in our lives for your glory.

2nd Journal entry November 29, 2010 6:40pm

Lord I am so tired and so ill. Don't let me be mean to my family. There is constantly someone on my computer when I need it, the tv is blaring country music, people everywhere, talking loud on phones, I am so tired and I don't mean to be ugly but, you would think they would be a little more considerate. Calm me Lord as only you can, give me peace to be able to deal with everything calmly and rationally, without yelling, ranting and raving. Don't let my blood pressure spike, don't let me have a stroke or a heart attack. Let me get my sugar under control, my kids need me right now. I am ready to go anytime you say, but if you can use me for your glory, then so be it.

I love you Lord

Journal entry November 30, 2010

Lord I am so tired and I have so many people coming in for Jerry. I can't believe it. Help me to cope and to be kind to everyone. Let me get done all that I need to and make me realize . . . .

Fell asleep and didn't finish

I was so very tired, and felt more like a robot then a person. There were so many things to get done. I am so glad that we talked about everything so that I knew exactly what Jerry wanted. I was still having a hard time believing that he was actually gone.

There were so many people around, the only time I really had time to think was in the mornings, before everyone else got up.

Its funny, I used to watch people in the movies, smell a loved ones pillow, or house coat or jacket, anything that carried the familiar scent they knew was their loved ones and I would think they were crazy. But you do, you will look for a smell, or a sound, or a certain item that will let you hold on to them a little while longer. After everyone was gone and the kids were back in school, I watched all of our home movies. This would help me while I was watching, but always made me sad when they would end.

My alone times were the worst, when the kids were at school. The house was so quiet, I didn't have a job or a business anymore to go to. Lord I wish I had the business still just to keep me busy and support us. I was facing more then I could handle. With Jerry I could get through anything.

One day, when we first found out that he was terminal, we were talking, and I told him that I couldn't get through all of this, he just looked at me and said "Yes you can, I know you can". I don't know how he could be so confident in me, or was his confidence in God?

I think it was probably the latter.

Journal entry December 1, 2010

Lord help me, I am tired and frustrated. I will do this for Jerry. I love you baby and I miss you so much. God help me to hold up and be a good witness. Satan is on me so bad right now. I need rest. Please get my son here tomorrow, I need him so much. Casey needs him. Let this day pass smoothly and quickly.

Keep all of our family and loved ones safe while traveling up here. I wish my baby were here and we were going on a trip. I can't wait until we are all together again. I wish the rapture would come tonight. Lord lay your healing hands on little Olivia, and Bud and Gene. Bless our troops who can't be home during the holidays.

In Jesus name
Amen

Journal entry December 6, 2010

Lord help me. Friday December 3, 2010 we had visitation and funeral service for Jerry. So many people came, right at 8:00, Casey wrote a beautiful Eulogy for his Dad It broke my heart to see him struggle through it Lord, but he did an amazing job. Janeen and

Amy were both sick but made it through "My chains are gone" with Mark. As always Debbie did a beautiful job with "Praise his name" and the choir sang "Victory in Jesus" David did a wonderful job, Jerry would have loved it.

Saturday, December 4, 2010 we had graveside service for Jerry, his military service he always wanted. We had gotten him a red, white,and blue spray. I wish I had taken a picture of it.

My baby is gone, my heart is broken Lord, I pray you mend it. I can't go on feeling like this. Heal me Lord. I miss him so much. I need you God, only you can heal our hearts.

In Jesus name
Amen

Journal entry December 7, 2010

Message from Jessica (my niece) left on my face book. You can't even begin to imagine how uplifting this was to me, how special it was. It was truly an answered prayer and I have peace in knowing the devil loses.

This note was precious on its own, but go back and read my journal entry on 11-2-2010

And you will understand why it is so special to me.

The note read as follows:

Dear aunt Jackie

I just wanted to let you in on a little special something and hopefully it will make you feel a little better. I firmly believe and always have that everthing happens for a reason, even death. When uncle Jerry found out that the cancer had spread, I prayed that his will be done, and that as his maker and father, that if it be Jerrys' time to go that it must be to help someone else out and to prepare that persons heart for whatever lesson was to come.

Little did I know, that at least one of those people would be me. Its hard to put into words this peaceful and beautiful thing that has taken over my life in such a sad situation. I prayed for a long time on the way back home about all of this and that if there was any way for uncle Jerry to know that through his death my faith has grown so much that God please let him know it. I used to always kinda question Gods existence, even up to the minute he died, that is gone now. I just wanted to let you know that. I know that you are hurting, no matter how strong your faith is, you loved uncle Jerry with everything you have and everything you are, and nothing will ever make that stop. I look at that as a good thing, you should love your husband even when he is no longer on earth.

The only two things I can offer for comfort is this: 1. How his death is helping others who did not have as strong a faith as he. And 2. That he is with our God, no longer tired or in pain. Not thirsty nor hungry or fevered. He is healthy and beautiful and is forever singing his praises to him. One day you will see him again. I love you so much aunt Jackie and I hope that through time and understanding you will begin to feel so much better about the hurt you are feeling now. I continue to pray for you and the kids and uncle Jerrys' brothers.

Jessica

This is one prayer in all of this that was answered, at least one person was touched by Jerrys death enough to change their life for good and God gets the glory. I know there are more, maybe not as obvious. My life is forever changed, my faith still strong but my body and mind weak.

Help me Lord,
In Jesus name
Amen

Since this day, I have had so many people tell me that my faith, through everything that we have been through has inspired them. I don't see it, but that was my inspiration for putting all of this down in a book to share. If this book helps even one person, like my nieces letter did me, I will be so blessed. I hope it leads people to know that when we go through these heartbreaking trials, that God is the only way to get through it. He is the only one who has the power to heal your shattered heart, and even then it will take time.

Journal entry December 8, 2010 9:28 pm

Lord help ! Heal my heart. It is shattered in so many pieces, I don't know if I will ever feel whole again. I barely made it out of the grocery store when I lost it. Crying hysterically, and it always hits me when I least exspect it. God I am so afraid of a life without him. I don't know what to do. I will just keep trusting you. Wrap your loving arms around me Lord, lift me up, out of satans reach. He is tormenting me right now and you are the only one who can stop him. I don't know what I am supposed to do, I will just wait on you.

In Jesus name
Amen

2nd Journal entry   December 8, 2010

Lord help me, now these stupid attorneys and trustee are trying to take the life insurance money. I don't understand. I paid these people $1500.00 to help me, but they have ruined my life. Help me Lord. I am so tired which is good, its 10:00 pm and I need to sleep.

Help me Lord,
In Jesus name
Amen

Journal entry   December 9, 2010

Lord I know Jerry is with you and he is far better then I, so please put a hedge about me and protect me from satan. Are we to lose everything, after we lose that which was so precious to us? We would gladley give up everything that we have to have Jerry back. I hate being without him. I could face all of this now if I had him to come home to, and talk to, and snuggle with. Lord I know your ways are not for me to understand, but I pray it gets better soon. This emotional roller coaster is exhausting and sometimes its so hard to breath that I actually feel like my heart will stop. Its already broken. I hate these waves of hysteria that I can't contol. Help me Lord, how many times do I have to ask. I am your child, and a child needs the love, protection, and comfort of their father.

I need to be held in your mighty and powerful arms, and to tell satan ENOUGH !

Jerry went through so much these past months, almost a year if you count headaches and sickness before we knew what was going on. Lord I wonder how long he knew something was wrong. I pray he forgave me for falling apart at times, and times when tired, I was snappy. Knowing him, he let it roll off his back.

I told the kids today that if I died tomorrow I can say I have been loved. That I have experienced and shared true love and that my husband was not only my best friend, he was my soul mate. I do thank you for the blessing of almost 30 years with that man and for the gift of our youngest son. He was Jerrys shadow from the beginning.

Lord I am hurting, but I would like to take a few minutes to pray for some others who are also hurting. Betty Watson, God bless her, she and Mayford were married sixty four years, over twice as long as Jerry and I. When she spoke to me at the funeral, I could see the pain still so deep and its been five months. Please heal her heart Lord.

Also the Jenkins family, they are suffering the same hurt as us, they are going through the same thing that we did with Jerry, so I want to pray a special prayer for Bud, because like Jerry I know he is worried about his family. Give him peace Lord, let him know that you have it under control. I pray for Gene and Charlotte, they have been through so much. Bless them Lord. So many in our church are going through turbulent times, I know its satan. He hates Gods children and our church is full of them. Lord help my family and let Mondays bankruptcy meeting with the trustee go better then I can ever imagine.

I pray in Jesus name
Amen

After making it through the storms of life, some that are so bad they leave us with nothing. We are walking around in a daze, just trying to get through one day at a time. We have no control over our emotions, crying out, screaming, or just sitting quietly with so many thoughts running through our minds that all we can do is sit there, saying nothing, seeing nothing, tuned out to protect our minds.

It is these times that I get my prayer journal and go into my bedroom or up to the gazebo, anywhere that it is quiet, and write and pray. I use this as a release and my time with God. I don't care what is going on, if I am faithfully praying, and surrendering it all to him, he will lift me up. I have never got on my knees, or in my prayer journal and not got up feeling 100% better then when I started. But let me say this, if you are just going through the motions of prayer, and not praying with real faith that God is in control, then don't expect to feel the spirit move on you as I have described. If you are not a true child of God, if you do not believe in prayer, if you are not earnestly seeking him, why should he help you? Also, you have to be willing to wait on Gods answers, and he is not always going to say yes, he will say no sometimes. God is not going to change his plans for anyone, and we are not always going to understand why he allows the things that he does, at least not in this lifetime. But this I know for sure, even when we think we can't make it, he gives us grace. He never, ever turns his back on us. He does want us to be happy, and if we are not, how much of it are we willing to take responsibility for? Are we doing all that we humanly can to help our situation. We can't just sit there and expect God to help us if we are not willing to help ourselves. I wish I had done more to help my situation with the business and finances.

One thing I am thankful for, and listened to him and my children, is that we got back in church over six years ago. I am so grateful for the prayers, help, money, food, and just knowing they are there if I need them. I know many times money has been left in the offering marked for my family just when we needed it. Always cash, and no name, so I want to thank my secret Angel(s) and pray

God blesses them for the blessing they gave me. There are others that I do know who it was, but I know they would not want me to call them by name. Thanks to everyone who has helped. There are too many to name. My mom and friend Katie did as much as they could at the store until I closed it, my family were all there for us when we needed them, I was especially glad to see my oldest son, we needed him. I am so thankful that he was able to get here. I know the family was happy to see him after so many years. So many prayers, and words of encouragement.

I remember one night, Jerry and I went to the alter and because of our health we sat on the front pew instead of kneeling. The spirit just over took me, I was weeping uncontrollably, and I think Jerry was also. So many of our church family surrounded us and David came over and ask special prayer for our family. I could feel Gods sweet spirit, filling me to the top with peace, comfort, and courage. There is no mistaking that feeling, you know when God comes down, words can't justly describe it. His Grace is sufficient. The last time I felt God move like that was when we were all on that same alter praying for Randy. I think that he is always there with us, but that he makes his presence known more, when we need him most.

Journal entry December 11, 2010

Lord I am humble, I am on my knees begging. Help me please. Our neighbor just came over mad as sin over Balto. Apparently he has been down at his house causing trouble. He ran the neighbors dog out of its house and stole his water bucket, tried to run off with his dog bowl. Lord help me come up with a way to keep Balto out of trouble, Casey loves him so much, he will be crushed if we have to get rid of him.

God I need you so much. Even the little things throw me into hysteria. You took

Jerry home, I don't question your reasons, but why does everything have to keep getting worse. I've lost my best friend, we may lose our home, business, even the life insurance.

I have no job, no way to take care of us. Lord its so hard and you said you would not put more on me then I could bare, well I'm there Lord. Please, I beg you to help me. I need you so much. Touch our lives in a good way please. I ask healing for my body Lord. My feet burn so bad at night from the diabetes and my sugar was very high. I am working on my diet and getting my sugar and blood pressure under control. My kids have been through so much, I don't want to add to that grief.

I vow to celebrate my saviours birth without saddness, and with Joy. I will not let satan steal that. I pray that these next years will be a continual climb back to the top of the mountain. It is a shame that I took so much for granted and didn't realize how blessed that I really was when things were going well. I had my soul mate that I shared my life with, our kids and grandkids, God allowed us a son together that gave us an opportunity to raise one in a loving home, wish we had done that for our oldest boys. We had a good business with good friends, and helped a lot of people. I wish I could go back and live the ten years over, and do it differently in some ways. But since I can't go back, I am going to go forward and make the best of whats left of my time on earth. I feel very alone and dread the next few years. I know you are there Lord, just please lift me up and lead me where you want me to be. I know if I stay in your will you will take care of us. I need you Jesus, help me please. Use these difficult times to let my light shine.

I pray in Jesus name
Amen

2nd Journal entry December 11, 2010 10:15 pm

Lord I ask grace and peace for Molly and her family. Bud passed away last night about 2:30 am. Like Jerry, Molly said he went peacefully. Thank you Lord for that and get them through these next few weeks.

In Jesus name
Amen

Journal entry December 13, 2010

God please have mercy on my broken heart. I don't feel like it will ever mend. I know its selfish, I know he is not sick, and his happier then he has ever been, but I hurt so bad. Touch me Lord in a way that only you can. Give me the strength that I need Lord. I don't want to bring my kids down. Bless us Lord with all that we need until we are all together again. Please touch the Jenkins family who have lost such an important part of their family. Its made even harder during the holiday season. Let us celebrate the reason for the season. If we focus o him and not our grief we will bring our joy to the surface. There is no way Jerry would want me to feel this down, so help me Lord, I'm not strong enough, I need you.

In Jesus name
Amen

Journal entry December 14, 2010

Lord I am sorry for not dealing with this loss very well. I know its selfish on my part. I don't like being alone. If you think about it, I guess in a way grief is selfish. My husband is not suffering anymore and I am grateful, But my heart is broken at the thought of not being able to see him, touch him, hold his hand, kiss him or hear his beautiful deep voice. I know I will see him again, but when I do, what will our relationship be like? I believe we will be as brothers and sisters, with you our father. Will we have a special bond with our soul mates, like we do here? Will he be my best friend as he has been for thirty years on this earth? I know it will be wonderful and that it will be different. I also know there will be happiness we have never known until then. Lord I really do wish the rapture would come. There is still snow on the ground and its cold. I don't like winter because its so cold and the cold and bare trees, no animals frolicking makes me think of death. Maybe that's why people refer to the last years of life as the winter years or some call it the sunset of their days. I hope and pray that Heaven is eternal spring. I love spring. It wraps you in the warmth of the sun, life is renewing and everything is green and there are colors of flowers blooming everywhere.

Lord I am going to try really hard to focus on moving ahead. I will do my best not to dwell on what I have lost, but rather, what you have planned for our future. I ask that you give us all that we need and keep satan from trying to steal our joy. Please Lord, let us have peace and healing. I beg you to let us get out of debt and stay in our home, and though I know the devil will make it hard, I will gladly accept whatever your will shall be with a faithful heart. No matter what I face I will always be your devoted child and will do my very best to let my light shine in all circimstances.

Help us Lord, give us wisdom to do the right thing, to follow the path that you have planned for us. If it be your will to start over with the business, then make it happen, I will not pursue it unless you make happen. I will work hard at whatever you tell me to do. Thank you Lord, I know I am blessed, even when my heart is broken.

In Jesus name
Amen

This was such a sad time for everyone. We had lost Jerry, The Jenkins family had lost their patriarch, Bud, and the Watson family had lost theirs, Mayford.

And the church suffered so much family loss, Jacque M. lost her mom. And later we would lose Miss Mamie, one of the sweetest ladies I have ever had the pleasure of knowing. I know there were other losses in the families, I just can't think off the top of my head who they were, I just know there are a lot of people grieving great losses right now. When we went to Buds funeral, we went back to his home to spend some time with the family. Bud left a good legacy in his children and grandchildren and even a few greatgrands, I'm sure, although I didn't know her well Ann had a lot to do with it too. They are an awesome family. I can say the same for the Watson family also, and they are all related. Betty who was married to Mayford was Buds sister.

We hadn't been there very long, had just finished eating when someone came in and said the roads and drive were a sheet of ice. We ended up staying the night at Buds, which was enjoyable because it was interesting to hear the family talking about their Dad and Mayford and others back in their young days. Anyway we got up fairly early, I don't remember the time, but the sun was barely up good when we started home. The roads were still covered which terrified me. Crossing the bridge across the lake was nerve racking as well as going Henderson towards our house. All that I could think of was sliding off into that lake.

Casey did an excellent job driving, he had no problems until we got to our road. SOLID ICE. Oh my gosh, I thought I would wet my pants when he started sliding on that drive. For those that don't know us, that is quite a drop down the hollow if you slide off the drive. He couldn't even get up the first twenty feet, I was screaming by this time. Me and Kaylain got out and Casey eased it back down to the corner and pulled it as far off the road as he could. Then we began trying to navigate our way up the driveway, walking on this was not easy at all. I had on slick bottom shoes that I had worn to the funeral and I was sliding everywhere. The kids were laughing so hard, and even though I was terrified at the prospect of breaking a hip or leg, it was good to see them laughing. I was holding on to Caseys jacket and he was trying to walk and drag me up this icey hill at the same time, we almost fell a couple of times. I don't know how long it took us except that it was a while. We finally got to the bottom of our drive, I cut across the front yard and waited for them to go through the house and come downstairs and let me in. My feet were frozen, not literally, but with no socks or hose they were real cold.

I changed and warmed my feet and hands, then sat down just to catch my breath. As I sat there I began to pray and thank God for getting us home safely. Although it was an adventure, we were safe, and we didn't suffer any injuries. I knew there were many opportunities that satan could have made this a tragedy, but God had his hand right there between him and us.

Buds graveside service was that afternoon, but I knew that I wasn't going back out in that. Casey on the other hand would not be deterred. He loves this family and thought the world of Bud and he wanted to be there for Anna. He hopped on his four wheeler and went, I knew there was no talking him out of it, so I just prayed. We as parents have to do that a lot when our kids are old enough to start venturing out without us.

Journal entry December 16, 2010 Happy Birthday Michael and Daddy

Lord thank you for getting us home safely this morning. We went to Buds house after the funeral and got iced in. Casey, Kaylain, and I stayed at Buds house and left this morning. We made it all the way to our drive and it was solid ice. Scared me to death. Casey got the car back down to the mailboxes and we walked up the hill. I nearly fell five or six times, but we got home safely. Casey did a really good job driving home, I was very proud of him, he is so much like Jerry.

I love the Jenkins family, they are good people. I pray that it is your will that Casey and Anna finish school and get married and have a family, he would be so blessed.

Lord my heart still hurts so bad, please heal it. Make me whole again. I feel like so much of me is missing. I miss him Lord, so much. I dread those special moments that he is going to miss, like Caseys graduation, first day of college, college graduation, his wedding, Kaylains wedding, and the birth of their children.

We won't get to travel and see the country in a motor home, but we did get to do a lot together. It didn't matter if we were sleeping in a tent or on a cruise ship, we had so much fun. I think its because we were together, not because of where we were.

Lord let things go well at the hearing next week, please let us keep our insurance money to get budget under control and manageable. Lord whatever your plan is for us, your will, we will be accepting and grateful because our faith is in you, our trust is in you.

Bless my little family Lord, we have been through so much.

I pray in Jesus name
Amen

2nd Journal entry December 16, 2010 3:40 pm

Lord I need you, I have this overwhelming feeling of dispair, fear, anger, and loneliness because my baby is gone. Being cooped up because of ice and snow doesn't help. Amen

3rd Journal entry December 16, 2010 7:20 pm

Lord this has been a sad day for me, except that its my oldest childs birthday.

Happy Birthday Mike. Its also my Dads birthday who died twenty one years ago. This is my first Christmas in over 29 years without my sweet husband. Its hard Lord, I am trying not to get too emotional because Casey is sitting here behind me on the computer.

It's all made worse by having to sit in this house day after day and I just sit and think about past Christmases with Jerry. Our first Christmas when he gave me my little diamond promise ring, then there were Christmases in Florida, some in Mississippi, some in Charlotte and Gastonia, and all of the wonderful Christmases here in the home we loved so much, that we may lose now. Please don't let that happen Lord. I want Casey to have many Christmases here with his family. But, if it is not yor will, we will trust in your plan for us and to faithfully go where you lead us. I need peace Lord, I need calm.

Its so hard to think about what we are facing. I'm trying not to worry about the future, but its hard not to. I literally feel sick to my stomach because, even though I have not doubt where my faith lies, its your plans for us that worry me, we have been through so much since 2001. Ten years of grief, and trials. Please God let these next ten years be good ones, especially for children. I don't care what worldly things we have to surender if its your will. Its our happiness and security that I pray for. Let me be the rock for my kids that Jerry was for me. You are my foundation but I know that you used him to calm me in the storms of our lives. No I am not afraid. I don't know why, I know I am your child and that you will take care of me. Please God help me, lead me, most important of all use me for your glory. Let Christmas be a wonderful celebration of your sons birth, let me stay focused on that and not let anything stress me.

Thank you Lord for loving me even when I'm not lovable.

In Jesus name
Amen

4th Journal entry December 16, 2010 11:27 pm

Lord help. The shamble that is my life right now is getting to me. Its been eighteen days since I lost the love of my life. I miss his voice, his smile, his calm nature, that twinkle in his eyes when he smiled. I will always love him, I hope he can feel that.

Lord help me get my sugar under control, I just checked it and it was 281, my head feels like there is a tight band around it, so my blood pressure is probably up. Just lay your healing hands on me Lord, help me. Lord if Rick and his family make it in, please let us have a wonderful time. Don't let me get ill and cranky.I want to have a wonderful celebration of the birth of my precious Jesus while enjoying family and remembering my baby. Please let the next week go well, help my Lord, I need you and only you. I feel like I'm stuck in mud up to my neck and can't move or breath, guide me Lord, show me the way, keep me in the center of your will.

In Jesus name
Amen

Journal entry December 17, 2010 7:24 pm

Lord thank you for easing my stress today anyway. We went and got Caseys flat screen for Christmas, he wanted one last year and we couldn't afford it then and really can't now, but with help from money someone gave at church, and him paying some of it himself, and money from my brother, and help from the rest of the family he got one. I am going to get Kaylains tomorrow. They won't get anything else, except some things that they need, but I think having that one big item will be special. They know how things are. So thank you so much Lord.

In Jesus name
Amen

This was such a stressful time for me and the kids. We were trying so hard to focus on Christmas, but we were so tired and still reeling from the loss of Jerry. Rick and the kids were supposed to come for Christmas and I am ashamed to say that I was dreading it. I was in such a state of mind that I just wanted a quiet, peaceful Christmas. But I didn't discourage it because I thought maybe he needed to feel close to his Dad, and Christmas is for family. He ended up calling and saying that they couldn't afford to make the trip, I guess God knew what was best for all of us. They are going to try instead to come up when school is out this summer. Maybe by then we can do some things with them. Casey loves both of his brothers and I hope they will all stay in touch and grow their relationships.

We didn't even decorate except for the beautiful Christmas tree that my sister Candace and her family and my brother Kyle had sent for Jerrys funeral and the beautiful arrangement that my brother Clay and his family sent that was a center piece on the table, I couldn't believe that it was still alive. Our Christmas was nice. I let the kids open their gifts early and we had Christmas dinner with my family. My sweet Casey went shopping and bought gifts for him and Kaylain to give to me. He is so tender hearted, and thoughtful. He was worried that I would be sad if I didn't have a surprise to open for Christmas.

I have to tell this story on him because it was so cute. Jerry Love hated to shop. Unless it was tools, or stuff for the garden, or something for his tractor, he did not want to shop. In our early years together Christmas shopping was as follows, make a list, go to the store, get whats on the list, go home. This was a mission to me, not Christmas shopping. I always like to stop and look at all of the cool stuff they have at this time of year. So the next few years, we tried getting what was on the list and then he would go to the snack bar and have coffee and in those days you could smoke. But after about an hour he was ready to go. So then I finally gave up and started shopping alone.

As a gift to him I started buying my own gifts from him and the kids. I would buy what I needed and give it to him and he would give it to the kids to wrap. We did this for many years, we also did this mothers day, and birthdays. We quit buying cards all together when they went up to four and five dollars a card. Except our anniversary and Valentines, this is the only time Jerry would actually shop for anyone and he always bought me the most beautiful cards, I still have everyone of them. They were never funny cards, or anything like that, but instead were so very romantic and full of love. I will always cherish them.

Anyway, one night Casey and Kaylain and I were lying on my bed talking. Casey looked at me kind of sadly and said "I guess I will have to go get you a present from us "

I said "why?" He said ' Because Dad isn't here to get it." I wish that I had a camera when I told him that his Dad didn't buy my gifts anyway. I hadn't seen that look on his face since he found out there wasn't a santa clause. He just stared at me for a few seconds and then said unh huh, (how ever you spell it). I then explained to him what we had always done and that it wasn't necessary for him to buy me a gift. Now I wonder if I should have told him that.

Anyway he went shopping and bought me a nice mixer and a shopping basket to put in the van and keep items in. He was so excited he wanted me to open it as soon as he got it home, it was still days away from Christmas. He was so proud, he gets so much pleasure out of doing nice things for people. His wife and children will be very lucky.

Kaylain is like that to a degree, but not like Casey. She is still more about what is she going to get, but that will change as she matures. She was emotionally drained during this time. She didn't get to go spend Christmas with her mom like we had planned.

She was so sad about losing her grandpa. She wouldn't sleep in her bed for a long time. Anytime Jerry was gone, like when he and Casey would have a boys weekend camping or doing something together that would require being gone at night, she was in the bed with me. She was never afraid when Jerry was at home. She is finally back in her room, I think she has decided to trust God to take care of her.

Journal entry December 19, 2010

Thank you for this day or as Jerry would say "Thank you for another day of life "

Lord I am grateful for my life and the many blessings. I wish I could feel better, feel alive, Jerry took a big part of me with him when he died, and I feel so alone. I miss him so much. I try so hard not to let these feelings creep in, but they do anyway. Its not for him, I envy him. Its me and I know that's so selfish, and it makes me ashamed. I want to feel alive again and enjoy whatever time you have planned for me that is left. I want to enjoy my kids as they go through their milestones of life, but what about when they are grown and out raising their own kids. Those are the years that I wanted to spend with my sweet Jerry. What now Lord, that's what scares me, I don't want to end up a bitter old woman who is rejected by her kids. Help me Lord, get me through this until we are all together again with you.

In Jesus name
Amen

Journal entry December 21, 2010 11:37 pm

Help me Lord, I am trying to wait on you, I don't know what you want me to do. I am so afraid and confused. That trustee wants to take the money from the life insurance and leave me with no way to take care of my family.

I'm angry at you and I'm sorry that I have these feelings. I know its satan but when your in the situation he can make you feel hopeless and alone and unsure of what it is that you want me to do. You took my sweet husband and I know there is so much more I can lose, I'm not unappreciative of what I have and I'm not bitter about what we have lost. I am frustrated because I really don't want to lose anymore. I feel like nothing is ever going to be right again. I can't stand to see my child hurting when he has been through so much. To see the anger, the fears and most of all the doubt in his eyes, is more then I can bare Lord. Help us, help him, keep satan from him. I keep telling both the kids to be strong, that we will be ok and that satan will use these times when we are weak and vunerable to get his foot in the door and use us for his evil, we can't let him.

I feel like I should try and drop this bankruptcy if the judge will let me. I don't feel like the attorneys have given me good advise and that I am being dealt with unfairly. I certainly don't feel like the trustee cares one bit about us, its not his job I guess. But I don't feel like I can have peace unless I try. I'm not saying I won't try to pay debts, I am saying I can do a better job.

They want me to sell the business and pay the business debts, but they want to claim the stock? I don't get this whole thing and I am going to fight it. If I am going to lose everything I will lose it fighting for it. I want to be a good example to my kids. Help me Lord, lead me, guide me and direct me. I don't think they even care if his funeral is paid. All of those attorneys have passed the buck. I have not gotten one straight answer about my concerns when I asked. Its been that way through this whole process thus far.

I have to fight for what I believe is right Lord, if I am wrong, then things will continue to go wrong if its not your will and I accept that.

Jesus, Lord, I pray for much needed blessings on our lives right now. We are all tired and weak. Put a hedge about us, especially my kids. Lord I don't care if you take me tomorrow, if you have no more use for me here. I just pray for my kids. In the words of Job as he stood in the ashes," here I am Lord." I am yours, do with me as you will. I am your child and I want only to serve you. Show me the way Lord. Use me for your glory, let everthing I say and do bring you glory.

In Jesus name
Amen

Journal entry December 22, 2010

Thank you Lord for this day. I enjoyed dinner with family at moms house then went to church and watched the kids do their Christmas program. I missed Jerry being there with me.

No matter what I am going through, no matter how sad I am, watching my kids raise up their voices to sing Gods praises always brings the joy in my heart bubbling over. Its hard right now Lord, but I still trust in you. I wrote a letter to the attorneys to drop the bankruptcy but if I am going against you then let them deny it. I want to be in your will and not be pulling against you. Let Kaylain have a good time with Amie and Haley tomorrow. And Lord please give the Cannon family a blessing for their kindness.

I pray that blessing be healing fo Ann, I think the world of her. She is one of the most Godly women that I have ever known.

In Jesus name
Amen

I was having a really hard time in dealing with this whole bankruptcy ordeal. The trustee handling it was the most arrogant, cold hearted person that I had ever delt with. Maybe like a doctor, he has to detach himself so that he can do his job. But to leave a family totally without any way to live, is too much. I understood that there were debts that we owed, but to not let me pay his funeral or catch up the house payments was just cold and evil. I was having a hard time letting the attorneys handle this.

Journal entry December 23, 2010 9:40 am

Been up since about 5:00 am. Casey got up early, he and Anna went to volunteer at the empty stocking fund this morning giving out baskets, I am so proud of him and I know his Dad is too.

Lord please let the decisions I make come from you and let things get better please.I am going to write a letter to Jerry now, please give it to him. Amen

My dearest love,

I miss you so much, we were supposed to grow old together and now you are gone. I wouldn't bring you back for anything, instead I look forward to the day we will be reunited in Heaven. I am happy that you are no longer suffering, as much as you tried to hide it, I could see it in your eyes.You were the strongest, sweetest, caring man I have ever known in my life and I am so glad that God put us together.We are soul mates forever.We were good for each other and I miss that.

I miss the twinkle in your eyes when you were happy or having fun. I miss having you to talk to, I miss everything about you. I see so much of you in our son, God truly blessed us with him.You always were so proud of him, you can be especially proud of him now. Don't worry about us, we will be fine, I'm sure you already know that God is going to get us through. It's three days until Christmas and it's a comfort to me to know your are with Jesus and your mom,dad, sister,our babies, my dad, grandma, our friends : Bud, Randy, and so many others. I love you so much my sweet love and I am so thankful for the years God gave us and I can't wait to see you again. Until then I will take care of our family with Gods grace and mercy.

Your loving wife

Journal entry December 24, 2010 Christmas Eve 2010

Thank you Lord for last night, we had so much fun. I cooked all day yesterday and we invited family and friends over to eat. I went ahead and gave Kaylain her wii because it has a dance game with it and those kids (and Melissa) had a blast. They danced until late. I believe Casey said four hours. It was a good time and the first time since Jerry died that I really had fun.

I miss him so much Lord, and I know that I always will. I beg you move this mountain Lord that we have had in front of us for so many years. Please make them let us drop this chapter 7, it is ruining our lives. They have no mercy on us. You are the only one who does, but then you are the only one who counts. So here is the bottom line, I pray for us to keep the insurance money and use it to :

1. Give 10 % to the church
2. Pay for Jerrys funeral
3. Get charity established
4. Get debt caught up including taxes, lights, trash, house, and car.
5. Get Casey into college
6. Refinance the house, get payments where I can afford them by myself.
7. Pay back my mom
8. Get repairs done on the house
9. (If its your will) allow us a family vacation

Lord I really want to do this, I can't lie to you, you know the main reason I want these things is for peace of mind. But I really want to help people, that is important to me, especially since I have been on the other end. I am so grateful for all the people who have helped us financially through this and I truly want to do it for others, even more so now.

Last, but most important of everything we have faced these past six to ten years, hardest being the loss of Jerry, is that I want people to see you Lord, to see that through our faith in you, your grace is what gets us through. If it is your will for my prayer to be answered, I pray everyone see your hand in it and we will most certainly give you the glory.

In Jesus name
Amen

Journal entry December 25, 2010 1:30 am

HAPPY BIRTHDAY JESUS

Yesterday I spent a good day with my kids doing last minute shopping and the afternoon and evening with our family, it was a lot of fun. Lord I miss my sweet Jerry and I pray that you give him my love.

Thank you God fo the gift of your precious son, born into this world of sin to save us from eternal damnation. I thank you for my many blessings and for your grace that brings me peace and comfort at such a difficult time. Please bless us Lord with all that we need.

In Jesus Holy name
Amen

2nd Journal entry December 25, 2010 10:01 pm

Thank you Lord for getting me through this day. Everyone is gone now and Kaylain is in there on the computer and Casey and Alex are down stairs hanging out.

I just went outside and walked around for about twenty minutes. The snow is gently falling. They are big fluffy flakes, so beautiful. I walked up towards the building that Jerry spent so much time in, he loved his building, he loved this home. It just seemed like the doors should be open and the lights on and him be in there working away on one of his many projects. But then I come back to reality and the tears start to flow. I prayed Lord, walking around out there I pleaded with you. Its hard enough to let go of him, let us please get our lives stableized. Let us prosper and do well and make wise decisions and do good works for your glory. Help me Lord, I am nothing, I am weak, only you can make a miracle and I need one right now. Whatever your plan, we will accept it with faithful hearts and trust in you.

In Jesus name
Amen

Journal entry December 26, 2010

What I posted on face book status yesterday

What I want fo Christmas Lord, only you can give me :

1. A mended heart
2. A focused mind
3. A strong will
4. A steady hand
5. And most of all a faith that grows more and more each day.

Today I would like to add :

1. The wisdom of soloman
2. The faith of Job
3. The love of Jesus
4. The strength of Sampson

I had made it through Jerrys death. After that I knew I could get through anything. Things with the bankruptcy was going bad and I didn't want to leave the house to buy groceries much less go to the store and start on that. I didn't know which way to turn or what to do.

Journal entry December 27, 2010 Happy Birthday Bobby

Lord, I wish you would rid me of this sinking feeling I have in my stomach, especially when I pull in the driveway and it feels like Jerry should be here. I miss him Lord, and I know its selfish because he isn't missing us and I'm glad. I look forward to the day when none of us will suffer a broken heart.

Lord please change our lives for the good, its so hard and its been this way for so long. I miss his deep voice, his gentle kiss, his strong hand and reassuring way. He could calm me like no one other then you. God I enjoyed that message yesterday on being slothful (Hebrew 6:12). I feel like you were speaking to me. If I have displayed a slothful spirit to you then please forgive me.

I have always hated wintertime, I hate it even more now being cooped up with all of the memories. The snow is beautiful but I don' like it. I love spring. I am so sorry when I disapoint you Lord, I want only ot please you. I hope to get the business going and to do well for my family, employees, and many, many more people who find themselves in our situation and just need a helping hand. Those who like us have worked all of their lives and can't qualify for assistance because they own a home. Its not fair the way working people are treated when they fall on hard times.

I had to call Casey to bring money to the grocery store Saturday because I didn't have enough, yet that trustee wants to take my life insurance money and leave me with nothing to live on until I can empty the store and get the business closed down and find a job. God please don't let that happen. Lift us up out of this hell we have been going through Lord. Give us peace, hope, and security.

In Jesus name
Amen

Journal entry December 28, 2010

Lord I am afraid. I know I shouldn't be, but nothing seems to go good for me. I have a huge hole in my heart, I am so down about our situation and honestly don't know what you want me to do. I feel so alone without Jerry, I know that I am not, but it feels that way. Help me Lord, show me the way you want me to go. Don't let me get angry and out of sorts when things don't go my way. Help me to know what is your will and what is not. Protect me from evil people who are not in it for my benefit. Help us Jesus. Lord I don't know how things go up there or what is allowed, but if it is possible give Jerry my love and let him know how much I miss him, and that we are ok. Help me Lord to overcome this awfull feeling, I don't even know how to describe it. it's the worst emotion I have ever known.

I ask these things
In Jesus name
Amen

Journal entry December 31, 2010 9:22 am

Lord tonight at midnight begins a new year (in this world). 2010 has been the worst year of my life. The worst being the loss of my precious husband. He was my everything, he completed me. We were not to good on our own, but together we were great. He was my rock and the only one next to you who could calm me in a storm. As long as I had him to lay next to at night, I could deal with the problems of the day. I know you are the one who can change things and that you are the one who will lift me up, brush me off and set me on the right path. Please continue to give me grace to face each day, each moment, show me Lord, I have ask you so many times to speak to my heart about what you want me to do. Evedently I am not getting the message because my life is in shambles, and Lord I know I do my very best to live right and I try to do what brings you glory and to serve you. So please show me where I am going wrong. I really do want to be the best I can be in your eyes, not everyone elses, just you. God I really am going to try and live better, to do good and to please you. I pray when I come to you this time next year I will have accomplished a lot for your glory.

Keep me strong in my faith
Keep me focused
Keep me on the right path
Keep me in the center of your will
Keep me faithful and hopeful in the eyes of my children
Keep me in line on improving my life and my health

Lord let me be able to stand even stronger every time the devil knocks me down, and while I am no match for him, use me as a light in this world of darkness.

In Jesus name
Amen

I decided to make these commitments or prayer requests, rather then resolutions.

2nd Journal entry December 31, 2010 11:44 pm

Sixteen minutes until the end of 2010, worst year ever. Lord I pray you will see it in your plan to give us a better year. I can't even grieve for worring about the store., the insurance money, the bankruptcy, our home. What are we going to do? And every time I give up on the store, something happens to make think you want me to move forward with it. I got an email from Jerry B today giving me until March 31,2011 to pull it off. I can only do it if we can keep the check. So if its your will let us get the money, if not we won't get it. I don't want trust my own thoughts right now, so this way I will know if its your will and I will accept it. Please help me Lord to do your will, not mine. Take care of us and give us what we need.

In Jesus name
Amen

P.S. Please tell Jerry I love him and miss him so bad.

Finally 2010 was over, the worst year of my life. We still had so much to get settled with the store and the bankruptcy, and the mortgage. I have to do something with the store and I have to get a good job somewhere that will support my family. I was so exhausted and wanted nothing more then to get my life back on track, to even have a life.

I was going through what I guess was depression, I would just sit for hours. I would spend some time on the computer looking for jobs and filling out applications.

What I really needed to do was get to the store and figure out what I needed to do there.

Katie and I and the kids eventually went and started trying to pack up the store, but it was so cold and damp in there we couldn't stay long at a time. And the mildew where the roof was pooring water in all of this time was unbarable.

I was losing my mind. I was shutting down, I began to withdraw, to not care. At this time I had to do a lot of praying and soul searching, I had two kids depending on me.

Satan was using every tool in his arsenal to make me miserable and it worked for a while.

Then I remembered who I was, who I am, A child of God, that's all that I needed.

CHAPTER 8

Shock

After the shock wares off, you slowly begin to feel again. Some pain, some joy, some fear, some hope. You start to live again, no longer do you want to just sit and push the world away. You still aren't there yet, but you know that you have to push yourself to move forward. The time comes whether we want it or not to start focusing on what needs to be done. This is especially true if you still have kids to take care of.

You still get distracted with memories, and periods of what to do next, but the key is to keep moving, keep praying, keep trusting. Challenge to get one thing a day done, even if its just cleaning out a drawer, or filling out ten applications, or cooking your families favorite meal. And anytime you feel the devil trying to move in on you, stop whatever your doing and pray. Get your Bible or if you use a prayer journal get that, or both, just get with God. He is always available and he wants to hear from you.

This time was especially difficult for me because when the shock of losing Jerry was new, I didn't care who came after me, they could do whatever they wanted to me. I had lost the most precious person in the world to me, my kids were the only thing that kept me from completely losing my mind. But now I was coming back to life. I started to think about all that I needed to do for the sake of my children. The bankruptcy was a real pain to deal with. I don't know when it will be over. I don't trust that trustee or the attorneys, I don't know if because I am suffering grief that I think everyone else is crazy and out to do what ever possible to destroy me completely or if satan has me in a panic and I am the one that everyone else is thinking is crazy. Either way I will be glad when its all over, it will be nice to know where we stand and what we need to do next.

If you think of something that you suddenly feel compelled to do, that you have never done before like writing this book is for me, do it. It could be something therapeutic and a good release. My hope that it will be something worthy of publishing for two reasons. First and foremost I want it to touch people who are dealing with grief. It doesn't matter if the grief is caused from the death of a loved one, the breakup of a marriage, the loss of a job that has been a part of your life for many years, it all has emotional impact on your life, some more then others. Second I pray that it will be successful enough to sell and to raise enough money to pay for my mortgage and settle all of our debt so that my children and I can start over. If I can't have the second, I still pray for the first.

One thing that has helped me a lot, is to not only focus on my grief and heartache but that of others that are suffering. When I pray for Gods help and intervention I also pray for others, and when I see God move in all situations, mine or others, I make sure to thank him.

This is a time we are starting a new life, a new chapter so to speak. While some things remain the same, because of our loss we deal with them differently. We tried so hard to hang on to our business and turn it around, but it wasn't meant to be. It always seemed so important to save it and it ruled our time for years until Jerry got sick.

I also found it very hard to wait on God during this time. I know I drove my attorneys crazy, but when it concerns the welfare of my family, I am very tenacious.

If I think for a minute that someone is not dealing with me fairly or jeopardizing our well being, I will fight hard to stop it. But I also will pray that if I am the one who is in the wrong, for God to set me straight, to put me and keep me in the center of his will. It is very humbling when God opens your eyes to the fact that you are wrong. And its usually because either you were not listening in those quiet moments when he was speaking to your heart or you are not waiting on him to move. He does things in his own time not yours.

Take these life lessons to heart and learn from them. Trials will do a couple of things. It will strengthen our faith and our relationship with God, and it will teach us. Share them with others to help them if they find themselves in a similar situation. Oh there is one more thing, if we rely on God faithfully, and earnestly trust in him, it will be obvious to those around you and will strengthen your witness and testimony. You don't know what this can do for another persons faith.

Watching Charlotte go through all that she has, really encouraged me years ago to seek a better, stronger relationship with God, her pain and how she dealt with it these past years has helped me in mine now. Randy was also another who touched our lives in a profound way. He was battling cancer and what struck me was how he was always trying to assure his family and friends. Because he trusted in God, the grace God bestowed on him was evident to those around him, I'm sure this helped Jerry in dealing with his. I have no doubt they are all having a good time in heaven.

This is what I want this book to do for all who read it. I want it to be a blessing to those who are struggling in the valley right now. I want people to understand that the only way to get through these times is your faith in God. Be open about what you are feeling, other Christians in your life want to help you, they want to be there for you. When I can say or do something that will be a blessing to someone, it blesses me more then it does them, and in turn when they see someone going through it they can share what God did for them and be a blessing to someone else.

Journal entry January 1, 2011 3:00 pm

Lord I am sitting here on my front deck and I think about all of the times Jerry and I or us and the kids would sit out here and talk and play. I look out at the beautiful view which hasn't changed much, only the people who view it. Sitting out in the gazebo yesterday also brought back memories such as company cookouts, Easter egg hunts, and the simpler more precious memories, like Jerry plowing his garden or bush hogging the yard. He loved the out doors so much. That's where Casey gets it from. God I miss him so much, and I try not to dwell on it, but I am so lonely, even in a room full of people.

I hope to keep this place and someday pass it on to Casey and his family. There are so many happy memories here for us. Lord please let us have an early spring, I hate these cold, gloomy days, it only deepens my despair. But even in spring I know I will miss him even more. I will miss him working outside, miss camping with him and the kids, and working with him in our business, or just lying together at night talking or watching t.v. while the kids were doing their thing.

Lift me up Lord please, I have faith, I have hope, please. I don't want to live in my memories, I just want to cherish them. I remember the first time Jerry and I came to this place. We loved it from the start. I can remember the feeling when Teresa called us to pick up the keys, that we had the house. We were doing good at the store and having so much fun, but I can see now that we did not honor you or give you the glory that you command and for that I am so sorry.

These past six years we have rededicated our lives and have walked so much closer to you, but things have gone so wrong. I hate losing Jerry, I know I have to accept and trust in you. I do trust in you but, God forgive me, I am angry and hurt and don't understand. I know I will when I get to heaven, but it doesn't help the pain. I am sorry.

I love you, I trust you
In Jesus name
Amen

Journal entry January 2, 2011 Happy Birthday Candace

Lord bless us this day with all that we need. Thank you for our many blessings, even the ones we take for granted. I am so thankful that we have a roof over our heads and we are not hungry. My children are healthy and happy.

This is a new year and I pray a better one. I pray I will be sitting here, still in our home this time next year. I do hope to be thinner and healthier. Lord guide me in every decision that I have to make. Let us keep the check to start our little diner Jerry and I talked about and pay off debts and refinance our home and make necessary repairs, and get a safe vehicle to drive. Its a lot to ask, but not to much for you to handle.

Journal entry January 4, 2011

Thank you Lord for my many blessings, guide me through my many trials. Speak to my heart, give me your will for my life, use me lord. If dealing with Becky and her charity is the way you want me to go, I will gladly do it, but only you can make it work.

I don't have to be an owner, I just want to be able to pay off all of our debts, keep our home please, and take care of my family.

I miss my husband so badly Lord, please let him know how much he is loved. Please help me to survive without him. God I trust in you, my faith is in you, please protect me and my family from the evil and wrong of this world. Use my pain and valleys to inspire others, let us be a light and a good example of a Christian. Lord give us peace, comfort, wisdom, and blessings to have what we need to move forward.

In Jesus name
Amen

Journal entry January 5, 2011 afternoon

Lord, I honestly don't know where my life is headed. I pray its down the path you have chosen for me to follow. I have a plan, that I hope is your will. It will benefit Beckys

Charity, the landlord, and me, so please make it come to pass. Its good, honest work and it still enables me to be in a position to help people. Please lead, guide, and direct me. Help me to do what it is that you want us to get done

Lord please help us to do the right thing concerning the insurance money. I can really use it, but if its not your will then please provide, as you always have, what we need. Keep us focused on your will and your plan. My faith is in you alone Lord, and my trust is in your plan.

In Jesus name
Amen

Journal entry January 7, 2011

Lord, please keep satan away. Let our plan work, if its your will, let things go quickly and smoothly. If you want me to keep the store, or work for Becky at the store or be at the store at all. Just please make it known to me what you want me to do. Please send me help and let me get the store cleared out, whatever plan you have let us get this done so that the landlord can get in there and do the work that they need to do. Lord I ask that they approve my unemployment and get it started, please let my marriage certificate get here so that I can get the social security money owed so I can catch up my house payment.

I am so tired Lord, and right now I am so sick. Please help me. Why can't I feel you, does satan have me so numb that I can't even feel the Holy Spirit? I know your there because you said in your word that you would never leave me or forsake me. I have hope if things would just come together. Ok, I just read the scripture below, now I know why I can't feel you.

The fruit of the Spirit is love, joy, peace, patience, kindness, goodness, faithfulness, gentleness and self-control. Galatians 5:22,23 OMG

Amen

I have been lacking in the virtues listed, is that why? Is it because I have only known anger, frustration, sadness, hopelessness, doubt, fear, and all those little demons that satan uses. I also have been slack in my spiritual life and for all of these things I am so sorry. I need you Lord and only you can change my life. I beg you to do so.

Lord I miss my husband so much, all I can think about are the looks of pain, fear and confusion on his face the last few weeks of his life. None was about his faith, that stayed strong until the end. His concern was always for me and the kids. I pray that he left with the peace that we would be ok, no matter what we have to deal with. And that while I am so tired and overwhelmed right now, I know that we will be ok, I just wish it were sooner rather then later, but its all according to your plan and not mine.

I pray in my sweet
Jesus name
Amen

As the realization of our situation began to sink in, (when my mind began to function again), satan used this time to beat me down. Depression is one of satans strongest tools. He makes it so inviting to just pull the covers over your head and hide until it all goes away. He will use your memories, he makes them pop in your mind at the most unexpected times, surprise attack so to speak. So no matter if you are at the grocery store or driving down the road, or trying to have a discussion with someone, you become so overwhelmed with grief that you just bust out crying. Just talking about your loved one can make it all come crashing in on you. But I promise that it will change, you will begin to feel complete joy when you think of them, just be strong and lean on the Lord.

I'm not saying you won't ever cry, but they will become tears of joy rather then pain. The joy that God put in your heart when you were saved will push out the despair and eventually you will be happy again. You will grow stronger every day. And while you miss your loved one so much, you can take comfort in knowing that you will see them again. I know that I am looking forward to that day.

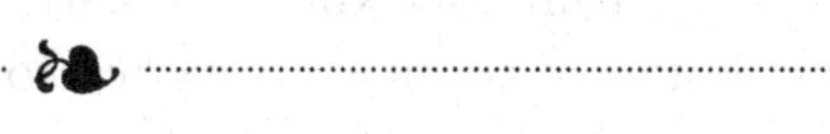

Journal entry January 8, 2011

Thank you Lord for all of our blessings big and small. Lord I pray that you are the one who sent me the information about the statue concerning the life insurance, I pray that it is all I need to stop them from taking all of the money and not paying Jerrys funeral or settling our mortgage so we can keep our house. I think greed is what moves that trustee because he gets a percentage and that's bull.

Guide me Lord in every decision, every step, I need your guidance because I sure don't know what to do. Please let me get the business cleared and sell all that I can to help settle the debt. Lord I beg your hand on these matters cause I don't know what to do. Help me Jesus, help me God you are the only one who can.

In Jesus name
Amen

2nd Journal entry January 8, 2011 4:30 pm

This has been the longest day. I am fighting depression. Lord you know where my heart is and where my faith lies. You know I trust in your plan. I am only human and I can't even begin to fight the devil. I have not had a job since the end of October, and losing Jerry after six months of battling cancer is more then I can bare. Add to that losing the business and dealing with the pressure of getting that cleared out, and dealing with the bankruptcy and attorneys who don't know what they are doing and a trustee who wants to take the life insurance money and leave me with paying the funeral bill, and the taxes and house payments and no way to pay them, he is nuts.

Lord I am not asking for luxuries or trips, or anything like that. I've lost Jerry, nothing else matters to me except you and providing for my kids. I pray that is your will for us. I also want to tithe to the church. I haven't in a while and they have been so good to us. I would like to use some to get tires and brakes on the van, fix the tub, sliding door and other repairs around the house. Allow me to send Casey to college, and send him on a senior trip. I pray that I find a really good job or start a new business that will support my family and take care of our needs, and will still allow me to help others. This is my prayer Lord, I pray that it is your will.

In Jesus name
Amen

Journal entry January 12, 2011

Lord thank you for all of my blessings. Thank you for peace and comfort. I ask so much, and I jump from one thing to another. I am feeling like your plan for me is not with Becky, she hasn't even called me to say she doesn't want to go with the plan.

I don't even feel like you want me at the store. If you need me somewhere else that is more pleasing to you, then put me there, direct me, guide me. All I ask is that I can work at something that is meaningful and helps many people, not just a job that supports my family. Although for that I would be so grateful.

I just hate leaving Jerry B. in such a mess with the store. But with no money, no help, now all of this snow and ice keeping me prisoner at home, I will probably be doing him a favor to just get out of his way. I need a job that will also provide health insurance. Please bless us Lord with what we need and maybe a little of what we want.

In Jesus name
Amen

Journal entry January 13, 2011

My precious Lord, my heart is so broken, my mind is too full of worry. My body is tired and run down. I beg your healing touch in each of these situations Lord. I need to feel your Holy Spirit, my comforter in every fiber of my being. I am so down and out, bordering on depression. I can't fight this Lord, I know its satan, so I need you to handle it. You are the only one who can.

Lord I have tried every way I can to save the business and every time something happens to make me think its your will, it doesn't work out. I quit. I don't think its your will so please show me your will for my life. What can I do to serve you Lord. How do you want to use me for your glory? Please open my ears to hear, my eyes to see, my mind to know, and my heart to lead. Lord I am so low and being stuck in the house because of snow is not helping.

My Father, my God, I ask that com March 22, 2011, we can keep the majority of the life insurance. I will give you, the church, (I am not making deals with you God, I know better), my 10 % tithes. I will pay Jerrys funeral, I will catch up house payments, make necessary repairs, pay Caseys college, refinance our home asap, get a better car, and send Casey on senior trip. I pray it be your will to let us take a family vacation. Nothing expensive or extravagant, just some family time away from everything. Lord I miss Jerry so much. The waves of panic and despair, are pushing me toward depression, help me Lord as only you can. I pray by spring as life renews itself that I and my kids can renew ours. We have to live life as a family of three instead of four now, help us to adjust. I am so looking forward to living again, to feel life again, because right now I don't feel like I have one.

Watch over my children Lord. Keep them focused on their school work and let Casey graduate and get into college. I pray that you have a bright future for him, he deserves it. I pray Kaylain starts high school here and while I pray she has a wonderful time with her mom and sisters, I pray she comes home to stay, this is where she belongs. Casey and I are her family, the only one she has known. But only you know what is best for them.

I would like to pray for Kylie, the little girl on caring bridge that needs you and for Gene and Charlotte, for Charles and Wilma, Kathy Haynes, Tammy Crowe, Robert Gibbs, and all of those who need your healing touch right now. Touch the hearts of all those who like us have lost someone dear to them. Watch over our military and their families.

Lord use me to plant seeds in the hearts of the lost, use my life for your glory, to be a light. I pray that the rapture is near and that you are coming to get us soon. I can't wait to be with you and my sweet husband. I pray for the time of your choosing when we will all be together again.

In Jesus sweet name
Amen

Journal Entry January 14, 2011

Lord please let the landlord respond well to my e-mail from last night. I am so helpless as to what needs to be done in this situation. I don't want to cause a big headache for them, but I am so tired just from the stress of everything all at once. When I feel like I will lose my mind and I think that I can't handle all of this, I don't have Jerry here telling me that I can. But then I have you telling me I don't have to.

So Lord here it is, I give all of my burdens to you. I am laying them at your feet and I will not pick them up again. (I will try). I pray for your will to be done and if its not what I pray for then give me the grace to deal with it. Whatever we face Lord, good or bad, let there be good come out of it for your glory.

In Jesus name
Amen

I Peter 5: 7,8
Matthew 6: 25-28

Journal Entry January 15, 2011 11:30 am

Lord please let today go well, let us get a lot done so the land lord will see that we are working hard to get out of his way. Let us have a good time with Candace and Jimmy.

In Jesus name
Amen

Journal Entry January 16, 2011 7:30 am

Lord give bro David the message you would have us to receive this morning. Let your holy spirit move like never before. Touch my body Lord and heal me. My back pain was unbearable yesterday and I only worked two and one half hours. I don't know why, but when I do anything repetitive with my arms, my back kills me. Bless me with better health Lord, please.

In Jesus name
Amen

Journal Entry January 19, 2011 9:30 am

Thank you Lord for all blessings, no matter how small. Thank you for my kids and for watching over us. Help me get as much as possible cleaned out so I can get things settled with the business and IRS and be out from under that burden.

Please let me get through this bankruptcy and still have most of the money left to pay bills, get our home where its affordable and sell this van and get something more dependable and economical. Let me send Casey to college, and go on a senior trip with his friends. And if its not too much to ask let me have some kind of little vacation away from everything to reflect, grieve, and plan (with your guidance) a future for my family.

Lord I miss Jerry so much, please tell him how much he is loved.

I praise your holy name
Amen

During this period of my life I was so overwhelmed I couldn't function. I have never at any other time in my life fought depression so hard, and that's saying a lot because I have been through a lot in my life. Its debilitating when you are in this frame of mind, you don't want to face life, this is why satan likes to use it. I used to say and still believe that I am too blessed to be depressed, but I am only human. I fight it everyday and if I think about it, I guess that I am too blessed, because if it were not for my being blessed by God, I probably would have crawled up in my bed and just waited for him to take me.

When I get really down, I go him in prayer. He will gently remind me that I am blessed with my children, my family, my church, and dear friends. That he still has a purpose for me and that when my time comes it will be at his choosing, and until then I am to live my life serving him. Death is a part of the circle of life, we are all going to face it one day if he tarries his coming. We are not promised tomorrow and it could happen at any age.

If God were to take me today, I can say that I have lived a good life. In spite of all the valleys, I have known the love of a good man, I have kids that I adore, I have known true happiness, and God has used me many times for his glory. There are so many who don't get to experience the joys that I have known, so I am very grateful. This is one thing that makes me want to move forward and make God happy with what he has planned for the rest of my life.

Writing this part makes me realize how good God has been to me. It makes me want to move on and find happiness in what he has waiting for me. I am confidant that he will lead me to a job that will support us, that my son will go to college, and that my children will have families and lives that will be happy. I know that he will use me in some way to help others. I am actually starting to look forward to the rest of my life.

Journal Entry January 21, 2011 Friday 8:22 pm

Lord my life is . . . . I don't even know what. I am so tired and so stressed. My heart keeps fluttering which scares me. I am on the verge of a nervous breakdown. Every time

I think things are looking better. Something else happens.

Today I was having such a bad day, very down. Then I got a call from the company interested in buying my racks and stuff,

I was feeling a little better then I got a letter from that wicked trustee, I do believe that man is demonic. Now he says I am uncooperative, what an idiot. I haven't touched a dime of that money even though I owe, Nov, Dec., Jan. house payments, my van needs tires, brakes, radiator and several other things fixed. I need to go to the Dr badly, my sugar is out of control and my blood pressure is also. I don't sleep, I can't think, I bust out crying without any warning. I have panic attacks so bad that I feel like I am having a heart attack.

Lord I don't know what I've done to bring all of this misery, but please forgive me. I am begging you. My poor Jerry, I remember him saying all of the things he had quit that displeased you and yet he still ended up losing to the cancer. Lord I don't care when you take me. I would like to stay a little while longer for my kids sake, but I know their faith is strong. I just don't want to leave Casey with this mess. God sometimes I just feel forsaken, I know that is not true because your word tells me different, but is so hard to believe sometimes. But my faith is always in you.

Kaylain has her computerized baby from teen living. She has it for the whole weekend. I think she got one that has a glitch, this thing has been going constantly since 5:03 pm., its only 8:46 pm and she has eaten five times and had diaper change four times.

Kaylain is already tired and she has it until Monday.

Lord I am so miserable right now, I know its not what you want for me, so please change it. I know I will understand when I get to Heaven, but I am so unhappy. What do you want me to do, I want only to be in the center of your will. Reach down and touch me Lord, have mercy on me. I am on my knees begging. I try so hard to be the best Christian that I can be and I feel so let down right now. Please forgive my lack of faith, but I am not Job.

My heart is broken, I miss my precious Jerry. People who say its better to have loved and lost then never to have loved at all, must not have lost love to death, because that is the most awful feeling ever. Touch my heart, my soul, my spirit.

In Jesus name
Amen

Journal entry January 22, 2011 5:11 pm

Lord please make my stomach quit hurting, it is hurting so bad and I don't know why. My Father in heaven, I beg you to make things good again. They never will be the same for me without my soul mate, but I pray they get better for the kids. I am so sleepy,

I am going to take a nap. We went to moms and hung out with her and Candace and ate some soup. Casey went shopping to get Anna a gift for their anniversary. He bought her a beautiful diamond bracelet in the X's and O's pattern.

God I miss Jerry so much. My life is such a mess right now, especially without him. Please help me, let me have a beautiful, realistic dream about him while I take a nap.

In Jesus name
Amen

Journal entry January 24, 2011 1:16 pm

Lord I need you so much, I am tired of the evil of this world tormenting me. Help me Lord, I plead with you all of the time, why won't you help? Well I should say help more, get us out of this. It's not that I am not grateful for all that you have done, its just there is so much more then I can handle to still be done. I don't want to set a bad example for my kids, I will not resist what the law says I have to do and I will accept your will for us, even if we lose everything we have. Just keep my family safe and don't let satan get his toe in the door. Heal my body, guide me in an effort to live and eat healthier. I pray it is your will that I stick around a few more years. As always Lord, I pray you use me, my family and our trials for your glory.

In Jesus name
Amen

2nd Journal entry January 24, 2011 6:09 pm

Lord I'm sorry for my thoughts, but I really feel abandoned by you. I know that I'm not, but when everything goes against me its hard to trust. It kills me to see my son worry and get angry and frustrated. He should only have to worry about graduation and getting through college.

God I just want to get through it all. I know its not fair, this world is not fair, it belongs to satan. What I don't understand is why you won't help me. Forgive me Lord, I know it's the devil. I know where my hope is, it is and always will be in you. Please let this be a life lesson for my kids and not a tool for the devil to get to my kids or me for that matter. I've said a few words today I'm not proud of and I am sorry. I won't pretend. I haven't thought of having a cigarette, but I won't, just calm and protect me. Let me live the lesson I heard last night about anger, wrath, and vengeance.

In Jesus name
Amen

3rd Journal entry January 24, 2011 11:53 pm

Lord please calm my mind, let me have a good nights sleep. Help me Lord know what to do. Thank you for keeping the devil from my kids. This difficult time in our lives has only made them stronger in their faith. They get angry and frustrated and scared just like me, but their trust is in you.

In Jesus name
Amen

Journal entry January 25, 2011 Happy Anniversary
25 yrs (29) gone
Eternity to go

Lord I miss my baby. I didn't get to feel his tender lips or hear his beautiful deep voice this morning waking me with "Happy Anniversary". Instead I have stress and pain that scares me. I am having pain and fluttering around my heart. I've had this before and it turned out to be stress. I hope that's all it is now. Lay your powerful, healing hands on me. God please let us get through this valley soon.

Amen

Letter to my sweet Jerry for our anniversary

My dearest love, I miss you so much and wish you were here. Remember when we used to do our anniversary get—a-ways. I remember so well the trips to Valley View Inn in Boone and Harrahs in Cherokee. The night I remember most, was the night we got married. We were already living together for over four years.

(sorry kids, God has forgiven us). That night, that wonderful night, was so special. We were broke, well we paid the bills, but nothing much was left over. We went to Red Lobster and then went home and made a bed on the floor in front of the kerosene heater and laughed, loved, and talked until almost daybreak.

I have been watching our home videos and we had such wonderful times together. I even got one of our spats on one when I thought the camera was off. I would even take that right now because they never lasted more then a few minutes anyway. I remember so well the sparkle in your eyes when we go married and how your leaned over and sealed each vow with a kiss. I didn't know what you were doing until you told me afterward, I thought you were just nervous.

I remember all of the special things you did for me, like the little church you were building me, but never got to finish. I remember how you walked the hospital corridors all night with me when I was in labor with Casey, and how you rubbed my back all morning through the contractions and never flinched while holding the bowl I was throwing up in. That is why I felt so bad when you kept apologizing because I was taking care of you in the end. We had that special love that is God sent, and that is what gives us grace when we take care of one another.

I often sit in the gazebo and wander back to the many springs spent here watching you on your John Deere tractor working your garden. I can see you coming down this hill with buckets full of goodies grown with your own two hands and Gods gifts of soil, rain and sun. I am really going to have a hard time trying to grow anything. Tomatoes I can handle.

I think about all of the wonderful weekends at the campground watching the kids, grilling out, playing cards, snuggling in our bed listening to the rain hit the roof or sitting on the deck late at night after everything had settled into a quiet, peaceful calm enjoying a cigarette and a cup of coffee. I love the picnics that we used to have in the mountains. I remember one in particular. You were scheduled for your first by-pass surgery the next day so we took off for the mountains, spread a blanket and ate our picnic, then just laid there for hours talking. I miss those times so much.

It didn't matter if we were with twenty people camping or just the two of us, we always had such wonderful times. I miss you baby and my love for you is still so strong, I can almost hear your voice. Lord tell him how much I love and miss him.

Forever Love

Journal entry January 26, 2011 11:19 am

Lord why won't you help me? Why won't you stop all of this, I am trying so hard. All I ask is to be rid of the business and the bankruptcy and all of the stress that comes with it. I pray that you let us keep our home and pay our bills. Please God change our situation for the better. What I wouldn't give for normal again. I will never again take that for granted. I am grateful for small blessings and answered prayers and maybe its selfish, but you said to cast my burdens on you, so here you take them. Please Lord let us have enough money to pay Jerrys funeral, taxes, house pmts, Caseys graduation trip and if its not too much to ask some kind of family vacation to get away for a while. Even a trip to the mountains would be wonderful. But I would be happy with house and bills paid.

Use me Lord for your purpose not mine and bless me with what I need to survive this world. I love you In Jesus name Amen

---

Journal entry January 27, 2011 6:39 am

Lord I want to thank you for my blessings. I also want to praise your name. I am tired Lord and weak and I need you. God I ask you to watch over my children, guide their steps so they don't stray. Lord give them wisdom to make good choices. Don't let them make a mess of their life like I have. Lord Casey wants to be able to stay here and someday raise his family here, don't punish him for whatever it is that I have done, make it so that we can stay here. I really don't care where we live as long as we have a home.

I can't deal with these attorneys and trustee. I don't trust them. Please Lord show me what you want me to do. Touch my body, heal me and make me strong. Use me to do your will. Allow me to be a help, a blessing to others. Let my light shine in this world of darkness. Bless me with what I need.

In Jesus name
Amen

Journal entry February 2, 2011 11:21 pm

Thank you Lord for another day of life. This was one of those freezing cold days and high blustering winds. I hate the cold and I hate being cooped up all day alone. I have days when I am so low, I just don't want to get out of bed and if I do, I don't feel like doing anything. I am so tired. I am tired of dealing with these burdens, please take them from me Lord.

Lord I wish Casey wouldn't go on the senior trip he has planned, I wish he would plan something that Anna could do also so they could have fun together. Show him why he should do this. Lord help me through these next months with the business, bankruptcy, and that trustee, and the modification on the mortgage.

Please Jesus, go to the Father, our Father on my behalf. I really need his grace more then ever.

In Jesus name
Amen

Satan was all over me about this time, he beat me and weakened me, but he didn't win and he won't. I couldn't get anywhere with the attorneys about the bankruptcy and the store was sitting there full of our stuff. I didn't have the money or help to move it and store it. I probably could have gotten help from church, but I had no where to keep it. I was feeling like Alice in wonderland when she shrank and felt so small in comparison to the world around her.

It was so frustrating to me that I was getting money that would help me get through this difficult time, but the trustee wouldn't let me keep any of it, I was having a hard time making up my mind as to whether I should hand it over. Listen you might think that because it's the law that you wouldn't hesitate, but when you could lose your house and the junk van you bought is falling apart and your kids need things for school, especially a senior, and you don't have a marker on your husbands grave because the funeral home hasn't been paid, trust me you will be tempted to fight also, I was willing to go to jail to keep it until I found out they would keep me there until I turned it over. My attorney thought I was a nutcase for sure when I ask him how long I would have to spend in jail if I didn't turn it over. I thought if it was two or three months that I would do the time for the sake of my kids.

I know those attorneys think that I am crazy, but I am fighting for my kids and their well being. That law needs to be changed. Insurance money should not be able to be taken when its made out to the spouse for the purpose of taking care of the children and bills until they are financially stable on their own. I am not a dead beat, I have always worked hard. I was trying to get debts paid, but, Jerry went through several health crisis' over the past five years. On top of that I had an uncle that I was trying to help who had Alzheimer's. In 2005 I made seventeen trips, seven hours one way, to Surfside to help my uncle. If they look at my credit report they will see that I have paid off 6-7 credit cards and several other debts. I was really trying, but with the business going down every day and taking care of Jerry, I couldn't get it all paid fast enough.

If you had told me ten years ago that I would be at such a dark place in my life, I would have said that you are nuts. Don't take anything for granted. Thank God everyday for your spouse, your kids, your home, your job, because he could take any one of them at anytime and it will rock your world. And know matter how strong you think you are, you are only as strong as your faith and even then you can be weakened.

This was not only a difficult time for me, but for my children as well. The devil was trying to overcome Casey, but he stands firm in his faith and trusts God, though there are times he gets angry, and frustrated. Kaylain has a little harder time dealing with the devil. She is so young and has so much to learn, but when she starts to stray off the path that God has set before her, he will yank her back to where she needs to be. On top of dealing with everything here she has her mom and sisters, and her dad and their family, and school. The teen years are hard enough to deal with, without all of these added pressures. All you can do is pray for them, listen to them, and lead by example. They feel your stress, your fear, your sadness. If you stay strong and keep God first, they will follow your lead.

One lesson that I feel God has instilled in my heart through all of this is that he is not trying to punish me for something that I have done to displease him, that will come on judgment day, but rather he is using me for his purpose. I don't know what that is exactly, I just know that he is. And I pray that what ever it is, that it will touch many lives for his glory. I want to leave a legacy of faith, love, and being the best child of God that I can be.

I really hope this book is one way that he can work through me, it would be such an honor.

As we go into February, I think you can see that this is probably the peak of my turmoil. At least so far. Its as if everything was coming to a head. I was at my lowest point I believe. I was tired and felt God was going to leave me here to suffer from now on. I began to have nightmares. I even had one that Casey had died, my worst life experience would be to lose one of my kids. I was slipping faster and faster into depression. But I also think that this was the time God chose to let me feel the Holy Spirit so strongly that I was finally able to say ok satan that's enough. I am a child of God and you can take everything I have, but you can't touch my soul. That was bought and paid for a long time ago and there are no refunds, no exchanges, Praise God.

❧

Journal entry February 4, 2011 8:53 pm

Lord I am so sad, I miss Jerry so much and I don't feel whole without him. I also found out tonight that granny (Eva H.) passed away. I had been wondering why I hadn't heard from her and I don't know why, but I looked in the obituaries for the last six months and there she was. What is so ironic is that she died within a week of Jerry. I will have to find Geralds address and send him a letter, not only to send my condolences, but to tell him what she meant to me and how special she was.

I can't believe this many people in my life have passed away in the last seven months. Jerry, Maford, Mamie, Bud, Granny, I hope this means you are getting ready to rapture the church. I am so ready, then we can all be together forever. Lord use me to win as many souls to you as possible. Let me be a light in this world of darkness. I know people recover after losing their spouse and in time find happiness again. Lord the devil is trying to make me believe that I will never find happiness again. I know he is a liar, but it is so hard not to listen. Lord if you are letting all of this happen for the benefit of lost souls, even one person saved would be worth it all. I pray that it has touched the lives of my loved ones in a way that will lead them to you Lord. I know where my strength lies. Only you could get me through this.

God heal my broken (shattered) heart. Heal my body, mind, and spirit, lift me up Lord as only you can. God also trust in you to carry my burdens and make things right according to your will, I just ask that you do not tarry. You said you wouldn't put more on me then I can bare, I believe that. I ask you guidance and your protection Lord.

In Jesus name
Amen

PS I pray for that trustee, his heart is evil

Journal entry February 5, 2011 Saturday 8:36 pm

Lord this is too much, when I see my son in pain, I'm at the end of my rope. He is so conflicted Lord over this senior trip business, he wants to go but he is frustrated because no one will listen and because Anna can't go. Lord I feel he shouldn't go with the group but rather plan something that Anna can be included in. God if there is anyway you could see your way clear to let me work out something special for graduation, that can include Molly, Melissa, Me and Kim if they want like a cheap cruise or a road trip to the New England states, something. Don't let all of this pull him and Anna apart. Open his eyes Lord to your will. Don't let him be deceived by others.

God reach down and lift up my little family in your arms and comfort us. I just came back down from the building, talking to Casey. He misses his Dad so much. He has cleaned the building and was telling me all of his plans for it. He also talked about their old pickup truck and the jeep.

Lord he and I sat there on those two old office chairs, where Jerry and I used to sit and talk, in front of the little heater just talking. Lord his eye lashes were wet and there is an underlying sadness about him. I have never seen him like this. Don't let satan get a hold on him Lord, protect him and guide him. He is special, not because he is mine, but because he is yours. I dedicated he and Kaylain both to you a long time ago. I pray that you use them for your glory. I pray also that you use me. Keep me calm in all situations Lord. Let me show strength and faith in all that I do, no matter what I am dealing with.

God let me find a way to keep our home and get Casey through college and Kaylain as well if she stays here. Lord let the flea market idea be what we need to survive.

Jimmy just got laid off too. I pray nothing happens to Candaces job. Let us all get turned around and headed towards recovery. Heal our broken hearts Lord and forgive our lack of faith when we are weak.

Lord I have never lost my joy, its always there. When I am down, I can spend time in prayer with you and feel the joy, but the devil has robbed me of my happiness, my security, and he makes it hard to be slow to anger. When I displease you Lord, speak to my heart, when I start to stray form the path of righteousness, just yank me back.

I ask special prayer for Katie, she is upset over her daughter and I can understand what she is going through, I went through it with Michael at that age. Katie is a good girl to be in the middle of so much wickedness. Reach down and show her the peace you give to me. Reach out to her Lord, I know she will reach up to you. I trust you Lord, my faith is in you.

I love you, I thank you
In Jesus name
Amen

Journal entry February 7, 2011 12:39 am

Lord help me to rest and get sleep and please no more bad dreams. Lord I had a dream that Casey died.The devil is tormenting me. Hold us tight in the palm of your hand. Guide us and protect us from evil. Help me to get through this week and please God let every day be better then the day before. Please let good things happen. Lord I pray its your will that we keep the insurance money so we an pay funeral, Dr bills, house (2nd mortgage paid off), taxes, church, get decent car, have good graduation for Casey, repair things around here and maybe if you could see your way clear, a little vacation.

Then Lord let me find the most wonderful job ever that I can work until seventy years old or until I die which ever comes first or hopefully the rapture. I know your not going to do all of this, I don't know why you won't, I do know you have the power and I have the faith and the trust. But know this Lord, no matter what your answer to these prayers, I am still you child.And my faith will never waiver.

I pray one day that my heart will heal and I will be happy again. I know I will have it in Heaven, I just need some now. Lord I had no idea little Olivia had been through so much. Touch that child Lord as only you can. Please take those horrible, painful memories from that precious child.You put them with the right family, just give them the strength that they need and the wisdom to deal with the situation. I also pray that Jimmys job picks up soon.

In Jesus name
Amen

Letter to Jerry

Hi honey,

I miss you so much. I know you probably don't get to read these, but I need to write them. I am trying so hard to take care of our family, but I'm not doing a very good job of it. I try my best to let God have his way, but I get scared and I get in the way trying to handle things. I don't know why I do that, I certainly can't do what he can.

Spring is coming, it was always our favorite time of year. I loved lying in my hammock, watching you on your tractor. But its different this year. We are just a couple of months from Caseys graduation and this is going to be so hard for me because we both had looked forward to it so much. I am so proud of the man he has become. He truly is good and he is a child of God. But I see sadness in his eyes lately and he is under so much stress. I am praying so hard for God to lift him up. I pray I can do something special for he and Anna for graduation.

He is so much like you. He has claimed the building and has big plans for it and he has plans for the truck, jeep, and smoker. I wish you were here to do it with him. I love you so very much. I am ashamed I took that for granted. I don't think I can fully comprehend that you are gone. I miss you so much baby. I hope you know how much I love you. You were the love of my life. If people had the love we had there would be no adultery, no divorce, no fighting (not bad anyway). I wish people had fun like we did.

We did so much together. I hope these kids have at least half the happiness and love that we did. I can't wait until God brings me home, so we will never be parted from one another again.

I know that you are happy, your in no more pain. You are there with people that you love, your mom, dad, sister, Dons kids, my dad, grandma, and our babies. Now you have a bunch of our friends up there with you, Mayford, Bud, Mamie, Randy, and I just found out granny is also.

Took a sleeping pill, passed out before I finished.

2nd Journal entry February 7, 2011

Lord please keep me safe and out of trouble this week. Put your hand over my mouth and Caseys also, so that we don't get into any legal trouble. I am, if they let me speak, going to tell the judge all that has been said or done to me by this trustee and these attorneys. Lord you know my heart, you know why I am fighting this. You know my needs, so whatever the judge decides, I will do. You know I am not trying to be difficult, I am fighting for my family. If it were just me, I would just say heck with it and go stay with family or get a camper to live in. I don't want to stay here for the same reasons that Casey does want to stay, the memories.

This was our perfect place, we both loved it here. Our happiest memories were made here. I can still hear his silly giggle. It would make me laugh every time I heard it.

And the crazy voice he made up to embarrass the kids. I have watched our home movies so much, just so I could hear that beautiful voice that I love so much. I miss him Lord.

Casey is growing up and is starting his own life and Kaylain wants to go live with her mom. I have no job, and more burdens then one person should have to bare. I have family and friends that care, but its not the same. I am so alone. I keep telling myself that it will be better when spring gets here, I can get out and keep busy, hopefully working.

Lord all I want to do is take care of and provide for the needs of my family, and do whatever you lead me to do. Please Lord lead us out of this valley. Let us have some happy times. Let me be here for the kids until they are married and take me home. I want to see you Lord, and the first face I want to see after you is my precious Jerry, he truly loved me in spite of myself and he loved me like no other ever has. He was the love of my life and I am so very thankful that you put us together. He was my best friend. We could talk about any and everything. We completed each other. Yes we had difficult times the first eight years, but these last twenty plus, have been amazing, a real love story.

I remember the playful times, whether it was just the two of us or with the kids, we had a lot of fun. I will miss you till my dying breath, then we will be together again.

Give him my love Lord, let him feel the love we have for him. Carry my kisses on angels wings and plant them softly on his cheeks, he will know it is me.

Watch over my children Lord, all of them. Set their feet on the right path and guide them always. Use them for you will, for you glory. Use me Lord until my dying day and even then use it as you did Jerrys mortal death to touch some ones spirit and draw them closer to you. While I fret over the things of this world, you know what is most important to me. I ask your mercy and your grace.

In Jesus name
Amen

Journal entry February 8, 2011 8:28 pm

Lord you said you would never leave me nor forsake me, so why do I feel like you have. I am going to give them that money even though I don't believe its right and its leaving me worse off then when I started this bankruptcy. I don't know what to think anymore. I can't believe you are allowing the devil to do so much, I don't understand. WHEN GOD ! Please make him leave us alone.

I can't even pray right now God. All I can do is say that I need you, I love you, I trust you, I will do my best to get through this in a way that will please you. But I can't hide the fact from you that I am doubtful, weak, and angry. Its just so wrong. I know I will understand one day but right now I am so tired and so weak that I don't even care any more. All I care about is the kids and my relationship with you. I want to be closer to you Lord, help me.

In Jesus name
Amen

Journal entry February 10, 2011

Lord I held $100,000.00 in my hand yesterday and I turned it over to the trustee, (even though I don't trust him). My lawyer said I didn't have any grounds to stop the surrender of it so I have decided I am going to step back and let you control it all, my trust is in you. I almost ran down town this morning to attend this hearing, but I keep hearing in my heart to trust you, so I didn't go. And even though I am behind on bills about $ 6,000. 00 And climbing, and could really have used that money, I will trust you.

Lord I am not going to ask why anymore. I remember when Jerry was in the hospital, him asking why after he had quit smoking, quit drinking, quit gambling and chasing women, (before me). He knows now and while I wish I did, I will not question your will for me anymore. I am going to trust in you, stay focused on you no matter what the devil throws at me. Lord I ask special prayer for my children, all of them. Mine and Jerrys all. Bless each one of them. I especially pray for my baby boy. Keep him safe and on the right path. I know he needs some time for himself, but I pray it doesn't cause a problem between him and Anna. He takes her for granted, I think he thinks it won't bother her and I know she wouldn't tell him if it did, so lead him to make the right choice. I love Anna, I know in my heart she is the right one for him.

Lord help me and my sisters family, help all of us. I don't need much Lord just a home, food, job, necessities to take care of my family. Please hear me Lord. I LOVE YOU, my faith in you is stronger then it has ever been. Amen

Journal entry February 11, 2011

Lord this is the last page of this journal, it covers the hardest, lowest time of my life and I don't know when it will change. But I am trusting in you. I want to keep pursuing this thing with the attorneys and the trustee, but I said that I would trust in you. Lord if there is a purpose in this to stop some kind of evil that is going on in the justice system, then use it to stop all people involved. If others have had their lives torn apart by people abusing their power, then use me to stop it. If I am wrong then forgive me, show me what to do. I am dazed and confused and want only to put it all behind me and pick up the pieces and with your blessing and your grace begin a new and better life for my family until the day comes that you bring us all home to be united with our family in Christ. Help me God, help my children. I pray.

In Jesus name
Amen

I had given my burdens to God so many times before. But now it was different.

At the hardest time of my life, I was giving it all to him, and this time I knew that I would not pick it up again. I don't know how to explain how I knew it, I just did. I think that I just answered my own question, "this was the hardest time of my life, the time that I have needed him more then any other time.". He had brought me to my knees and while there, I saw how much I needed him.

I believe that this is what he wanted me to see. I had been trying for so long to do everything I could to make things go the way that I wanted them to instead of laying it at his feet. When I finally took it to the cross and left it there, I felt a peace that I had never known before. And this is when I started to feel happiness little by little come back into my life. I am still struggling, and I still have moments of sheer anguish, and grief, but I am no longer fighting the depression that satan tried so hard to wrap me in. I can't fight the devil, but I have a Father that is far stronger who will do it for me, I just have to let him.

CHAPTER 9

Starting to rebuild

As I started a new journal, I was praying that I was starting a new chapter of my life. My world had been in a tail spin for so long that I didn't even know what it was like to be normal. The one thing that I did know was that I would have to trust in God more and quit trying to do it myself. I also was going to have to learn how to be one individual instead of a part of a couple. This is going to take some doing, I have been part of a couple for so long that I will have to do a lot of adjusting. I will have to make decisions on my own, although I do include the kids, its their lives too. I just pray that God doesn't allow me to use them as a crutch. They have their lives to live and I don't want to add to their stress.

I pray that when I get to the point that I become a burden to my kids, and that I can no longer do for myself, take care of myself, that you will just take me home. As long as you can use me Lord for your plan, I want to be here. In fact I want to do more for your purpose now then I ever have. I would especially like to do more for my church and all of those at church. They have blessed me so much and I want to be a blessing to them. Give me a mission Lord and the wisdom and strength to follow through.

Journal entry February 11, 2011

This new journal begins a new chapter in my life. I am starting it on the day that I finished my last journal. Lord I pray that your will is to change my life for the better. Let me please get on my feet and be able to keep my family in our home and taken care of. Let me be able to provide them a college education.

I also want you to use my pain, my frustration and anger. Take the fear and uncertainty and use them some how for your glory. My kids and I belong to you, you know this Lord. Please let there be a lot of good come from this. Help me Lord, please lift me up, hold me, reassure me God. I need it so badly right now.

In Jesus precious name
Amen

2nd Journal entry February 11, 2011 6:57 am

Lord thank you for my many blessings, no matter how small. I am so grateful for all that you do for me. Lord I praise you and give you all of the glory for any good in my life. I ask your guidance Lord, give me wisdom to do the right things in my life. Please keep me calm and focused when dealing with any aspect of this bankruptcy. Protect me from those who seek to do evil against me. Protect me from satan, he has caused me so much pain. Heal my heart Lord, heal my mind. Pry my hands loose from the selfishness, anger, and evil that I hold on to. Please carry me Lord when I am weak.

Watch over my kids. Please walk closely with them through this valley. They are vulnerable right now Lord, as am I. Satan will use this to weaken our faith, I pray for a hedge of protection around us. Lord please guide me to a job that is your will for me. Please let it be one that allows us to stay in our home. Give me a miracle Lord, it is what I need. I need the store gone, the bankruptcy settled and stability back in my life.

Thank you for giving Jimmy work, I pray it becomes permanent.

I pray our family day at church goes well and everyone is touched by the Holy Spirit. I pray that we all have a good time of fellowship. Bless all who are sick and give them healing grace.

I LOVE YOU LORD, I PRAISE YOU, I THANK YOU, I GIVE YOU ALL OF THE GLORY.

In Jesus precious name
Amen

This was the Bible verse at the bottom of the page that day and what I wrote beside of it.

The Lord himself goes before you and will be with you; He will never leave you nor forsake you. Deuteronomy 31: 8

I need you Lord,
I need to feel you
Amen

Journal entry February 12, 2011 Saturday

Lord that trustee is going to make me lose my mind. He told me in December that he had no interest in the store assets and now the attorney is again telling me not to sell anything until he hears from the trustee. Lord please get me out of this mess, they are driving me crazy. I am not going to argue. Lord watch over my kids, keep them calm, this is so scary for them.

In Jesus name
Amen

Journal entry February 13, 2011 Sunday 8:29 pm

Lord thank you for today. I really needed it. It was bitter sweet because it was our first family day at church and Jerry wasn't here to enjoy it with us. But, it was still so much fun. After church we had dinner with family at church, then music by the Blacksferry Boys. Then the kids and I took our dogs, Balto and Missy and went walking at Melton Lake. Then we came home and went out to dinner where we talked and talked and laughed. I enjoyed it so much. I pray this is the beginning of better times, healing times, peaceful times.

I love you so much Lord,
In Jesus name
Amen

Journal entry February 15, 2011

Had a nice valentines day yesterday. Got resume done, fixed some pretty flowers and took them and put them on Jerrys grave. He is my eternal valentine. I can not see to write this, I can barely see the line, everything is blurry, I hope I'm not going blind.

Got Missy groomed today, she looks so cute.

Can't see to finish

Journal entry February 18, 2011 Friday 10:10 am

Here I sit Lord, at the department of human services waiting to apply for Tenncare and food stamps. I never thought I would see these days. We worked so hard to build a business and did well for a long time. I guess we got to wrapped up in worldly things. The strange thing is when we started going back to church is when everything started falling apart financially. I guess we really made the devil mad.

Everything is such a mess, but I gave it over to you, my trust is in you. Guide me Lord in what you want for me and guide my kids. Don't let satan get to them during this time in or lives. Touch me with your healing hand. Please tell Jerry that I love him

In Jesus name
Amen

2nd Journal Entry February 18, 2011 1:30 pm

Well Lord I couldn't get tennecare for me, but I can get it for the kids. Can't get food stamps unless me or Casey lose our check. Still don't know if we get any money back from trustee. Don't know if I can hold on to the house or pay the bills. I can't get tenncare to see about my diabetes and feet and back. I am a miserable mess Lord, you know I am trusting in you, I am just having a moment, first hysterical moment in almost a week, that's an improvement. Must be getting a little better.

Sitting here looking at Caseys Cap and gown picture and I can see Jerrys face just smiling ear to ear if he were here. I wish he could have been here but I am going to do my best with your help to make sure it is a happy day for him. Please don't let me break down, I don't want to spoil his day.

Please let me find a good job that will support our family and one that is pleasing to you. Lead me to where you want me Lord. I accept your will and trust in your plan for my life. To you be the glory.

In Jesus name
Amen

Journal entry February 19, 2011

Lord, WHY? Why do you keep allowing these things to happen to us. I am so sick of all of this. What am I supposed to do? I am so angry at you, and I feel so ashamed of it. Its so hard just to trust when nothing goes right. I am trying to be a good and faithful Christian, but I feel so beaten down by a judicial system that is supposed to protect me and be just.

Tell me God, please, what do you want from me? What do you want me to do? Why can't we have some peace and stability in our lives? Why is that too much to ask? I have said more cuss words in the last five minutes then I have said in the last five years. It hurts me when I give in to satan, especially in front of my kids. I hate showing my anger, it only upsets Casey and it just isn't fair.

God I am mad and I am mad at you. I can't pretend that I am not, because you know my every thought, but you also know how bad it makes me feel and how sorry I am. Forgive me Lord, I am sorry, earnestly sorry for my feelings. I know I disappoint you with my lack of faith. I will try hard to be stronger in my faith and to trust in you, but please forgive my shortcomings when it gets to be to much. Guide me Lord, help me. You said ask and I would receive. I am asking Lord, I am trusting.

In Jesus name
Amen

Bible verse that day read :

The Lord your God is with you. He is mighty to save. He will take great delight in you. He will quiet you with His love. Zephaniah 3:17

I wrote : Where are you Lord?, I need to know that you are here!

Boy did satan have his way with me that day, looking back I can't imagine being so bold as to yell at God and question him in that way. The things that were running through my mind could have only been put there by the devil himself, and I gave in for a brief moment, in a state of weakness. This is what he wanted me to do, this is how he works. He will throw all of the woes of this world at you to weaken your faith and even the most faithful can be weak in these situations and if you think for one minute that you are above it, think again. The devil is powerful.

He still tries to provoke me and he will as long as I draw a breath in this life time. He can't touch my soul because I have been forgiven and washed in the blood of my Lord and Savior Jesus Christ. What he can do though is use my weakness to affect others by weakening my testimony, my witness. A lost person thinks that as Christians we will never sin, that is so far from the truth. We all sin and all fall short of his righteousness.

The Bible tells us that we are as filthy rags, and none are righteous in the sight of God. We won't earn that right until we are in Heaven.

God expects us to sin, he knows that we will, what he also expects is for us to be the very best Christians that we can be. When we do sin, if we don't feel remorse and ask forgiveness then we need to search our hearts and be sure of our salvation. As true Christians, we can not sin and just go on about our lives, he will not let us. At the same time that I was screaming at God, doubting him, and thinking evil things, I was feeling guilt that I was allowing satan to use me that way. I immediately asked for Gods forgiveness.

He made me remember what Jesus had suffered for me, and what I was suffering was nothing in comparison. When I think of what they did to him, how they tortured him, and even those close to him turned their backs on him, I am ashamed that I ever let the devil use me. I have more right now then he had his whole life as far as worldly goods.

Forgive me father when I fail you. I look forward to the day when the needs of this world will fall away and we are with you in Heaven. That wonderful, glorious day when I can look on your face and be reunited with Jerry and the people that I love who are already past the needs of this world.

Journal entry February 20, 2011 Sunday 8:12 am

Lord, I don't understand your ways, or the whys of my circumstances, but I trust in you. Even when I let the devil weaken me for a moment, I know you will reach down and lift me up. Keep me mindful of my many blessings while in the midst of my trials. Keep me on the path that brings you the most glory.

Amen

Journal entry February 23, 2011 Wed. 8:30 am

Thank you Lord for another day of life and for all of my blessings. I need your guidance, I need to feel your Holy Spirit. I feel numb and without happiness. I don't know why I let myself get into these hopeless feeling moods, I guess I am just overwhelmed.

God, my almighty father, I ask you to lead me through this valley. Fill my mind and my heart with your will for me. Keep me focused on your voice so that I don't drift from your plan for me. Lord forgive my shortcomings lately that I know disappoint you. I am truly sorry. Lord fill my heart and soul with so much of your spirit that satan can't get to me.

I know the choices are mine, and I know I have let you down. I am going to do better and not let my faith waiver. I know you have a plan for me and your plans would never include anything to harm me or bring me down. Please help me Lord. Bring me up out of this hole I have dug for myself.

God I also ask that you touch my kids. Guide and direct them Lord. I am concerned about Casey and his relationship with Anna. I think he takes her for granted too much. Please make him see that even though she doesn't say anything, he does hurt her when he puts his friends first. If he loses her, he will be devastated, but it will be his fault. I really don't want him to go on this senior trip. I don't feel good about it. I hope something comes up and he doesn't want to go. I want him to plan something that will include Anna and Samuel.

Lord guide my baby girl this year. She has big decisions to make. I want her to be happy. I also want her to stay in church and be loved as much as we love her. Don't let her get hurt Lord, she has been through enough already.

Lord please help me, guide me to a job that will allow me to keep our home and support my family. Please, I am begging you. Let me make the right decisions according to your will. Let my precious Jerry feel the love that I will always carry for him. I miss him, but I know that he is happier and stronger then he has ever been.

In Jesus name
Amen

Journal entry February 24, 2011 2:45 pm

Facebook status this morning:

Even though things look hopeless for my family right now, I know that's not the case. God has a plan for us and though I don't know what that is right now, I am excited and trust in him. Our trials will only serve to strengthen our faith and our resolve and make us better Christians. I love you Lord.

Amen

Lord I need you to lift me up and keep me focused. I need to get three years worth of tax information together. I have no idea where to start. Let me get through this along with everything else I am dealing with. I know everything will be ok, I just hope its soon.

In Jesus name
Amen

Journal entry February 25, 2011

Lord thank you for this day. I feel like we made a dent in the mess at the store. Thank you for a beautiful day and the many blessings. The kids just went to a party and I am sitting here thinking about

Jerry, thinking what if my sweet husband were here. He would have spent the day plowing his garden, cutting grass, and any other outside project he could find. At this time of day, just as the sun is beginning to set, we would stroll up to the gazebo, coffee in hand and just sit and take in all the beauty you have blessed us with. You led us to this place Lord, I am sure of that. What I don't know is since you took Jerry home three months ago, is if you intend to let us keep it.

I try to focus on the good that is left in my life, my kids, my church, my friends and family. I know I have so much to be thankful for, and I am. So why do I let the devil have his way and feel angry and bitter about what I have lost. My precious soul mate of almost thirty years, my business, numerous things we worked so hard to pay for. Then there are the people in my life right now that satan is using to torment me, like that arrogant, evil trustee. I pray for his soul Lord, I know he can't be a Christian, he couldn't do this to us if he were. Lord I would give everything I have to have Jerry back. I would love to just have normal again. I don't know how long you plan to let this go on but I know I will never take anything for granted again. Even if you plan to keep me in this valley forever, I beg of you, don't put my kids through any more. Let me get them through college and with families of their own.

Give them good lives Lord, full of love and joy and happiness. Use them for your glory, for they are willing. I know I disappoint you a lot these days, I am weak, but you know my faith is in you. I love you.

In Jesus name
Amen

It was along this time that I began to tear through the veil that satan had shrouded me in. He had been way too much influence in my life lately and I was beginning to see it. This is when I really started to rely on God for my day to day needs. I started to think about what my life is, rather then what it was or what it will be. I couldn't dwell on the past, I couldn't change anything about it. I wasn't about to borrow sorrow from tomorrow. So I had to focus on the day that I was living. It was at this time that I really started to take myself out of the situation and hand it over to God. Best thing I ever did.

Journal entry March 3, 2011

Thank you Lord, even in the storm, I know how blessed that I am. Went to CMS today to get Kaylain set up for high school. I know its selfish, but I hope that she stays here.

Tried to get tax transferred to fafsa for Caseys financial aid, but its not ready yet. Hope its soon. I will be so relieved when we have everything ready for college. Thank you Lord for a nice day with my sister yesterday, we had a good time. I think she enjoyed her ride on the four wheeler with Casey. They went looking at the property for sale around here. I wish my family did all live on this hill that would be awesome, as long as we all had our own homes to retreat to.

Thank you so much for this beautiful day. I enjoy being out here on the deck while spending time with you. "Hilltop Heaven" that is what Jerry and I named it when we moved up here all those years ago. We have made so many memories here Lord. I pray we will be allowed to make a lot more while we are still on this earth. Bless us with all that we need. I love you so much, I can't even describe it, but you know. Use me Lord until my dying day, I want to serve you.

I pray these things
in Jesus name
Amen

Journal entry March 4, 2011

Lord I love you so much and I know how much you love me in spite of my shortcomings. If you had told me a year ago that satan could get to me the way he has, I would have adamantly denied its possibility. I can not believe how, in less then a year, my world has changed so much and not for the good. I have lost the love of my life, my business, and I am at this time, while trying to deal with my grief, having to deal with a legal system that seems to be controlled by satan himself.

Looking back at February nineteenth. I read the words written in anger, fear, frustration and hopelessness. I can't believe I was so angry at you that I almost screamed out that I hated you for putting me through this. I hate myself for letting the thoughts even cross my mind.

I am not through this valley yet, still have months maybe longer, unless you have a different plan. But I do know that since I've decided to step back and take my hands out of the situation and put it totally and firmly in yours, that I have peace. I don't know what will happen these next months, but what ever happens I know that you are in control and that I will never let the devil weaken my faith or my testimony again. I trust in you Lord. I ask your mercy and forgiveness in my time of weakness. I know you want the best for us.

(bottom of that page, the Bible verse read) :

"you will call upon Me and come and pray to Me, and I will listen to you. You will seek Me and find Me with all your heart" Jeremiah 29:12-13

And I wrote beside of it: With all of my heart. Amen

(continuation of March 4 2011)

God my father, who gave what was most precious to you for my salvation, I am so sorry, I love you so much. I am going to write this story, for two reasons. One, I want to share my testimony so that others won't feel alone in their circumstances, and to show what a real relationship with you will do for our lives. Two, I want people to open their eyes to the evil in our world. To see that it is not about the good, hard working people of the world, its about money, big corporations, and the wicked evil ways of satan. I pray that you give me the words, the guidance, the wisdom to write a perfect story that will be a testament to you and bring you much glory. I pray that it will touch many lost souls in such a way that they sincerely seek you out. If it can lead one lost soul to salvation, then it will have been worth all the strife.

I love you Lord,
I am your child,
I praise you and honor you
And to you be the glory.
In your precious sons name
My Jesus My Lord

Amen

March 5, 2011 Saturday 5:25 pm

Calm my heart Lord, I just spent a long while up at the building with Casey. The memories are in every inch of that place. It was Jerry, his place, his quiet place, work area, get-a-way. Now it belongs to his baby boy. Who loves it just as much as his dad did. It was all that I could do to keep from having a full blown panic attack. There was a feeling in the pit of my stomach that I had never known before. Never had I known such pain and I hope that I never will again. It has rained all day, it seems like I feel down and sad on these days, don't want to do anything or go anywhere. My life is such a mess. Please Lord, get things on the right track, let us get back on our feet. Let me breath again.

Jessica and the girls are supposed to come up and live with us a while. I will enjoy having little ones around again. You know, I can be surrounded by family and friends that I know love me, but I still long for Jerry. I didn't realize how empty I would feel. I knew it would be hard and that I would miss him, but this is so hard.

I wish you would come now Lord, and take us all, I am ready for the rapture. If you are going to tarry much longer, then please get us through this valley. I got through things so much easier when I had Jerry to lean on, now I panic, get scared, cry, and scream. I just can't bare anymore. Please help me Lord.

In Jesus name
Amen

Journal entry March 8, 2011

Lord thank you for Sunday, I enjoyed lunch with the Hensleys and the Watsons.

Then this evening we enjoyed a nice dinner with the Kegleys. You have truly blessed us with good people in our lives. They are a God send.

Yesterday was one of my bad days. There was so much that I needed to be doing, but I just couldn't make myself move. I sorted the laundry but never washed any. Didn't do anything all day except cry and sit and sit and cry. I didn't even want to talk to anyone. All I could do was think about Jerry being gone and what a mess my life is. Casey went to Wasabis with Anna and some friends, so Kaylain and I went to get my medicines and I took her to eat and then we went to the grocery store. When I got home I felt like I was going to have a panic attack, I couldn't breath, so I took ½ of a nerve pill, I did relax enough to get some much needed sleep.

Felt a little better today, got two loads of laundry done, cleaned the kitchen, and cooked a pot of soup. I also started my book over. I am writing it about this past year and what its been like for us. I hope it will be good enough to sell, wouldn't that be a blessing, at least good enough to pay off the house and pay our debts. It is raining again and of course its dark and gloomy, but working on my book today did lift me up. Even if its not good enough to sell, its good therapy for me and I really need it right now.

I found four more old videos and I watched two of them, one was our cruise we took with the kids in 2005. We had the best time we have ever had. I wish I could go back to that time and stay there forever. I miss my baby so much, I can't stop crying. My heart literally flutters and acts up when I think about him being gone. It is so selfish I know, but I hate being with out him. God please help me. I pray Lord so hard for our lives to get better. Please heal my broken heart and let me get my life turned around and back on my feet. I am no good to others if I am no good myself. I pray the time of your coming is at hand. This world is so bad and I am tired of satan making me miserable I hate feeling this way.

I want to get away somewhere, but there is no place that sounds fun anymore without Jerry. I don't think I could enjoy a vacation without him. I would love just to get away from it all for a few days. I pray for peace of mind. I said I would stand back and let you handle it, so that is what I am going to do.

I ask for strength Lord, I am so weak right now. So many times lately I have thought about smoking to calm my nerves, or wondered if a glass of wine at bedtime would help me sleep, and I have thought about buying a lottery ticket, maybe I could win enough to pay off my house. I know it is satan putting these thoughts in my head and the choice is mine, so I choose to say no to him, and that feels good because now I am aggravating him. I will stay strong in my faith, even when my body and mind are so weak. I can only do it with you Lord, so please keep me in the center of your will and give me the peace that only you can give me.

In Jesus name
Amen

Journal entry March 11, 2011

Lord, first I want to pray for the people in Tokyo who were hit by an 8.9 earthquake today and then a tsunami. It is awful, so many dead. Please protect the Friske family, the wife and child of the marine who was killed a while back.

I thank you for letting me get my tax refund and getting some bills paid. I also thank you for the sale at the store this morning. I sold all of the bagged clothes and some racks and hangers and made $300.00, You know how much I need it. I paid the January house payments and property taxes and caught up some other bills. Lord let me sell a lot more and get as much as I can out by April 1. (this is when the landlord takes over the store so he can so the renovations) I feel so bad leaving so much undone, but I can't pay bills, much less hire people and pay out money to have bails and trash hauled off. Jerry B. has been so good to me, I pray you bless him in some special way.

Lord I am trusting in you. I have not contacted those attorneys or trustee as much as I have wanted to. Don't let them hurt us in any way Lord, only you can stop them. Please don't let this drag out past July 31st 2011, I can't believe he got it moved back from March

22. I told that attorney to file a motion or whatever to stop him and he didn't. Lord if they are doing wrong, I pray you stop them. The statutes concerning this should be changed. Because Jerry died within 180 days of the filing they have the right to take the insurance proceeds. And they took it all, that's what isn't right.

Now let me get away from praying about my situation and turn to more important things. First I have had two people on my heart all day and I want to pray for them. I pray for Katie, she lost Ronnie two days ago and even though they were not together it has crushed her. Help her Lord as only you can. I also ask special prayer for Amie, she has a hard road to walk with her Dads cancer. I pray that you cure him Lord, but if it is not your will, not your plan, then give her and the family the grace to get through it. I especially pray grace for her father, I know what Jerry went through and it was hard. I really don't think I could go through what that man did. I don't want to put the kids through that. Please don't let me ever be a burden to them.

I also pray for the lost Lord, use me to touch peoples lives, to plant seeds. I feel in my heart that your coming is not far away, I want my family with me in Heaven. God if I never get another thing, please let us keep this house and afford what we need, get the kids through college. Please let me get a good job.

In Jesus name
Amen

Journal entry March 13, 2011 Sunday 2:50 am

Beautiful spring afternoon. Thank you Lord. Sorry I am missing church today, my back hurts and I am worn out from working at the store yesterday. I did manage to get a good dinner cooked or I should say me and Casey. After they got home from church he grilled the pork chops and fixed the mashed potatoes along with that we had fried okra, buttered corn, carrot salad and garlic bread with herb butter. Anna spent the afternoon with us, it was such a peaceful and relaxing day, I wish Jerry were here to enjoy it with us.

Casey rode Anna to the top of the hill on his four wheeler. This is his special place. He and his friends used to camp up there and Jerry would drive the jeep up there and sit around the camp fire with them. I think he is on all of our minds right now, we all miss him so much.

Today is Dons birthday. I sent him a framed copy of the picture and poem that I have of Jerry sitting on my secretary here in the living room. I hope that he likes it. I wish that I could look out our back door and see Jerry on the hill working his garden. God I miss him so much. Thank you for letting me put one foot in front of the other, I know without a doubt that I couldn't do it without you.

Some days I don't even want to get out of bed. I need purpose in my life. I am no longer a wife, a soul mate, a business owner, an employer, a help. I am still the most important things in life. I am a Christian, a true child of God. I am a mother and grandmother who loves her kids very much. I need more Lord. Use me, I need to have purpose and security. I need to be useful and a blessing to any who need me. Help me God, as only you can. I am going to keep working on my book because I want this dark time in my life to inspire people. I pray that you use it for that purpose or all of this would be for nothing. I love you Lord. I beg of you to change my life now, for the good.

In Jesus name
Amen

Journal entry March 14, 2011 Monday 9:25 am

Lord as I sit here watching the news my heart goes out to the people in Japan. Last weeks devastating earthquake followed by the tsunami came six miles inland and destroyed everything in its path. So many are dead, injured, and missing. People all over the world looking, trying to contact family members who were there. Now there is a nuclear meltdown going on, many exposed to radiation. I feel so helpless and that is true in a human sense, but the one thing that I can do, that is more important then anything thing else I can do, that is pray. I pray your mercy on the people involved Lord. Put a hand of protection around them. Give them peace, comfort, and most of all grace. Let them find any who are still alive and help them. This will be a long recovery, heal them quickly Lord. Rebuild broken lives as your rebuilding mine now.

Lord my head hurts so bad. I finally fell asleep about 4:30 and woke up at 7:19 am

I am exhausted. I am going to try and get a few hours sleep now that the kids are gone to school. When I wake up I pray for the energy to get my certification done, and Caseys fasfa done and some laundry done. I pray that you help me get what I need out of the store and everything else sold. At least I will be over this part of my life by April 1, 2011. Lord I ask that you move the attorneys to get all of this mess done with the bankruptcy finished, finalized, and leftover money back to me. Let us heal Lord and move us forward to a better place where we will find happiness again.

I don't know all that is going on with all the kids and why they don't seem to be as close as they used to be. I knew they would branch out as they grew older and left high school, but I hope they all remain really good friends for life. I love them all and pray that they all have long, healthy, happy, successful lives. I miss seeing them.

And finally Lord I ask that you heal my heart, I miss Jerry so bad. I miss his giggle, his voice, the sparkle in his eyes when he was happy. I miss our life together, working together, playing together, just being together. We had so much fun, even in the hard times. As long as we had each other we did fine. I pray you come soon Lord so that we can be together again.

Lead me to a good job that will pay our bills and let me take care of my family. Bless us with all that we need. Get Casey through these next few months. Let him pass all of his classes and graduate in May and let us get extra money s that he will have fun at the prom and on senior trip Lord I don't know what is going on in Kaylains mind, but help her, guide her, and comfort her, I don't know what to do. Only you can help her.

In Jesus name
Amen

Journal entry March 15, 2011

Lord my baby boy, the one I always brag about is just about to kill me with a heart attack. Last Friday he and Kaylain were both gone. He was at Annas. I was on the computer typing my book, the dogs started barking and then I heard a car come up the driveway and it wasn't Caseys. I freaked out and ran into the bedroom and called him and ask where he was. He said he was at Annas, I told him to get home that someone was here and then proceeded to load my gun. I told him to get home and hung up, I cracked the bedroom door and started to yell "who is it?" when someone grabbed the door handle and as I put the bullets in the gun and yelled, Casey yelled "its me mom" because I had the chain on. Lord if he had not yelled out to me I would have shot him. That scared me so bad I couldn't breath. He was laughing so hard, until I started crying and went into a full blown panic attack when

I realized that I could have killed him. Then he was trying to calm me down, I was so angry.

Then last night after I told him not to, he decided to cut down this huge tree in the front yard, (there is a reason it cost a fortune to have this done, its called danger). Three hours later and no sun he had a big gap cut in it and couldn't get it down. I had to call Jimmy over to help him, it took them forever to get that tree down. For four hours my heart was beating out of my chest, I was terrified that the tree was going to fall on him., the neighbors house, or our house. God he is going to kill me if he doesn't start using that brain. Now him, Curtis, Samuel and Jeffery are up at Norris in a cave. Please God give him a healthy fear of things.

I pray in Jesus name
Amen

Journal entry March 18, 2011

Lord thank you for another day. I worked on my book today so I didn't get much else done. I hope it will be interesting enough for people to want to buy it. If not, I just hope it touches people in a way that makes them aware of you. But I won't lie, it would be nice if it sold enough to pay the bills. I want to try flea marketing and see how well that goes. If I can make a living at it, I would rather do that. It is similar to what I am used to only on a smaller scale with a bigger customer base.

The little squirrel that was in the tree that Casey, Jimmy, and Curtis cut down, died today. I tried hard to care for it Lord, it was so cute, but too young to make it I guess.

I can't believe my baby girl will be fourteen next week, oh my gosh, that just creeped up on me. I just spent twenty minutes talking with Kaylain, evidently she talked to her mom for the first time in a month and now she is very upset, they both are. Her mom thinks I don't want her to have a relationship with Kaylain, but that is so far from the truth. I would not have tracked her down if that were true. I did say Kaylain could not go out there right now because she is so upset with Kierra and feels like they don't treat her right. I know it has a lot to do with being a teenage girl and there is probably a little jealousy on both their parts.They both want a special bond because they haven't been with her in a long time. For her to think that I do not want her to have a relationship with her is so far from what I feel about the situation. I know what it did to Mike not having a relationship with his Dad, I would never want her to feel that way. She gets so upset with Kierra and feels like her mom favors Kierra more, that makes me uncomfortable letting her go right now. I was more excited about them getting together them she was. I do think she needs a little more time before going out there. I want this to be a happy experience for all of them.

I only want all of my kids to be happy and if I feel something is going to interfere with their happiness, I am going to say something. Just like with Casey, I probably stepped on some toes because I felt like he took Anna for granted. I know there are a few girls that are close to him, I know he has a special friendship with Brooke, they have always been close, but I want him to always put the woman in his life first. They are all friends and always have been, I pray that they always will be. I don't know why all of a sudden there are problems, but I am going to speak up when I think something is not right.

What they are coming to realize is that as they grow up, their relationships change and they tend to spend more time with their girl/boy friends then with the group. I pray that they will always be good friends and spend time doing things together as a group. I love them all and I hope they know this.Also I just found out from Casey that Nathans father passed away. Bless him Lord and give his family the grace that you given us. I know how hard it is for Casey.

Help us these next couple of weeks get as much sold and everything that I need to set up a nice little place at the new public market. Bless us with what we need to keep our home and get a decent vehicle. Forgive me for my short comings. I love you so much.

In Jesus name
Amen

We were doing what ever we could to start to rebuild our lives. I was trying to get a job, but no one seemed to be interested in hiring me. I was afraid that this is what would happen. This is why I wanted to try flea marketing for a while. Maybe I could make enough to support us. There was a new one opening in the near future and close to where we live compared to the other ones in the area.

It had been about a month since I had given the burden of the bankruptcy over to the Lord. I know I drove my attorneys and everyone else crazy. I was obsessed and a little paranoid that they were all on a mission to destroy me. I wasn't in my right mind. But I didn't believe it was being handled properly. I guess we won't know until its all settled, whenever that will be. The one thing I do know about it, is that no matter how it turns out, I will accept it as Gods will, because that is what I told him I would do. Since I did this, I have had peace about it. For that I am so thankful.

Journal entry March 22, 2011

March 22, Today was supposed to be the deadline for creditors to file a claim. God you told me to keep my hands and my mouth out of it and let you handle it and I am. Please God stop them, don't let them use all of the money, let me at least pay Jerrys funeral. If these lawyers and trustee are being dishonest and doing this to benefit themselves at the expense of my familys well being, then use me to stop them. Especially if we are not the only family. If its too late for me, then use me to stop it from happening to them.

Let me say this for any who might be thinking about going through a bankruptcy, If you or your spouse (if filing jointly) have an illness that has the slightest chance of taking your life and you have life insurance, DO NOT FILE. The law states that if you die within 180 days of filing, they can order you to turn the money over and they don't even have to pay your funeral. Our judicial system, in this case anyway, does not look out for you. God I know this is satans world when they can do this to us and then spend millions, probably billions on the wicked people of the world.

Lord I pray for that trustee, who definitely needs you in his life. Touch his heart Lord, even if it doesn't help me, I would rather see another soul saved. As a matter of fact, I pray this same blessing on everyone involved in this case. That is enough said about that. I woke up again with the anger building about this again and now I feel better just talking to you.

It is going to be a beautiful day, let me get something accomplished today. Please give my baby boy strength, he is working so hard. I am very proud of him. Kaylain told me he is a little sad about graduation because his Dad won't be there. Bless his heart Lord, let him take comfort that his dad is ok and that he too will be ok. This will be hard I know, it will be hard for me too.

But he knows how proud his dad and I both are that he has reached this milestone in his life. Keep satan from him. Don't let him keep adding to his pain. I don't care what you allow him to do to me, just don't let him use my kids. Put a hedge of protection about them.

Watch over my little Kaylain, she is so conflicted about going to her moms. Gina is upset with her because she is not ready to have a relationship fulltime, living together. She and Kierra are fighting and I don't understand that, they have not even seen each other yet and she feels her mom takes her sisters side. I am sure there is some jealously on both girls parts, but I don't understand Gina. She thinks that I am trying to turn Kaylain against here. Why would I track her down if that were true. I don't know what is going on between the three of them, I have not read their messages or texts, I have stepped back and let them get to know each other and now this. Until now I have let Kaylain make her own choices, but these past couple of months I have seen a big change in her and not for the good. Now I have made the decision not to let her go out there this summer because I don't think it's the right time. Gina has a lot on her right now, she jus can't deal with the drama of her two teenage girls right now. Her husband is in the Navy and was recently deployed to a dangerous part of the world, her oldest daughter who has just come to live with her is stressful in more ways then one. Plus she has two little girls who are trying to adjust to having to share their mom with a new big sister and dealing with their daddy being gone. I am doing what I think is best for Kaylain, her mom and her sisters. If they don't like it I am sorry.

I do want to ask a prayer of protection for Justin (Reginas husband) as well as all of the men and women in harms way while protecting our freedoms. For the families of all involved in these wars who have lost loved ones, heal their hearts. War is of the devil and is caused by greed. I will be so glad when you come to get us. I ask you guidance Lord, lead me down the path you would have me to take. Please let me get a good job and be able to support my family, I pray these things in Jesus precious name

Amen

P. S. Lord please let me get a job at the insurance company if it is your will and if it will be good for us. And if I can be a help to them and a blessing.

Journal entry March 23, 2011

Thank you Lord for all of my blessings, I don't know if you are moving in my life or if satan is again tormenting me with false hopes. I pray that it is your hand Lord. First of all I went to my meeting with Mr. Atchley at Turkey Creek public market. I reserved three booths at three hundred dollars a weekend. Then on my way home KARM on merchants rd called and I have an interview in the morning. Now last but not least my attorneys office called and I have an appointment tomorrow, something about the insurance money and also to go through the bills and determine which are mine, which are Jerrys, and which are joint. Lord I said as late as yesterday that even though yesterday March 22, was the original deadline I would not call or contact them. I kept my word as hard as it was. Then today they called me. I pray that it is you and not the devil teasing me.

I thank you for these things Lord, I pray they are your works. If it is your will for me to do any or all of these things, that you give me what I need to do a really good job so that many will benefit. I love you Lord, my faith is in you alone. I pray that I finish my book and that many read it, love it, and get a blessing from it. Even if its not your will for it to be sellable, I pray it will still be a blessing to any and all who need it. I am so thankful for your grace, if I did not have you in my life, I would have lost my mind. I thank you.

In Jesus name
Amen

Journal entry March 25, 2011 Happy Birthday baby girl

Good morning Lord. I thank you for better news yesterday. I really pray it is not the devil messing with me. I went for a job interview, but all she did was walk me through and show me everything and answered a few questions I had. The whole thing was over in ten minutes. I don't know, its your will Lord, so if this is where you want me, show me. If I don't get it, its ok. I still have the public market. I am actually kind of excited about it.

I went to see the attorney yesterday and for once got what I hope will be good news. I am sorry Lord for being impatient and not waiting on you. Since I took my hand out of it and stepped back and let you work, its much better. He said that of the claims that were filed, most he thought would be dismissed because of the statue on life insurance money. I pray Lord that this is the case and we will have enough money to start over. He did have a claim for the funeral home in there, he wanted to know if I wanted to object to it because it was post filing. I said no, if nothing else in that pile gets paid, I want that paid. The funeral home was so good to us when Jerry and I went to make our funeral arrangements, and also three years ago when uncle Hugh died. I pray that the trustee doesn't object, even if he does I feel confident that there will be enough left to pay it. I pray that is the case. Then we can get his marker put down.

Lord I ask that you provide the means and the help to get what I need out of the store this week. I pray you guide me in what I need to keep for my booth a the market. I pray that if this is where you want me, where you can use me best, that everything goes well and I can still make enough money to pay our bills, pay Katie to help so that she can take care of her family. I am grateful for all that you do for me and I am sorry for not trusting sooner, please forgive me.

Lord today is my baby girls birthday, let it be a good one. I hope her mom calls and tells her happy birthday. I hate the way things are going between all of them. I don't understand why Kierra is being so mean to her and why her mother is acting so childish with her.

I have explained to Kaylain what her mom is going through, but I still don't think Gina should just dismiss Kaylains feelings and be so impatient with her. After all Kaylain is the child. I have tried to stay out of it, but now my baby is hurting and I will do whatever it takes to protect her and I will not let her go anywhere unless I am sure it is in her best interest. Watch over Casey Lord, he has been working so hard and he has so much coming up. They have prom, all kinds of senior stuff, and graduation, then his senior trip. This last one really scares me. I'm not worried about them doing things like drinking. Its driving all the way to Daytona and no adults at the condos, so I really hope they are all mature enough to act like the adults they are now. I hope they use good sense when in the water and not act like a bunch of rowdy middle schoolers. I really want him to have a good time.

I pray for our little church. We need you Lord. Build us up. Each family has been touched this past year, I pray this is a better one. I pray we have a good vacation Bible school. I pray these things in Jesus sweet name.

Amen

This was such a hard time in my life. I was still feeling so much grief and sadness, and also the fear and frustration of my financial situation. I believe this all stemmed from worry for my children. I have been through hard times, never anything so painful though, and I could live in a tiny apartment if I had to. The financial problems while a big concern could not touch the fear I had for my children. I was so afraid that all of this would allow the devil to worm his way into their lives.

I felt bad for Casey then because on top of losing his dad, I felt he was being stretched to the limits in some of his friendships. This was so unfair, he loves all of his friends, but Anna is his heart. Next to God and his family, he loves her the most and this should not be a problem. I knew the time would come (as it should) that his time spent having fun would shift from his friends to his girlfriend, this is normal. I can't tell you the times my heart went out to Anna when Casey would jump in the car with friends and take off when she couldn't go. Until now she has sat quietly by and waited. My prayer is that when they all develop relationships with the special people in their lives that they will renew and strengthen their friendships and spend time doing things as a group again. I love all of these young men and women and hope they will always be a part of our lives. Do I always approve of the things they say or do, no, but I am not perfect either. I have watched them grow up and I know them to be good, God fearing people and I am so happy to know them.

I know that I have stepped on a few of their toes and I hope they will come to understand my actions. I want Casey to always put his girlfriend first because when he gets married he is commanded by God to put his wife first after God. I pray that each of these young people find their soul mate and be very happy and that their spouse will put them first.

I am a talker, and I often say things that can be misconstrued, but people who know me, know my heart and that any hurt or anger I may cause is not intentional. If I intend to make a point or voice my opinion in matters that are important to me, I will do so. I guess I am one of those people that you either hate me or love me. But only the opinions of those that I love and most of all how God views me, are what matters.

This was a stressful time but it was not as scary to me as the previous weeks had been. I think that I had finally, sincerely handed it over to God and had not picked it up again. There were still times to come that made me want to cry, but the hopelessness was gone and hope was taking its place. I was beginning to realize that my life was not over it was changing and the life that I had known was gone. I have never liked change, now everything was changing. I hope that the changes I am facing will make me a better person and that I learn from all that I have been through.

I was starting to see God moving in my life, as I often sit and read through my prayer journals from years past, I can see how God handled situations in my life, how he answered my prayers. This reminds me of his power, his grace and his love for me. I was regaining my trust and strengthening my faith. There are lessons to be learned everyday of our lives and we need to apply them to our lives so we don't walk through the same valleys again.

CHAPTER 10

Clear Skies New Beginning

The storm is over, you have made it through, your lives are forever changed. A new beginning. As good as that sounds a part of you wishes you could go back to your life before, when you still had your loved one and things were good, but that's the circle of life. Gods plan never changes, but his plans can change us. I believe that's why he allows the devil to have his way with us sometimes. God already planned what would be Jerrys last day on this earth, how his plan played out before his death was to forever change our lives.

We have learned so many life lessons through all of this. We are stronger in our faith and have learned that no matter how bad things are Gods grace will see us through. We have learned the importance of a relationship with God and the love and help of a good church and a caring Pastor and church family. We have learned to never put our selves in financial jeopardy again, if we can't pay cash then we don't need it, a mortgage and college tuition will be the only exceptions. I personally have learned that working all of the time to make more money for my family is not as important as more time with my family, don't wait until someone dear to you is gone to learn this lesson.

I have heard this before, but it is so true," live everyday like its your last." Put God first in everything you do, live as if you could be standing before him in the next minute because you could. Tell your spouse and your children everyday that you love them and show them how much they mean to you. Work to never let harsh words leave your mouth, not only are they the devils work, but if the person receiving your wrath should die you could never take it back and even if they don't, words can be forgiven but the hurt will always remain. Pray everyday, get in Gods word constantly to see what he wants from you, what he expects from you, and what he demands from you. This is a big one for me, think before you speak, I am just beginning to work on that one and its hard. I know my attorneys and friends think I am a nut case. Don't be so quick to judge, get to know someone before you decide not to be a friend to them. There is always a reason for peoples actions, good or bad.

I am coming to terms with the fact that my life is forever changed and that this is the beginning of a new chapter in my life. I didn't want a new beginning. I wanted Jerry to live, I wanted to save the business, I wanted to retire and travel with my husband, I didn't want to have to worry about bills or how to send the kids to college. Guess what its not about my wants, its all about what God wants. In this next chapter you will see how my new beginning starts out and how God is there for me through it all, I hope you have come to see that he was here all the time, even when satan had me so blinded by grief, anger, fear, and hopelessness that I couldn't feel Gods presence. And just when I had given up and didn't care if my life went on, he picked me up, brushed me off, and told me :"Child I am not done with you yet."

Journal entry April 4. 2011

Lord I am sorry I haven't spent my time with you like I should. I was sick last weekend (as you know) and this week between cleaning out the garage and moving stuff from the store that we can use in our booth, I was just too exhausted. You know if I can't focus and give my full attention to this journal, I won't do it. I pray for strength and energy these next few days to get my house cleaned really good, including cleaning out my closet the laundry room. I pray also to get my tax number and business licenses Obtained and get everything ready to open at the market.

My Lord, I am continuing to trust in you for the out come of the bankruptcy, Mr. Burroughs gave me hope that things may turn out better then I thought. I know if it does that it is because of you and you alone. I will continue to pray for all involved and ask your guidance.

Just got a prayer request for Bethany R. Lord I ask your healing touch on her, and Megan P, and Kathy H. Lord I want to take a moment and both thank you and praise you for your blessings. I pray for your protection from the storms coming in tonight. I ask you to bless our church. There are so many gone who have left to go to other churches. I love my little church and want to see it grow.

I ask your blessing on my book Lord. I pray it will be your plan to make it a help to others facing trials and feeling defeated. And I don't want to seem selfish, but I pray it will be something that will sell, so it can get me out of debt, keep us in our home, get the kids through college, and get a safer car. I need a truck to carry things to the market.

I pray for my family, friends, and church family who are dealing with illness, financial problems, and uncertainness about their futures. Last but not least Lord, heal my broken heart. I miss Jerry so much, please let him know how much I love him and what he means to me. I thank you Lord for Casey, I will always have a part of Jerry here with me.

Thank you Lord
In Jesus name
Amen

Journal entry April 8, 2011 7:54 pm

Lord thank you for this beautiful spring day. When I got home late this afternoon, after running errands, I went up to the gazebo. The sun was starting to lower in the sky and as I lay in my hammock, there was a gentle breeze dancing across my face as I swung gently back and forth. I felt like a baby being rocked in its fathers arms.

I began to think about Jerry. I could almost see him on his tractor there on the hill. So many times in the previous years, I had lain in that hammock and watched him cutting grass or plowing his garden or hoeing the rows of corn and other goodies. Then I started to daydream about Casey and Kaylain, Taylor, and Kierra playing out in the yard. I could see them all laughing, running, squealing, and chasing each other around. I have had so many good years. I thank you for them, for the memories.

So much has changed, so much is gone. I miss him Lord, please heal my heart. Clear my mind and show me what you want me to do. God, I ask that you lead me to a lot of things to sell at our new business. Please let this go well enough to support my family. I don't want to lose our home. I am so tired and so weak and I haven't done anything except run to get flowers for Jerrys grave, and try and find stuff for Caseys graduation party. I took the first six chapters of my book over to Vickie to read. Mom started reading it, she got to the part when I was having a lot of pain and was so low mentally, I thought for a brief moment I was going to die. Of course being my mom she flipped out. I had to assure her that I was fine. That was months ago when I was taking care of Jerry, trying to save the business and going through bankruptcy. All of that while dealing with the normal day to day things of being a wife and mother.

I am not depressed or suicidal or anything like that, but I envy Jerry. He is happy, healthy, and strong again. He will never again know stress, worry, anger, pain, and frustration. He is where satan can never torture him again. All he has to do is wait for us and that won't be but a blink of an eye to him. Lord I can't imagine the time when I will see you and there will be Jerry and others I love also. Jerry and I shared a lot of good memories, a lot of wonderfully happy times. To think that these times are nothing compared to the happiness we will know in heaven. I try to focus on these times, it helps me to cope during these trials in this world.

Lord there are so many that need your healing touch right now. Please lay your hands on them. Kateys mom, Amies dad, Gene, Charles, Bethany, and Megan. I am glad we are coming up on Easter, I love this time of year. I pray that you fill me to overflowing with your Holy Spirit, I need you so much Lord, I can't function without your grace. I pray you put a protective hedge about the kids as we go into the time of prom and their graduation. So many changes for them right now. Casey will be going to college, Kaylain will start high school. They are growing up so fast.

I pray love and happiness for the both of them. I pray that this time is happy for them, that they get past the sadness that has been surrounding us these past few months. I pray these trials we have been through these past few months will only strengthen them and that you will not allow satan to use this time to weaken their faith. Use these trials to draw them closer to you Lord, this is most important.

In Jesus name
Amen

Journal entry April 11, 2011

Thank you for this beautiful day and for all of my blessings. I am sitting on the back deck and its so peaceful listening to the birds singing, there is a gentle breeze blowing, the bees are buzzing, and the sun is shining. Casey bought a really cool fountain at a yard sale and I love the sound of the water flowing through it.

I just finished addressing the rest of his graduation announcements and have to go mail them. I am so excited for him, but at the same time my heart is saddened because his dad won't be there to see him. But if God allows you to witness the happy times here, from a peep hole in heaven, he will be there. Lord lift me up right now, I miss him so much. But I am getting stronger. Now when he is on my mind, more often then not it is the good times I am thinking about. I try not to dwell on him being gone, its enough to live it everyday. I want to write Casey a letter to give him graduation day and tell him how proud his Dad and I both are of him and that his Dad would not want him to be sad, this was Jerrys wish. I was sad going through my address book looking up addresses. So many in there are gone now.The circle of life goes on, but one day we will all be together again with you in Heaven.

Lord let me find a job that pleases you or let the market do well for us. I pray that my book will be successful, and be a blessing to others. I would considerate a blessing if my gift could be writing books of inspiration for a living. Could that please be the job I have prayed for?, that could support my family and bring you glory, while helping others. I pray that this could be your will for me and that satan not be allowed to interfere.

I pray Jimmy likes his new job and things settle down for him and Candace. I pray good times for all of my family. I ask these blessings for Katie also Lord, she too has had such a hard time. Heal here mom and settle her daughter down. I wish I could do something to help her, she was such a big help to me with the store right up to the end.

Kim just called to see if the church would help her pay her light bill. I pray everything is ok. She gets a lot from social security for her and the boys and she doesn't have a house payment so I don't know what is going on, but you do. Help her Lord. Let me help her in some way. I fear the problem she is having and you know what it is. Keep evil people away from her and the boys. Guide her, she is a sweet and gentle soul

Lord these are the times I wish I had money. Please let me get on my feet and be a blessing to others and a obedient servant to you. I have learned so much and I know I will come out of this valley a stronger, wiser, more faithful Christian and for that I thank you.

I pray healing for Gene, Charles, Bethany, Janeen, Megan, and any who need it. Bless our church Lord, we need you.

In Jesus name
Amen

Journal entry April 13, 2011 9:24 pm

Thank you Lord for such a nice day. The weather was beautiful and my mom, sister, and Anna came over and cooked out. Things are moving so fast, Kaylain has T-caps the next few days so she went to bed early. Casey is in there writing an essay for a scholarship. In a few days, well a little over a week he and Anna will be going to their last prom, and in just over a month they will be graduating from high school. OMG next year Casey will start college and Kaylain will start high school. Lead them Lord, keep them on the right path and always in the center of your will. Its been a tough year, so keep us close to you Lord. Bless us with all that we need. Keep us in our home and let us get our little business at the flea market going and let it make enough to support us.

I am excited about the flea market because it lets me deal with used items, its what I know. Please let it be a success, we just want to work hard and pay our bills. God I feel myself getting stronger and though I know the pain will always be there, I know it will not be quite as sharp a pain as time goes on. I pray that you keep me busy with our little business and that things begin to turn around for my little family. I pray this is your will Lord, because I can't even get a job at Karm with twenty eight years of experience.

Another thing I have a burden for tonight is our church. Lord we are losing members right and left, I don't understand. Some according to rumor left because of hurt feelings or didn't like the way someone spoke to them. I think these are just excuses. Now if you are leading someone to go elsewhere then that is different. We must listen to your will for us. We have lost three members to death this year, a couple of members are now home bound, a couple of young people are getting married and moving to other churches, and some have just been led to go else where. I love my church, I am so thankful that you led my family here. There are good families here. Brother David is a good man and tries to teach good lessons and preach good messages, and though sometimes I am a little lost, I have learned from him. He is a caring man and loves our kids. Jerry thought the world of him. If it were not for my church, I could not have made it through all of this. Since I have been going there, my faith is so much stronger and I enjoy a much closer relationship with you and I have gained so much spiritually.

I am among true children of God, faithful and committed members. I pray you use me in some way to help the church. I don't know how or in what way, but guide me to do good for them while bringing you glory. Sometime since yesterday, someone stole the wiring from our air conditioning unit. It is a sad day when evil doers will steal from a church. I pray they catch them and that they punish them and that the experience will change their path. Whoever did this is deep in the hands of satan, I ask that you grab them by the heart and set them straight. If this is someone just trying to feed their family, maybe someone who has fallen on hard times like me, then lead them to our church to be fed spiritually as well as physically. They don't have to steal, we would help them.

Lord help my mom and my sister. Touch them Lord as to help them to get along better, especially my sister, she can be a real pill when she gets upset and she is too sensitive and obnoxious when she is like that. I don't deal well with that kind of attitude and satan will use that to make me get in the flesh real quick. Touch her Lord, I don't know why she is like this. I love my family, but I sure couldn't live with them.

I pray these things
in Jesus precious name
Amen

Journal entry April 16, 2011

I need your help Lord. I am getting stronger and the devil doesn't like it. Now my car won't start, I broke my bed, and its cold and rainy yet again. Lord provide me with what I need to sell some of these vehicles and have enough money to get a truck or let me get some money back from the trustee please. I also ask that you let me get lots of items for our new business, I am missing three good yard sales today. I will wait on you and trust in you.

This is Brent and Erins wedding day, please clear up this nasty rain and let them have a beautiful afternoon for the service, and let me fit into something to wear. I ask your healing touch for Megan P., Gene H., Charles S,. Amies' dad, Bethany, Kathy H, and all others I may have forgotten. Oh yea, Howard and Lisa. I pray your blessings on my family, mom and Vickie, especially right now. Watch over our oldest boys and their families. As for me and the kids just give us what we need when we need it. Please let our little business take off and thrive. Let it do well enough to pay all of the overhead and support my family. I ask you now Lord to please provide me the means to buy a pickup, a good one that will last a long time. I thank you Lord for your many blessings and please let me get better, don't let me slip back into despair.

In Jesus name
Amen

❧

Things seemed to be getting better. I don't know if it actually was or if it was just made better mentally because I was again trusting totally in my sweet Lord to take care of everything. I still had so much on my mind, but I felt relief in prayer and my faith in God.

The church was really on my mind, I couldn't understand what was going on, still can't. I do know the devil has his hand in it. He hates the fact that we are Gods children and he is trying hard to destroy our church. But I was praying hard as were many others who could see things were not what they needed to be.

❧

Journal entry April 17, 2011 2:30pm

This day has been such a blessing. Jennifer said she was inspired by my book. I hope it will be an inspiration for many. I pray it would be good enough to sell, but if not just let it help people as much as it has helped me by writing it.

Kaylain and I had nursery at church today, we had more kids then I have seen in a long time. I am so tired, but it was so much fun watching them hunt eggs after dinner. I love our church Lord, I love our Pastor, I love our church family, but something is wrong.

We are losing members all of the time. I feel like you only get out of church what you put into it. I am talking spiritually. Our pastor can preach, the teachers can teach and we can be there for each other, but its all about God and not what he can do for us, but what should we be doing for him. You can do all of the good deeds in the world, you can be in church every time the doors open, you can tithe thousands of dollars, but if you are not saved, if you don't do these things for Gods glory, and as I like to say if you do not walk the walk and not just talk the talk then its all for nothing. I see David getting discouraged and sometimes I don't always agree with the lesson or understand it, but I love him and believe he is doing it for God. I think sometimes he over analyses because he wants to be the best shepherd he can, all he needs to do is relax and pray and listen to God. Touch him Lord, let him know that you are there for him and then guide him in what it is you want him to give us. He is a sweet soul who wants to do good for his church, Bless him Lord. My almighty God, Satan is trying hard to destroy our church, please put a hedge about the church and Angels to guard it. Let us reach out to the lost and encourage more people to come. In every family there are going to be times that you will butt heads with a sibling or parent or child. Do you run away and pout or do you discuss it and work it out. The same is true in your church. Do not think for a minute that there is a church that has never had problems, don't think that there will be a church who can attend your every need, only God can do that and its up to you to seek his guidance.

Four or five times that I can think of people have quit their church because of hurt feelings. No one came when they were in the hospital, no one called after my surgery, no one came to the hospital when my brother was in there, it goes on and on. Do they ever really sit down and think, when did I go see about sister so-n-so when they were so sick?

Have I ever taken a pot of soup or a meal to a family going through a crisis? Have I even just picked up a phone to let them know I was thinking about them or sent a message on face book to let them know that I was faithfully praying for them? If not, why should I expect anything more then what I have given? The answer is because we are to strive to be Christ like. Think about this, Christ lived his whole life giving and never did he expect anything other then your faith, nor did he turn his back on us when we needed him. And he never ask anything of us except to trust God and accept him as our savior, to be washed in his blood.

My church or rather the people of my church family have done so much for me, but that is not why I stay. I stay because they are a kind, loving, and most importantly a God fearing people. I will faithfully pray for the revival of my church, my pastor, and our family. Let us Lord instead of running away and weakening our church, help us through faith and prayer to build our church up. I could not do Brother Davids job and I know he has a lot on his shoulders so I ask you to lift him up Lord, fill him with your Holy Spirit and let the joy overflow from his heart.

I pray these things
in Jesus name
Amen

2nd Journal entry April 17, 2011 10:35 pm

Thank you Lord for the nice evening with the Jenkins and Hughes families cooking out and making plans for graduation. It is sweet of them to include us in their family graduation festivities. I am thankful yet again for money from our secret angel (s)

At church. I know who one was but not the other, but I am grateful for every bit I get. I need a blessing Lord of a decent car or preferably a truck to drive. One that will last a few years instead of a few months. Help us to come up with enough money and lead us to a good, reliable truck. Ease Caseys mind and don't let him get impatient and ill.

I thank you Lord
Amen

This was such a bitter sweet time for our family. So much was going on, so many milestones and Jerry was not going to be there. As much as I was dreading it, as each day passed, it seemed to go by without a lot of grief and pain, God was truly answering my prayers to let this be happy occasions for all of our families, as the Jenkins and Hughes family and Nathans family had also suffered a great loss.

We had broke our backs, Casey, Jimmy and I, trying to get stuff moved out of the store before the deadline. Now I was not looking forward to moving it all again in a few weeks (or so we thought). I don't have the strength that I used to have, and my back and knees are not what they once were. My mentality was definitely off kilter also, you just don't realize how draining mental stress is until it hits you full force, but God always gives me enough of what I need to accomplish what has to be done. I don't know if my plan to open a business at the market is Gods will for me, I am just trying to find out where he wants me while at the same time trying to support my family. I daydream of a better time to come. I pray it is Gods will to allow us good years to come. Every time I think of going on a trip or doing something that I used to consider fun, I just can't seem to get into the mood for it. It just doesn't seem like fun without Jerry to share it with. I know I can have fun with the kids, but its different. They are growing up and want to do things with the people in their lives now.

Journal entry April 19, 2011 7:45 am

I need your healing touch this morning, my back is really bad. I need healing before I have to start loading and moving all of this stuff again. I hope when we get it open that it does well. I hope and pray that it stays busy enough to support my family, pay the overhead, afford us insurance and be able to hire Katie to help her out. I think it will be fun to meet a lot of new people and I am glad they have church service on Sunday mornings if I have to open on Sundays, I would rather be at my own church.

Lord let everything go well for all of the kids prom this weekend. Then in a few weeks when they graduate and on their senior trip. I pray that Brandon wins the T shirt design contest, his really is the best. He is a good and faithful young man, bless him Lord.

Bless our church, grow us and help us. Let us fill the pews with new families, teenagers, kids, seniors all. Give us the means and wisdom to teach and guide. Continue to open our minds to the messages you want us to have when we read your book. Lead David Lord, help him, I know he loves you, but he is struggling. He wants to bring you glory, show him how. Bless our deacons, our teachers, and all who do work for your church. Let us all as members come together and bring our church out of this slump. Help me Lord financially, I pray we get at least half of that money back and that I can pay the debts, refinance the house, and get a reliable car or truck. I hope to get a truck so that I can use it to carry items to the market.

I ask your healing touch on all of those who are sick. Bless those who are grieving, including myself. I especially pray for Ms Betty, she seems to be doing a little better, I see her at church more. I love you so much Lord, I can't even say, but you know. I pray that as I do my Easter fast this weekend that you will purge my body and especially my mind. I pray that I listen attentively when you are speaking to me. I pray you give me the message you want me to have and that you will reveal to me what it is you want me to do. I pray you use me Lord, I want to be a light to others.

I especially pray for the lost this morning Lord. There are so many, some even think they are saved, but don't live it. I pray with everything I have that all of mine and Jerrys family are saved. I miss him Lord, my heart is still hurting. I know I will see him again, but it doesn't fill the loneliness. I guess being stuck at home with no job and no car doesn't help, except it does let me spend more time with you, maybe that's the reason for it. Thank you.

In Jesus name
Amen

Journal entry April 20, 2011 12:52 am

I can't sleep Lord, I know it's the devil pestering me. Another day is gone and still no word from the attorneys, so no money, if there will be any money left. I need it Lord my van broke down almost a week ago, the jeep is trying to die and there is no insurance on the truck. I have no way to go to the bank or store. I need to shop for the new business.

I have hardly been out of the house. I am going nuts. Please God let there be money left and let it come tomorrow. Let us get started with a new beginning. Lord I need your healing hands on me this day. My back and side are killing me, I mean bad. Please heal whatever this is. I ask these blessings in Jesus' name Amen

Journal entry April 22, 2011 6:45 am Good Friday

I can't sleep this morning Lord, but its not from worry. The kids are out of school and I wanted to sleep late but couldn't. I have been lying here thinking about "Loves Corner" our little thrift store we are opening at the new Turkey Creek Public Market. It doesn't open until May 21, but I hope to get in there soon and start setting up. I have to thank you for not letting me wake up sore. I fell off a ladder yesterday trying to fix moms gutter and hurt my back, my arm, and ankle. Lucky for me I didn't go down the steps, I was only inches from it, but you put your hand there and stopped me. While I am a little bruised and sore, its nothing like what I thought it would be. So I am grateful.

This is Good Friday, I am about nineteen hours into my Easter fast. I am looking forward to this weekend. I feel so close to you this special time of year. One because I am so very thankful for what you did for me. I don't take it likely what you did for me, what your son went through for me even though he didn't have to. I know this debt can never be repaid but I will do my very best to make sure others understand his sacrifice. It brings tears to my eyes every time I think of what Jesus suffered for me. That is why I get so emotional every time I hear our youth sing "The Last Blood".

Even in these, the darkest months of my life, I still have the joy in my heart that you put there the day I was saved. As hard as the devil has tried, he can not rob me of it. He tries so hard and he steals my happiness a lot and puts fear, sadness, frustration, and anger in my mind, but all I have to do is come to you and you give me grace to overcome and strength to face each day.

Lord I have always ask for you to allow me to have a job that will help many people and I just this moment realized I already have that job. Sharing my testimony, being a witness for you is more help to those in need then any worldly thing I can do for them. I will continue to help others any way humanly possible, but I can see how that any way I can help them spiritually would bring you more glory and please you more. Use me Lord for your purpose, for your plan, for your will, not mine.

I miss Jerry so bad, but I can feel myself getting stronger everyday. I pray for grace and guidance these next couple of months as we go through graduation and getting our new business started. I pray you bless us with all that we need until you take us all home to be with you. I look forward to that day. Let my sweet husband feel all the love we carry for him and tell him that I miss him. My life has changed so much since this time last year. I am now starting a new chapter of my life. God whether I have two minutes or two decades left of this life, I will spend them serving you. I love you so much, I thank you, I praise your Holy name, in the sweet name of Jesus

Amen

Journal entry April 24, 2011

The sun is coming up, Casey left about 20 minutes ago for sun rise service. I wish I had gotten up in time. Forgive me Lord for breaking my fast, I am weak. I don't feel that clean, beautiful closeness that I usually do and I regret that. I beg you to please fill me to over flowing this morning and move among us at church, touch each and every person there. Bless our kids and all those who stand up for your glory this morning. I didn't realize what a difference not completing my fast would make in how I feel. When I fast I am so happy and feel so good, touch me this morning Lord. I need to feel the Holy Spirit today. I am weak but you are strong I pray that you touch David this morning and bring his joy to the top and overflow through his words. Give him the message you alone would have us to receive. I love you so much. They are playing one my favorite songs by the Cathedrals, I have always called it "I

Thirst" but I can't find it anywhere, I am going to look under "He gave me water" Now I feel you Lord, I feel the Holy Spirit, I am ready for the day.

I wish Jerry were here, he loved to get in the kitchen with me to fix big family dinners. Casey likes to do that too. I miss him Lord, but I wouldn't bring him back for anything. Instead I will look forward to the day that we will all join you in Heaven. I know that he is far happier then I am right now.

I will live for you all the days of this life and witness to the lost about what my Jesus did for me. Thank you God for the most precious gift ever given. This has been a long hard year. This is about the time everything started last year with Jerry. It was the saddest year of my life. But nothing is as sad as the thought of what Jesus endured for us.

Because he suffered, Jerry didn't. Through his salvation, God gave him dying grace. Yes he felt pain, and was sick and weak, but God took care of him and took him home to suffer no more. I pray for us to get through the next couple of months with joy and happiness. Jerry would not want us to be sad at such an important time for Casey. Let our family dinner go well today and let us enjoy each other. No stress. I thank you so much Lord for all that you do for us. Please bless us as you always have with what we need, when we need it. I love you Lord.

In Jesus name
Amen

Journal entry April 26, 2011

Lord I have a lot on my heart right now. I am so upset that Harold is trying to get a big chunk of the insurance money. That man knows what he did to us and that company, I have never seen two people more greedy then he and Bette. He knows we have lost the business and to try and get sixty six thousand dollars is insane, what an idiot. Please Lord don't let that man get one thin dime. I have never seen anyone do a 360 like he has. Keep him away from me, away from my family. I don't think I could control myself if I ever saw him again. I do pray for them Lord, I know they used to be good people, a little selfish yes, but not evil, not like now. They need to feel your Holy Spirit Lord. I pray they turn their life around, I thought they were saved, and I guess they are but they sure have let satan get his foot in the door. My brother-in-law said they always knew what kind of man he was and couldn't understand why I couldn't see it. I know that he used to be a good person. We used to have bible study at lunch and he was like a big brother to me. I guess I always want to see the good in people instead of the bad. Either way I pray for them. I pray that they find the peace and joy that Jerry and I did.

Lord, I feel like my interview at Goodwill went well today. I pray that I get the job if it is your will for me to be there. And that I can be just as much a blessing to their organization as this would be for me. If I do get it Lord I pray that you use me in a way that pleases you and that I can do a really good job so that I can make enough money to take care of my family and keep us in our home. If the market is where you want me then don't let me get this job. If we can do both, then work it out for us. Your will Lord that is all that I pray for, use us where ever you put us.

2nd Journal entry

Lord thank you for a nice time with my kids tonight. We went to see Heavens Gates at Calvary Baptist in Oakridge. I enjoyed it, but it was a lot different from the version we had at Riverview a few years ago. This was more of a musical version with video sequences rather then an acted drama. It was touching and one of the video clips was scenes from the "Passion" and I always get overwhelmed with grief when I hear how my Jesus was tortured, much less watch a realistic reenactment of what he suffered. But it was a beautiful production and the singing was amazing and the spirit moved people and there were several on the alter.

I pray for all who are in the paths of these storms coming across tonight. Watch over my family, whether in Mississippi, Tennessee or North Carolina protect us. Keep my children safe at school and coming and going to school. I ask peace tonight Lord, calm my mind, ease my heart, let me sleep and relax.

I pray in Jesus name
Amen

Journal entry April 27, 2011

Watch over us and protect us right now Lord. We are down stairs in Caseys room, there have been tornado producing storms all day. We are under tornado warning until midnight. Casey went to church because it had calmed down, now its getting bad again. I told him when he left to stay at Annas after church until all if these storms pass. Put a hedge about all of us Lord, protect those at church, protect all of us. Be with all those who have been devastated by these storms.

Keep Michael and his family safe and protected. Watch over my mom and sisters just protect all of us Lord. Like Paul on the ship in the storm, I don't care if we lose the ship in the storm, just don't let us lose any lives. I am calm, the only worry I have is Casey being out there. Protect our little church, and please keep Jerrys flowers right where they are. I wish he were here now. He would always sit on the porch and watch it come across. If it was real bad he would stay inside so that it wouldn't scare me. Casey just got home from church, guess where he went, right out on the porch. He is his fathers son.

I pray Lord for the blessing of financial freedom. Let me get a good job or let the market do well enough to support us. I will work hard for what ever you would have me to do. Just let me earn enough to keep our house and pay for our bills. I am lying here on Caseys bed and I can hear the rain pounding on the roof, the lighting is streaking across the sky, and thunder is rolling for so long that I listen to see of it's a tornado. I usually am terrified, but I'm not now. Lord I ask grace and calm for all of those who are going through these storms. Greenback Tennessee is not far from here and they were hit bad last month, now they are in shelters waiting out this one.

I know those children are scared. Please touch their little hearts and let them know that you are there. This has been a dangerous day for many states across the south, last count was twenty two dead and I don't know how many hurt. God bless all who are suffering because of these storms. There will be so much sadness, give them grace. God watch over mom and Vickie as they make their way to Candaces. Put your hands around them.

In Jesus name
Amen

Journal entry April 28, 2011 9:00 pm

Lord give me strength to stay where you want me. It will be at least another 30 days before all of these claims will be answered and then only you know when it will all be settled and if there will be anything left. All I can do is sit here and wait on you. It is so hard when it just goes on and on. I am really upset about Harold and Bette, how could I have been so wrong about them, especially Harold. I just can't believe that I busted my butt helping to build our business that put his kids through college, one of them twice and that evil man is going to try and take the life insurance money. What a deceitful man he is. We could have been doing a million dollars a year if he hadn't started back sliding. That man is an idiot. I know he was a better man once, but satan certainly got a hold on him. I have seen first hand how evil can work, I will never have anything to do with these people again, but I do pray for them Lord. I know he was good once, he inspired me in a lot of ways when it came to learning more about your word. I just don't understand how he could turn on me and have such venom towards me. I really considered him one of my best friends. Shake him Lord as you have me. Do whatever it takes to get him back in the center of your will. Now last, but not least, I am not going to worry about all of this again. I pray that you deal with the attorneys. I know that what ever happens will be up to you.

In Jesus name
Amen

This time of my life I was just starting to get into writing this book. As you can see it starts out slow. At first the prayers are repetitive and can slow the beginning down, but if you have stayed with it, you can see the spiritual growth that I have experienced through all of this. God has a mission for me, I don't know what it is, I just know that it is and I am excited. It may not be to lead, but to follow and to be a help and support for someone else who is doing important work for the Lord. I want to make a difference in peoples lives. I want to do work that brings lost souls to the Lord.

I am Gods little wild child and I don't always please him, but he uses this to relate to others. Those who know me, know my short comings and my weaknesses, and also know my faith and my love for the Lord. God knows my heart and that is all that matters.

Journal entry May 5, 2011 9:10 am

Lord, I know its been a few days since I spent time in earnest prayer and I am sorry. But I have spent time with you while writing this book. I feel your spirit moving within me as well as all around me. This book has been so good for me. It has been like therapy with you as my councilor. If this book doesn't get any further then a few friends, if it will help even one person as much as it has helped me putting it on paper, it will be worth it. On the selfish side of Lord, I pray it will be worth selling so that I can pay bills and take care of my family. It is totally up to you. I just want to be in the center of your will.

I have several things on my heart this morning Lord, I have a place on my face that is sensitive to the touch. I also would like to learn better eating habits so that I can lose weight and get healthy again. I ask that you mend my broken heart, help me to move forward for the sake of my kids. I pray Lord that everything will go well with the bankruptcy and that whatever your will is in this situation that you will let it be over soon. I just want this nightmare that has been my life these last few months to be behind me. I pray Lord for a better life, happier life for my kids, all of them. I am in a better state of mind these days then I was six months ago. I have fought through the depression, fear, and anxiety that consumed me. With your grace that is. I don't know how lost souls can get through these times with out you. I guess if they don't know you they don't know real love, for you are love. Therefore they don't experience the loss of a true love. I truly understand the verse in the marriage vows where it says, what God has put together let no man put asunder, and what until death do us part means. I think death only parts us physically and true love goes on forever. I feel sorry for those who have never experienced this kind of love. I will say this, the greater the love, the bigger the hurt. I wonder if because Gods love for us is so great, if he feels emotional pain when we let him down. My mission is to bring him more joy and glory. He is always there for me, even when I push him away, even when satan pierces my heart with grief, anger, fear and all of the negative emotions he can, all I have to do is call on Jesus. He will mend my heart, clear my mind, strengthen my back, and give me the courage to face another day.

Thank you Lord for giving me the grace to get this far. I do feel myself getting stronger. I do pray for financial stability whatever way you see fit. I do pray that what ever I end up doing, it will be useful to you, that you will use me to not only help my family, but others as well. I would also like to be able to help my mom financially, and give more to my church and youth group. Lead me Lord where you want me to be, its all that I want.

Jessica and the girls will be here in a couple of weeks. Lord use this time with her and the girls to help her get on her feet. I pray that you will take hold of Mike and give him power over satans demons that is destroying his happiness. Let my family help and inspire theirs. I can't wait to get them in Sunday school, they will love it. They will be here for VBS, I know that they will love that.

I also want to pray for my sister Vickie. Lord I know she is saved by her word, but she gives in to the devil to much. She yells and screams like a lunatic when she gets angry and that's all of the time. She has an evil tongue when she is mad she tries to blame everyone else, that we look down on her. You know Lord as well as I do that I have no right to look down on anyone. I think she has a very low self esteem and that she tries to build herself up to be more then she is. She needs to humble herself and accept who she is. She needs to focus more on what pleases you rather then those around her. She is smart, beautiful, and loves you, now she needs to live for you. Use me Lord to help her.

Maybe working to help her will help me to be a better listener, this is something that I need to work on. I talk to much. Please don't let her have anymore out bursts with mom, I will put her on the ground if she does. I won't stand by and let her give mom a heart attack. That wasn't very Christian of me, I am sorry. Ok Lord, here its yours, you handle her.

Help my children get through these next few days of school. I can't believe my baby is graduating in just over a week. Guide him and all of his friends as they move into adulthood. Surround Kaylain with your love Lord, she is an emotional wreck. She lashes out when she is hurting, show her how to handle these emotions better. Show me Lord what I can do to help her. I love her and can't stand to see her hurting. Bless her with peace, comfort, love and wisdom. Tap her on the shoulder, let her know what your will is for her. The devil is trying to claim her, keep him away from her. Thank you for this beautiful spring day. I am so grateful for all of my blessings. I would especially like to thank you for Riverview Baptist Church, for our Pastor, he is so good with our young people, he takes a real interest in them and for that I am grateful. Thank you for my church family, the are such a blessing to us. Grow our church Lord.

In Jesus name
Amen

Journal entry May 6, 2011 8:40 pm

Thank you Lord for a peaceful, beautiful day. Worked on my book in the a.m. this has been such good therapy for me. They called from Turkey Creek and soon we will get to go in and tell them what finishes we want on our spaces. Lord I am praying hard that this will work out good for me. I pray I can do enough to support us. No one will hire me Lord, I honestly don't know why. I guess I haven't found the place where you want me yet, so I will keep searching.

Tonight is Kaylains eighth grade formal and she looked beautiful, she is growing up so fast. Casey and Anna went to their prom last weekend and they looked so handsome and beautiful Time is going by really fast. Next week is graduation, I am really looking forward to it. Four months ago I was dreading it because Jerry wouldn't be here. Now I just keep reminding myself that I am missing a lot more then he is right now.

As happy as these occasions are, they are nothing compared to the joy we will know there. It will be the ultimate celebration. I know that I will shed tears for Jerrys absence, and joyful tears that my baby is starting his adult life, but I am going to make sure that this is a wonderful, happy day for him.

Now on a serious note, I have some special requests. I pray that they drive safely and cautiously to Daytona. I ask that you put a hedge of protection about them while they spread their wings. Bring them home safely and then let him have the best time of his life in Alabama with Anna and her family. He is a good boy and he works hard, please bless him. I pray Lord that the claims are settled soon ad that there is a lot of money left to catch up bills and make things easier for my family, and to get a decent truck. Bless us Lord with what we need.

In Jesus name
Amen

Journal entry May 7, 2011 Saturday am

Satan is on me Lord and for a brief moment I was letting him win so I figured I better get with you. I woke up so happy this morning, Kaylain had a wonderful time at the dance and she looked beautiful. I got word that before long we would get to go in and see our space at the new market. And would hopefully be getting to open first week of June. I am trying to hang on until then, but it is so hard. After I checked my account this morning I found I only had $11.43 left to buy food for next week. I sat in the recliner mulling this over, thinking about what to get that would stretch my money enough to provide lunch and dinner until my next check. The devil had me feeling really low and I was getting discouraged. Then I decided on what I could buy and was quite pleased that you gave me so many ideas. Then I went out and got in my van to go shopping and what else? My van wouldn't start. James and his uncle worked on it for two days and it did fine up through yesterday, now its not starting again. I just walked back in the house and there was that terrible feeling again. Not anger, just aggravation and sadness that evertime I start to feel good, satan takes a jab at me. So here I am Lord, I am giving it to you. Let me add this, the attorney has a paper for me to sign. He was supposed to mail it, that was about ten days ago. Please make him send it so that I can get it back to him so that all of this can be settled and please, please let us get some badly needed money to survive financially.

Lord I am excited about next weeks graduation and the festivities starting tomorrow with the special program at church. I am also concerned about the senior trip the week after. Keep them safe Lord, and slow Casey down when he is driving, he makes me nuts. Thank you for this beautiful day and for all of my many blessings.

In his name
Amen

Journal entry May 8, 2011 9:04 am Mothers Day

Lord thank you for this beautiful day. Church was good this morning and we went over to moms and spent the afternoon and ate. We watched a movie and talked. We went back to church, it was the night we have every year that is dedicated to our graduating seniors and this year my young man and his special young lady are the two honored. It was an emotional but wonderful service. I had to speak in front of the church about my child. That was not hard because there was so much good to say about him. I made reference to Anna also because I love her so much. I am so proud of the both of them. You know you expect us as parents to say nice things. But when the Pastor and the youth director and friends get emotional and proud when talking about them, you know you have good kids.

I made it through my words, though hard when talking about Jerry, I had to let Casey know what his Daddy had on his heart to tell him. Jerry wasn't up to writing a letter for this time, he always was a man of few words, but two things for sure he wanted me to let Casey know was that he was so proud of him and that even though he wouldn't be here physically for him, he would be spiritually. He said to tell him that he (Casey) was his heart and a real blessing from God. No parent was ever more proud then his Dad and I are of him. One more week until graduation and party and two weeks until his senior trip. I pray Lord he has a wonderful time and the best time when he goes to Alabama with Anna and her family.

I ask Lord that he can find a job for his money and bills and that I can either get a good job or do well at the market to support us. You have brought us through so much Lord, I pray these next couple of months will continue to improve our situation.

I pray these things
in Jesus name
amen

May 9, 2011 10:30 am

My precious Lord, I again just tried to make a trip to the grocery store and again that van won't start. Lord I have needed groceries for a week now, please let me get there.

God I pray with everything that I have that I can get some of the insurance money to help our situation. I need a decent car that won't be such a headache, I need to refinance the house so we can afford the payments and I want Jerrys funeral paid and tithes paid. But whatever the out come, I will accept your will. Its easy to trust you now that I have quit letting satan interfere, you have never failed me. Hind sight is easy, trusting for the future is hard sometimes, but I know that you will take care of me. I feel that I am getting stronger and that my faith will see me through what ever lies ahead of me.

I want to ask special prayers for my mom and siblings and their families. I don't know why we always argue if there are more then two of us together. I am going to try and focus on my own and pray for them all as well as for mine. I pray for mine and Jerrys boys and their families. I pray that they find the love that we shared with each other and the one of a kind love and joy that can only be found through salvation and a relationship with you. It is such a beautiful day, sitting out here on the back deck is so peaceful and serene, that is what we have always loved about this place and why we pray that you allow us to keep it. Casey dreams of buying this 15 acres that surrounds us. He wants to build a home at the top of the hill. I would love to see that happen for him. Please let the van start now and get me to the store and back. I love you Lord and I praise you

In Jesus name
Amen

Journal entry May 10, 2011

What a beautiful day, thank you Lord. I don't know why I can't make myself get out and enjoy it. I don't even feel like getting dressed. I don't feel like I am depressed, it feels more like the blues.

I am not sad about Jerrys death because I know he is not suffering anymore. But rather it's the loneliness and emptiness that makes me sad. It paralyzes me. I don't want to get out because I hate doing things by myself. I don't have a car right now so I can't go anywhere and even if I had a car, I don't have the money to go anywhere. There are a thousand things to do around the house but I just can't seem to get motivated to do them. Please help me Lord to snap out of this state of mind. I am ok when the kids are home, enjoy doing things with them, but they have their own lives. In fact I need to find something outside of home and school for Kaylain to do, she is fourteen years old and is at the age where she needs to spread her wings socially. I want her to be well rounded and have fun.

As I said before Lord, I need purpose in my life. Not only am I facing empty nest syndrome, it is also empty house syndrome. Women and some men feel loss when their children grow up and don't need them any more. When you get to this point in your life your focus shifts to your spouse. You make plans as a couple and look forward to doing things with the two of you. It might be traveling, or maybe an activity you can enjoy together, like camping, fishing, golfing, dancing, whatever. Jerry and I planned to come up here to Tennessee and along with our partners start a business, build it up, hire a good manager and go home to North Carolina and live and when Jerry was old enough to retire and Casey would be starting college, I would quit work and we would travel. There is a lot of truth to the saying, If you want to make God laugh, tell him your plans.

Lord I have been through more in five years then a lot of people do in a lifetime. I am tired and I am on an emotional roller coaster. Some days good, some days bad. Please lead me, help me, give me what I need to get my life going again.

In Jesus name
Amen

Journal entry May 12, 2011

My precious Lord, I need motivation. I have sat around all day doing nothing except going to get moms car and going to the bank. I just got up from lying on the bed watching t.v. and I decided to clean my kitchen, put on a load of laundry, get all of the trash out, and spend some time working on my book until the kids get home. Then after five I am going to take them to chic filet and eat to help Youth for Christ raise money.

The sun is shining, the birds are singing, I am alive and I am not going to let the devil hold me down. Bless me Lord Jesus with all that I need. Use me for your purpose for I am your willing child.

In Jesus name
Amen

These days were such bitter sweet times. How my life was changing and so fast that it made me dizzy. I sat staring at Casey and my mind was running away, he was a man now, not my little baby and he would leave me soon to start his own life. I didn't know what Kaylain wanted, one minute it was to be with her mom, the next she was mad at them. How I kept my sanity during this time could only have been by the grace of God.

People take their normal lives for granted, not even giving it a second thought, oh what I wouldn't give for normal. Just to have the security of a job and financial freedom. To be able to go to work and be productive and be with other people. To crawl into bed at night and snuggle up next to my husband. To laugh and enjoy just being together. Just being able to go out and get in a car that would start seemed like such a luxury. Everyone was so good to us. So many friends hired Casey to do work around their yards to earn money for his senior trip, I was so grateful. He had been through so much and I wanted him to get away from everything for a while and enjoy himself. I was wishing that I could do the same, I don't know why its not like you can run from your problems, but I sure wasn't dealing with them very well. I tried to strain every moment of happiness I could out of every happy event that I could. Graduation and all the festivities were a distraction for a little while, then reality sets in. How am I going to make it. Even if we get the insurance money and get caught up, what about when its gone.

Journal entry May 13, 2011 9:30

Friday the thirteenth, no different then any other day. I am so tired Lord, I didn't go to sleep until almost 4:00 am and got up at 7:00 am. I hate these nights when I am so tired but the devil is running around tormenting me. Today is my baby boys last day of high school. He graduates on Sunday. I pray Lord that everything goes well and that it will be a happy occasion.

I want it to be special and I pray that you keep satan from ruining the day with grief. I know his Dad is on his mind as he is on mine. Take that sadness from him Lord so he can enjoy this time. Put it on me, I would rather take it all then have his day ruined.

In Jesus name
Amen

Journal entry May 16, 2011

Yesterday was graduation day. I want to thank you Lord for answering my prayer beyond what I expected. In the weeks leading up to it, I was afraid that we would be so emotional that it would be to hard to focus on having fun. But you didn't let me down Lord, you pushed the grief so far down and filled our hearts with so much joy that it was impossible to be sad. I don't deny that I shed a couple of tears and that Jerry didn't cross my mind several times, but they were happy thoughts and good memories and I know it was by your hand. You have walked so closely to me these pasts months and brought me through so much and I am so grateful. I ask that these blessings continue through the bankruptcy and getting a job or starting a business. Whatever you want me to do Lord that's what I'm here for, I want only to serve you and please you. Bring us up out of this valley and set us on the mountain top for a while. I pray that things go well with the bankruptcy and that things are settled soon. Lord I paid CUB, water, internet, phone, and car insurance today and that will only leave me with a couple hundred dollars to make a house pmt. I need about $1200.00 more. I trust in you for what I need Lord, I thank you.

Lord I got Jeremys name at our breakfast the other morning, whatever is going on in his life, if its not of you Lord, I pray you fix it. I also pray for all of those with health issues, pray for healing. Guide us Lord, show us what to do to be in the center of your will.

In Jesus name
Amen

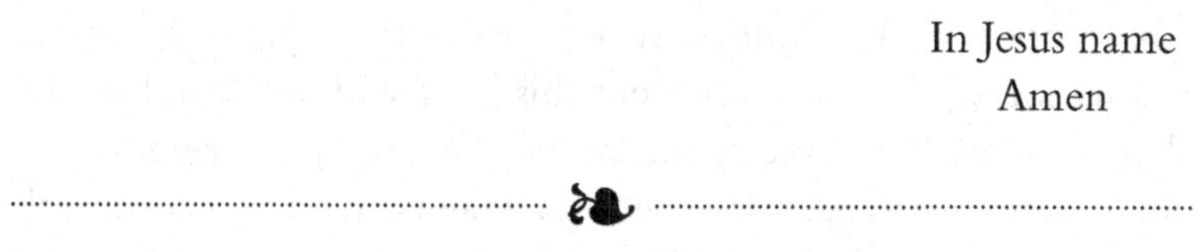

Journal entry May 17, 2011

I need a job Lord, or a business of my own. I don't care which one as long as I am able to support my family. Please let the money from insurance be in our hands by the end of the month so I can catch up my house payments and refinance our house. Please let me get a dependable car soon so I can get to interviews if anyone calls.

I ask that Casey get everything squared away with Pellisippi today, I don't want to worry about this all summer. And if it could be your will, let us soon take a little family trip together, we really could use it. We haven't had a fun vacation since we went to Orlando with the youth group. I wish I could get my timeshares caught up and banked so that I could provide another place for a retreat.

I am so grateful for all of the wonderful times that Jerry and I had on our vacations. We were truly blessed to be able to do a lot and see a lot I will cherish these memories always. Please allow me to make more good memories with my family. I also want to thank you for the people that you have put in my life and how much my life has changed spiritually. I pray that you use me in some way to enrich peoples lives for your glory. I would love to be a blessing to others as many have been a blessing to me. I pray for Jeremy Lord, for whatever need he may have. Put his feet upon the right path and bring him back to the way he was raised. In Jesus name Amen

❧

Journal entry May 31, 2011

I ask forgiveness Lord, I know I have disappointed you by not spending my time with you in prayer and study. I don't know why I have not took the time to seek you out these past two weeks. I don't know if I have ever went this long without spending my alone time with you, please forgive me. I am so empty right now. I don't even want to get out of bed and its all I can do to make myself do even a little around the house. I know a part of it is depression and stress but I also know its partly my diabetes or at least now I know, I checked my sugar 3 days ago and it was 533, not good. I am sure that has a lot to do with my loss of energy and always being sleepy. I have to get my life and my health under control. Kaylain and I are going to start walking every morning over at Melton Lake. We started yesterday and walked almost two miles. We didn't go today because we are both sick. I took her to the Dr. because I thought she had strep. They sent off a throat culture to see anyway, I have done good with my eating this week. I have had 1 Debbie cake and 2 Dr peppers, that's good for me.

Casey has been gone somewhere since graduating almost everyday. I don't get to see him much these days, but I want him to enjoy this time. He had a fairly good time on his senior trip, but I was disappointed that he didn't get to do a lot of the things that he wanted too, like deep sea fishing or parasailing. But the day he got home, he turned around and went to Alabama with Anna and her family for a family reunion. I am convinced he really enjoyed that more. You could hear the excitement in his voice when he talked about all that they did. The only bad thing was they went swimming in a river only to be told after that there were alligators in it. I bet next time he will ask someone before he jumps in a river he has never been in. Both of my boys are so adventurous, it scares me.

We all went over to moms last night and had sandwiches and visited, it was nice. We are all having to pinch pennies right now. We are going to go to titanic museum Thursday to take mom for her birthday. it's the last place Jerry and I went to together before he died. God love his heart. He went as long as he could go. I miss him so much. I tried not to dwell on him being gone all weekend, but its hard when your not working and your car is broke down and you are stuck at home. I thought a lot about how we would take the long weekends and have family and friends come up to the camper to cook out and play cards.

I wish that we still had our camper so that we could at least escape up there on the weekends and all it would cost was some gas and groceries. But then again I don't think I could enjoy it with all of the memories lingering there. Maybe someday I can get another camper at a different place so it won't be so sad. I know the kids and their friends would love it.

Lord I pray a special prayer for Jeremy, touch his life Lord and keep him in the center of your will. I pray also healing and protection for Rodney Pointer, and healing for Kathy Haynes and grace for them all. I love you so much Lord and I am sorry for being so slack with my prayer time and for not getting in my Bible the way that I should. I will do better. I realize that I have let satan have to much control, the choice is mine and I choose to make the decisions that I need to based on what you want me to do. I pray for the blessings of financial freedom, good health and the means to help others. Use me Lord, I am you child and I am willing.

In Jesus name
Amen

I was so low at this time and was fighting depression everyday. I felt like such a failure. I couldn't find work, the bills were stacking up and I knew my kids were afraid, that was the worst thing of all. Its bad enough to go through all of this, but when you can't protect your kids from it its heartbreaking. I prayed so hard everyday that God would change our circumstance, but nothing changed. I don't know why he let us go through this for so long, but I thought I would go crazy.

I was spiraling fast down into depression, I didn't talk about it because I was afraid that people would think that it was a lack of faith on my part. I was the one that always said that I was to blessed to be depressed. I have come to realize that it wasn't that I wasn't blessed, but sometimes God puts us on our knees because thats where we should have been all the time, on our knees in prayer. And I will never again pray for patience, because he didn't give it to me, he taught it to me. When you are dealing with lawyers, insurance companies, the IRS, bill collectors, trustees, you name it, you will learn patience.

Journal entry June 5, 2011

Here I am Lord to serve you show me what you want me to do.The day before yesterday was moms birthday,June 3.All I could think was that one year ago Jerry had his first chemo treatment. He was so sick the next day. So much has happened since then, its hard to believe. I lost my sweet husband six months ago and while I am getting stronger, my heart is still mending. I still can't believe that he is gone. Next week would have been his 65th birthday, and things didn't even come close to what we had planned for these years.

The business was supposed to be thriving and Casey would be in college and Jerry and I would be looking for a motor home, getting ready to travel. Instead its almost the opposite. Please Lord, let me get my life to a place where you can use me the most and where I can feel happiness again. I am tired and weary, I need a mission of some kind. Provide what I need Lord for every situation.

Jessica and the girls will be here next week (maybe). It will be a good distraction to have little ones around again. I think, I'm getting old, but I am looking forward to it. Kaylain leaves tomorrow to go on a beach trip with her friend.Watch over her Lord, and let her have fun, she needs it.

In Jesus name
Amen

Journal entry June 9, 2011 Happy Birthday my love

This day would have been Jerrys 65th birthday. I miss him so much. I didn't have a chance to be sad because Jessica and the girls arrived today and there hasn't been a dull moment. I enjoy watching them play and listening to them, they are very entertaining to say the least. I don't know if Casey has thought about it, didn't want to bring sadness to his mind. I bought some pretty flowers to make a nice arrangement for his birthday. The girls are so funny, they are scared to death of my cats. They were walking up the drive with me to take Missy for her last outing before bed, it was dark with only a little bit of light from the porch light. We were walking back down and right when we got beside the cars Tiger attacked Boo and oh what a ruckus. Kenzie screamed to the top of her lungs and took off running, when she realized she was running straight towards Balto (Caseys Siberian Husky) she turned and just started running in circles. I finally got her and we all headed for the house. They are good girls and I can see that Mike and Jessica work with them to be good and to love God. This afternoon while talking to mom I said oh my God, Kenzie immediately told me, "don't say Gods name like that, say oh my gosh." I was so embarrassed that I had been scolded by a child, but so tickled that she was taught not to use Gods name that way. Once everyone gets settled in, I think this is going to be a good adventure.

Lord I want to thank you for getting them here and also the lawyer called today and said he was going to go over the report from the trustee with me, he had just gotten it. I missed the call so now I will be up all night wondering about what was paid and what is left. He said it looks pretty good whatever that means. Please let it be what I need. Also orientation Saturday for the new market. Please let us get moved in and set up nicely. Let our little business do well and let us pay bills. I hope all goes well and I can meet a lot of people and share my testimony. I thank you for allowing me to help Jessica while at the same time helping myself. Things are looking so much better, please don't let satan ruin it.

In Jesus name
Amen

Journal entry June 16, 2011

Thank you God for all of my blessings, I know that they are many. I appreciate you keeping me busy with Jessie and the girls on the ninth so it didn't hurt so much thinking about Jerrys birthday. I pray Sunday (Fathers Day) goes just as well. We have been having vacation bible school this week and its always fun to watch the faces of the little ones, especially when the puppets are singing. I hope we have had at least one saved, but pray there will be many. Riley and Kenzie have really enjoyed it and Jessica has got to be a helper in crafts, this has allowed her to get to know some of the people in our church family. I am glad they are here, it's a bit crowded and its been a while since I have had little ones around and its definitely taking Casey and Kaylain some time to adjust, but the over all picture is a blessing. I pray that my family be a blessing to Jessie and her girls. I know they are one to me. Use each of us to help each other grow in our faith and in our walk with you.

Lord I ask healing, love, and strength for Jessica as well as courage. I had no idea what this child has suffered growing up or I would have went and gotten her years ago. Now she is gong through a life change that is hard for her because she loves here husband so much. I know you have a plan for her, so just guide her Lord, let her trust in you for her choices. I pray you use me in anyway that will help her to grow as a women, a mother, and most of all a Christian. She is a good little mommy and her girls are precious. Let her overcome her fears of being afraid, don't let this hinder her.

In Jesus name
Amen

Journal entry June 17, 2011

Last night ofVBS. Had six saved and one rededicated this week, that's amazing since our average was 112 per night. That's counting teachers and helpers. Had a good time, but I am so tired. There were a couple of times that I was a little overwhelmed. When we took the kids out in the field to play and I would look over and see his grave I would get a little sad and think about the wonderful times he and I would help cooking for the kids and then sit on the grassy hill and watch all of the kids playing games. We would come home exhausted but so happy. I miss him so much God. I was just sitting here thinking about the insurance money, we are getting back 80 % of it, then I realized that they called us with the good news on Jerrys birthday. I didn't get the call until after they had already closed, I had to wait until the next day, But it will be enough to pay the rest of the taxes, get a reliable car or truck, and refinance my house and hopefully hold us over until I get a job or start a business. I am so thankful. And after acting like a crazy women and fussing about the trustee and attorneys they actually worked out an amazing settlement. Jerrys funeral was paid, the IRS was paid and the trustee only charged $2500.

So we are lucky. I had to apologize to my attorney and even though I never talked to the trustee except at the first hearing in December, I apologize to him for all of the mean things I said about him.

But I do think they should change the law, I had to wait six months to get it and my house payments are behind four months. But God does things in his own time, not ours.

So far God has answered all of my prayers these past couple of months, which is a blessing after he said no to healing Jerry and saving the business. I pray Lord that you provide me with a job or business to make what I need to take care of us. I am certain you will provide me with what I need. I love you Lord, I know I haven't told you enough lately so please forgive me.

In Jesus name
Amen

Jessica and the girls had finally arrived. I was so excited, but as I learned and so did Jessie, this was going to be harder then we thought. I have a little tiny yorkie that the girls were obsessed with. I was constantly on them to leave her alone which in turn stressed Jessica out. I understand her frustration with me, but I can not let them hurt Missy. Most of the time things were fine. I would watch the girls while Jessie and Kaylain went to workout. I enjoyed time with them we had fun. Kenzie would say she was my little buddy. She would come lay on the bed and do my makeup and hair for hours while I watched tv. Riley would often join us. And if I was cooking or unloading the dish washer, or mopping, they always wanted to help. They would set the table for me. They were good kids, they would just get bored being inside all of the time. Once when the girls were gone to the gym, Casey got the water hose and made a big mud hole with some clean dirt left by the power company. We put the girls in old t-shirts and shorts and took them out to play in the mud. At first they just looked at him like he was crazy. I don't think these two had ever been dirty a day in there life. Once he got them dirty though and they started fighting back, they had one heck of a mud fight and I have got the pictures to prove it. They were so funny. When I called Kaylain and told her to tell Jessie, she didn't believe it. Then there were the times we took them out at dusk to catch fire flies, I couldn't believe they had never done this, even Jessica got into it.

As hard as we tried to make it work, it was just too stressful for all of us, she ended up going back to Florida which I hate because I really miss them all. I think if we had gotten them a house of their own from the start they would still be here. They had started church with us and everyone loved them, they still ask about them all of the time. But Jessica seems so happy and so do the girls, so I am happy for them. I just hope they know how much I love them and how much they mean to me. I hope that she will bring them up for visits, and we will be going down to see all of them, that is where most of our family lives. I love to visit, but I am always ready to come home to my mountains. I have always been a country girl that loves the mountains. To me there is not anything more beautiful this side of Heaven.

Journal entry June 21, 2011

I love you so much Lord, and I thank you for my many blessings. I pray Lord for us to get the money soon, I hope I don't sound ungrateful for getting any back at all, I just want to get things paid. I am so grateful for the many answered prayers. Please let Jerry know how much I love and miss him. These past few weeks I have really had him on my mind, his birthday, fathers day, and especially vacation bible school. We really enjoyed that as a family over the years. Jerry loved our church so much, and all of our church family and he was so fond of David. One comfort I have is that he has people like Mayford, Randy, Mamie, Eva, and several others in heaven with him as well as family.

I am enjoying having Jessica and the girls, they are a good distraction. Please don't let it be costly having them here, and use us to help them get to a good place in life. Jessica is guiding the girls down the right path, just guide her Lord. Fill her with your Holy Spirit. I also ask that you touch Candace and her family. They are going through difficult times. Don't let satan pull them apart. I also pray for the rest of my siblings and their families. Touch each and every one of them. Watch over my two older boys and their families. I pray that we all get on our feet.

God bless my kids here at home. Guide them through the evil that they deal with everyday. Keep the devil away from them. Lord I ask your blessing on our annual camping trip. This year we are finally going to venture across the mountain to the KOA in Cherokee, NC, Keep us all safe, let everyone have a good time, but most of all let us use this time to fellowship, worship, and lift up your name and be good witnesses to all those we meet. Let this be a life experience for Jessica and the girls that will bring them even closer to you. I want all of my family to have the joy that I carry in my heart, there truly is nothing like it. Thank you Lord for my blessings, your grace, and the strength to move forward. I am so grateful for the fulfilling of my needs.

In Jesus name
Amen

Thank you Lord for another day of life. I can still hear that beautiful deep voice of my love beginning each prayer with that. Thank you. I never realized how much we take for granted. Because God never promised us another day. I imagine It becomes more important when we are at deaths door, but what we should keep in mind is that this could be the day God calls us home and that we should thank him everyday for every blessing, for every breath we take. I am so grateful for them all. We should also ask forgiveness each day for our sins and short comings that we know displease him. He knows we are going to sin, but as Christians we should live the very best life we can according to Gods word and when we do slip, we should be remorseful and ask forgiveness, God gives us new mercies every day. If we don't feel sorry when we know we have went against God, then maybe we should evaluate our salvation and make sure we have it nailed down. Just because you go through the motions doesn't mean you are saved, only you and God know that for sure. If you have any doubt then you need to get on your knees right now.

You don't have to be perfect to be saved. All it requires is that you know you are a sinner and you are truly remorseful of the sins you have committed against God. There are no sins too big. You ask forgiveness of these sins, ask God into your heart, You believe Jesus died for you, and that you change the way you live and do your best to win other lost souls to God. Now get ready to experience a joy that can be found no other way but by the blood of Jesus. Remember God never said we would not experience hard times because we are his, in fact it may get harder, because satan goes into a rage when he loses another soul, but God gives us grace to face whatever situation we have to. Gods word is true and he tells us in that word that he will never leave us or forsake us. I have had many times these past few months that I felt like he had turned his back on me, but when I took my hand out of what I had been praying for, he took care of it. I am still guilty of doing this, even though I know that he will handle it.

Journal entry June 23, 2011

Thank you Lord for my many blessings. I know that they are many. Thank you for Jessica and the girls, I don't know how we will fair financially but spiritually it has been good for me and I think for her and the girls.

Church was really good last night. We only had a few there because many are on vacation. The lesson was on the witch of Endor which I have never studied before, but it confirmed what I have thought all along that satan has demons who work evil just as God has angels. I also know satan is powerful and even though he is not as powerful as God, he is far more powerful then we are. He will attack us and weaken us to make us look bad to those who are lost. I thank you God for giving me grace, strength, peace, and comfort through my darkest days. I could not have gotten through these past months or even years without you. I ask Lord that you allow us to get our money soon and that we get our truck and be able to make a trip down to see Mike and his family. Watch over all of my kids and grandkids, guide their every step. I feel like Jerrys death impacted a couple of family members and I pray its for your glory.

Lord I ask that you move in Candaces life, I know she is saved but she lets money rule her life and its destroying her family. Make her realize that money and things will not make her happy, but her family and her relationship with you will. Candace has a good heart, but she needs you to take a hold of her life and bring her family back close together. I don't know what is going on with her but she didn't have one nice thing to say to me when she was here the other day. I don't understand what is wrong with her, but help her. Spread a little over to Vickie as well. I have never seen anyone fly off the handle as easy as that child does and it makes everyone around her stressed, help her Lord. Watch over my mom, keep her calm and let me be able to do more with her when I can afford to. God watch over Casey and Kaylain, keep them on the right path.

In Jesus name
Amen

Journal entry June 25 2011 3:12 am

Lord I can't sleep. I don't know why. I have a lot of things running through my mind. Mostly thinking of what to do and when, nothing bad really. I just keep hoping the trustee will release the money that we so desperately need. I put a deposit on a truck that I pray you led us to and will last us at least four or five years. I need to catch up the house payments and bills, pay employer tax from business, and I also desperately want to take a little get away trip with my kids, I would like to go see Michael and maybe go down to see the family for a couple of days. I pray these things are your will. I ask for guidance and direction in trying to figure out how to support my family. My niece and her two babies moved in for a while. I am renting her a room to help make my house payment, but I am afraid that will be eaten up in added utilities, but that's ok Lord because I feel like you have a bigger plan. I think in some way you are using my family to some how help hers spiritually. I pray that is the case. I pray she and Mike both will seek your direction and that you heal and protect them and put their marriage back together and raise these two precious little girls in a Christian home. These babies are adorable.

We had a tornado touch down less then a mile from where Casey was house sitting, I was so afraid for him and mom and Vickie. That crazy child tried to drive home before we were sure it was safe enough. He did not like being alone through it all while house sitting for Annas family. Then when he couldn't get home, he went back there until rain slacked off then took off to Candaces. He is going to give me a heart attack with some of his antics. I thank you so much for keeping him safe. I ask Lord that you guide us through yet another camping trip, we always enjoy them so much. I pray we get through it safely and have a wonderful time and that friendships and relationships be strengthened This will be our first campout without Jerry, so please don't let it be a sad time, in fact please use this time to let us heal and grow stronger so that we can move on. Let us get started with our new lives or rather our changed lives. Give us normal again please. All I ask is for what we need and that you use us any way you see fit that will bring you glory. Help me Lord, I know that I am so much stronger then I was a few months ago, and I am no where near as afraid, but I still hurt so bad and though its not a constant pain like it was it still breaks my heart when I get it on my mind. Help me Lord as only you can.

I pray in my precious
Jesus name
Amen

Journal entry June 28, 2011

Lord calm my mind and my heart. I called the attorney today and they have no idea when we might be getting our money. Three weeks ago he thought it would be soon. Lord please help us. I put a thousand dollars down on truck, it only holds it until day after tomorrow then I will have to put more down. July 1, two more days, I will owe five house payments, not to mention the utilities and car and home insurance.

I am fighting the devil to stay calm. I can't fight him, I gave it to you Lord, I will wait and I will trust, whatever you want for us, we will trust in your will. I am so sorry I missed church tonight, I didn't realize until 6:42 pm at the grocery store that it was Wednesday. Remember my family and all of those who have prayer request.

In Jesus name
Amen

Journal entry July 1, 2011

Lord tomorrow is Caseys first birthday without his dad, I don't know why I think of every occasion as our first without him. Anyway I am having a birthday bash at the chimneys because its one of his favorite places and I pray he has the best time. Please let everything go well and let us have good fellowship and a lot of fun.

Please Lord let us get our check soon so we can get bills caught up, refinance the house, buy our truck and start a new business, only after we pay our tithes of course. If we can help someone in the same situation then show us who you want us to help. We are your willing servants Lord and want only to please you and bring you glory. I forgot my glasses and I can't make out the words so I hope this is legible. I pray things continue to improve and we can get back to normal again. I thank you so much for such a nice day at

Cades Cove yesterday. The girls, including Jessica and Vickie had such an awesome time. Casey took the girls down to wet their feet and of course they ended up sitting in it. We hung their clothes in the car windows to dry and put one of caseys t-shirts and Jessica's tank tops on them. They reminded me of little house on the prairie running through the grass. They got to see deer, and old houses and churches and just had so much fun in the fresh air. So many good memories came flooding back as we rode through. Jerry and I spent many hours there and it will always be special to me. Please let Jerry know how much I love him and look forward to seeing him again one day.

Now Lord I ask healing grace for Tammy and Kathy, and for Amie's dad and Gene. Please bless all of those requests that have been made through church. I pray healing for Caseys leg and Kaylain's health issues and mine as well, we have so many at church right now who really need your help Lord, bless us all with what we need.

In Jesus name
Amen

Journal entry July 4, 2011

Ninteen years ago today, Jerry and I brought our sweet little boy home from the hospital, thank you for him Lord. I would be so crazy without him. While Jerry loved all of our kids and grandkids, he was definitely closest to Casey. They were two peas in a pod. I am so thankful that it was your plan to allow us to have a child together born out of our love for each other. Thank you for eighteen years as a family. You could have taken Jerry in 1997 but you answered my prayer to let Jerry at least live until Casey was grown and you did. I thank you for the wonderful years that you gave us and for getting us through the hard years. I look forward to the day we are all together again, I can't even imagine how joyous that will be.

Lord I don't know what to do about earning a living. I saw today where Becky is selling out, I really wish she and I could have worked together and made a good business that would support a good cause. I honestly don't know what your will is for me so guide me please. Watch over my kids, let us get through the next two weeks in camping and retreat without anyone getting hurt. Let it go smoothly, let me please get the insurance money before July 16th so we can get on track and get a business of some kind established or put me in job where you can use me the most.

In Jesus sweet name
Amen

Journal entry July 6, 2011

Lord thank you for a new day and all that you have planned for it. Thank you for yesterday. I had a good day with my family. Me, Vickie, and all the kids went to Wasabi's and then watched a movie, it was fun. I want to ask special prayer for Vickie and her children. Satan had wreaked havoc in their lives for years and its all coming to the surface. Bless them Lord with the grace to face the ghosts of a tumultuous past and give them all healing and allow forgivness among them so they can grow as a fimily and grow in their faith. Use me Lord anyway you can in this situation, especially with Riley and Kenzie. They need stability and church. They are precious and Jessica is doing good with them, they are so smart. I am really enjoying them.

I ask guidance for my kids as they embark on new phases of their lives. Casey is starting college and life as an adult. Kaylain is starting high school and is crazy about a young fellow named Skyler. They are both adjusting to having little ones around and overall are enjoying it. Kaylain likes having Jessica to talk to and Kenzie is my" little buddy" Lord thank you for leading me to the cash register stand for our booth, I pray Lord you lead me in this venture and that it will be successful, I just am not quite sure how to use it. As a thrift or gift or what. I think gift might be a better fit for the market atmosphere, but I need the insurance money to buy what I need to fix it up nice.

I am thinking I should sell the thrift stuff off and use the money to establish the gift shop, lead me Lord, show me your will. Whatever it is, let me be able to get out of debt, keep bills paid, and help my church and youth group and any you lead me to help, which I pray are many. I love you so much Lord nd I am so grateful for your grace through the lossof my precious husband, and the strength to move forward.

In Jesus name
Amen

Journal entry July 15, 2011

So busy since last Thursday. Thank you Lord for a wonderful retreat at brother Davids this past Friday and Saturday, and for the good service Sunday. Great time at our annual camping trip with the kids. I thought of Jerry often, but it was sweet memories, not bitter grief. The only bad thing was that I ws bitten by what was most likely a brown recluse spider, boy it looks nasty. Went to emergency room the night we got home. The Dr. cut out some tissue and packed it with guaze. Mom took it out and cleaned it for me today it looks a lot better than it did. Lord please let them finish this bankruptcy on the 29th and send our money. I so look forward to getting my truck, catching up bills and making a nice little business at the market. I pray this is where you want me and that everthing goes well with it and I build a good customer base and a good reputation. I ask your guidance Lord, if its not where you want me then show me where to go.

School starts soon Lord and both of my kids are worried about what and how they will do. Give them the knowledge to do well and to accomplish their goals according to your will. I pray for Jessica to be able to get into culinary classes and business and her two little ones to get a good start in the whole education process.

In Jesus name
Amen

2nd Journal entry July 15, 2011 6:54 pm

Lord watch over my baby boy and the other guys that went on the ten mile back packing trip. Keep them safe, I am worried about flooding. Let them enjoy this trip and I pray that you use it to strengthen their faith, their resolve, and help them grow. Don't let them get lost or hurt.

Amen

Journal entry July 16, 2011

Lord the hospital just called and said the culture they did shows strep B. This is a bacteria that can lead to sepsis or meningitis, that scares me. I pray that you lay your healing hands on me and heal me Lord, top to bottom.

In Jesus name
Amen

Journal entry July 18, 2011

Thank you for watching over Casey and his friends on their back packing trip. They made camp on a bed of copper heads, they saw six. If one of them had been bitten they would have died before they could get help. I am so grateful for your protection. Now they are all broke out with some kind of mystery bumps. I pray its not anything serious. Lord let them find some not so dangerous hobbies. I pray Lord I get my booths ready for August 12th. Opening and that we do well. I hope it will at least pay for itself and support my family and church. Please let me get the insurance money next week so that I can get my truck and get started. I pray for Jessica and Mike and the girls. I would love to see them become a family again and grow in love, faith, and happiness. Those girls are precious and I would love to see them stable and happy and brought up in church. Bless them Lord with the love and happiness I once had with my sweet Jerry.

I ask grace and peace for Mikes Dad and Amies dad and their families. I know only to well how comforting your grace is in these difficult times.I know the pain they are feeling, but I also know that your are the only one who can dull it, so touch them. Tell my precious husband that I love him and miss him. Bless and strengthen and grow our church Lord. Bless our pastor and every member. I pray better times for Georgia and Durell and my family as well.

In Jesus name
Amen

Journal entry July 23, 2011

Lord watch over Casey and Candace and Taylor on their way to Florida. I hope he has fun, cause he is gonna work when he gets back and help me get some kind of business going. I need to be useful. Charlotte requested prayer a little while ago. She said Gene is not doing well, God she has been through so much these past seven years. I know we all go through things but it seems like she has had to endure so much. She is strong Lord, I know this, but even the strongest in faith have their moments. Be with them Lord whatever your will for them, give them grace. I pray the same for Amies dad and her family.

I also ask for Katie and her family, Katie has been going through her struggle for over a year. I ask we all get through these difficult times and that you won't tarry too long before coming to get us. I look forward to that home coming. I wish it were right now, I am so ready, this world is wicked and satan rules it. I pray for the lost my sweet Lord, use me to plant seeds that will grow into a beautiful relationship with you through salvation. I don't know how bad it would have been these last few years, especially the last few months, without you. Thank you God for your son and your mercy.

In Jesus name
Amen

July 31 2011

This time last year, Jerry was going through reatments and we were trying to hang on to the store and had filed bankruptcy. What a difference a year makes. Now he is gone after losing his battle with cancer, we lost the business, and I can't get a job, the bankruptcy still hasn't been completed and we have not received the proceeds left from the life insurance money. The house payments are six months behind, we put 3000 of Caseys money on a truck we both like because we thought we would have that money by now, so please Lord don't let us lose that. I let Jessica move in for a couple of months until she could get a place for her and the girls, I think they may have one, if they get approval. I pray it be your will Lord. Jennifer and her family and Josh and his girlfriend and her brother are up visiting, they leave tomorrow.

Lord I am so tired and so stressed and so beside myself I pray you reach down and lift me up into your loving arms and comfort me. I thank you for getting me through this year, I am thankful its behind me instead of ahead of me. Lord I know its selfish but please allow me enough after I get paid to do a family cruise next year, unless it is not your will, at least let us do some kind of vacation as a family, we really need it.

In Jesus name
Amen

Journal entry August 1, 2011

August already, wow. I can't believe that Jerry has been gone eight months.I miss him so much. I am lost without him. Lord thank you for all that you have done for me, even when I am ready to give up.You have always given me grace when I needed it, along with peace and comfort. I pray these blessings for Charlote and Gene and Amie and her family. I know they are tired and satan is working on them while they are weak so put your loving arms around them. God please let us get our money soon so that we can breath financially and get a business going. Or get a job one. I really need to work and make money Lord. Please make it happen. Let Mike and Jessica get that house and put their little family back together.

Please let me get both of my idea's for business off the ground. Let me do well financially and be able to do good for others for your glory. Use me to serve others as well as take care of my family. We have had such a hard road these past forteen months, last seven years for that matter so please let us have a few years of peace and calm, use us to be good witnesses to the lost. Bless us Lord with all that we need

In Jesus name
Amen

August 2, 2011 8:12 pm

Lord thank you for getting all the kids back to Florida safely, and for getting Mike up here safely, I know Jessica and the girls are excited to see him. I pray that they get the house they are looking at and that things work out well for their little family. I pray for financial peace Lord, please let us get our money this week and get our booth set up and ready for opening day. I beg you Lord to let it do well enough to support my family and to be able to do good things for your glory. I pray for our church, use my family to help grow it. Unite us Lord and bless us with new families and new members. Lay your hands on David and bless him with the messages you want us to have. Lift him up Lord, he needs you. I pray that things really turn around for our church and that we will be stengthend by your grace and your mercy. I pray for all of those who are facing illness, Gene and Charlotte, Amies dad, Missy Smith, Joanne neeley, and any I may have forgotten. I pray for wisdom and understanding in my day to day life. Keep my eyes ears and heart open to what it is you want me to do, what direction you have planned for me. Give me the strength and stamina to accomplish it

In Jesus name
Amen

Journal entry August 5, 2011

THANK YOU LORD ! !! !

Just got a call about twenty minutes ago, our check is on the way. I keep hearing that song four days late. The words talk about Lazarus, when Jesus was four days late, after Lazurus had died, he was still on time because he rose him from the dead. I was down to literally a dollar and some change when my hot water heater went out. I owe seven house payments and need to catch up so many bills, now I know that I can and I can get what I need to open my little business. Thank you God, I know my faith was shaken and satan weakend me at times, but I always knew your were in control and we would be ok. I don't know what your plan is for us, but I know you will take care of us. I ask that you lead us as to how to use this money, let me start making money so we don't waste this. I am going to give my 10 % to the church first thing. I pray for guidance and wisdom as we move forward with our new lives. Keep us always in the center of your will, and use us for your glory.

In Jesus name
Amen

Dear Jerry,

We are getting the check soon and hopefully will get the house situated and a profitable business started. We are ok but miss you terribly. We would rather have you, love you And miss you.

Your loving wife

Journal entry August 9, 2011 7:24 am

I thank you lord for all of my blessings. I ask your comfort this morning Lord. I have been through hell and back this year and even though things seem to be getting better and I am getting stronger, I still miss Jerry so bad. I am having one of those crying moments where I just can't seem to calm down. I need you God. I am listening to "oh what a savior" on tv, by the Cathedralls, and its talking about how your heart was broken at calvary, so I know that you know how I feel. I miss him, I ache for him. I know he is happy and not suffering anymore. I am happy for that, but you know I would be lying to say I would not want him back here with me, (but not with cancer).You have brought me through so much Lord. I ask you to please mend my broken heart. Let me enjoy the love and happiness my kids give me and not make them sad.They are doing well.You have answered so many prayers for me during this difficult time in my life and I know without a doubt that you have always been there for me, even when I didn't think so. I ask your forgivness for the times of weakness and doubt. I pray that the loss of Jerry and all that my family has been through will some how touch someones life who may be feeling weak or lost. Use my pain Lord so the devil doesn't gain from it. Make it for your glory.

Show me Lord which way to go and what to do. I want to do your will Lord not mine.I just want to be able to take care of my family. I tried to help Jessica and the kids out Lord, but either I failed miserably or it wasn't meant for her to be here. Help her Lord guide her. I pray things work out for her little family and that you take hold of her and Mike both and show the happiness they could have through you.Watch over my kids and grandkids as they start a new school year. Keep them focused on their studies and let them do well so that if you tarry your coming they will be able to have good careers and take care of their families. I pray Lord that since they have had such a hard life in their young years that you will let them have good adult lives. I pray Casey has a marriage like

Will and Mollies that is always happy and easier then most. I hope they both find the love that I shared with Jerry.

God my mighty and powerful father, I ask you to reach down and wrap your healing hands around Gene and heal him. I pray for Amie and her family and Rhonda as she goes through her health problems. She looks so frail, heal her Lord. I pray your blessing on all requests made. It amazes me how I feel better after spending time with you. Thank you Amen

---

Journal entry August 10, 2011

Lord thank you for this day and for your many blessings. I ask you Lord to please let this be a good day, let us get our space set up and filled to the top for this weekend and let us have a killer business weekend. Give me strength and stamina to get all that I need to accomplished. Let us make a lot of new friends use us to reach the lost through this adventure and let thins go well.

Bless our church Lord, grow it, strengthen it, and bring us many families who need a good home church. Our church has been so good to us, we belong to an awesome church. Watch over and lead our pastor, our youth, and all of our members. I wish Jessica and the girls had stayed, it would have been so good for them. Everyone loved them and will miss them. As stressful as it was, for their sake, I wish it would have worked out. I pray that you watch over them and guide them, especially the girls.

I pray that you lead me down the path you want me to take. I pray your hand is in every decision I have to make whether big or small. Use me for you plan so that my life has purpose again. What I mean to say is, I know I have purpose as a mom, now give me purpose as your servant, to do good in your name. Let all that I say, do, or write be for your glory and don't let the devil interfere. Help me Lord a only you can.

In Jesus sweet name
Amen

Journal entry August 14, 2011

Thank you Lord for all that I am blessed with. I started to the market this morning but couldn't bring myself to miss church so please watch over my booth while I am not there and please let me do enough sales after church to pay for my rent. I pray your spirit move through our little church this moning and touch every person there. Lift up our pastor and give him the message you would have us to receive. As the 2012 election nears, please keep it out of our church. I don't think politics should be brought in to church.I believe we should pray about it and ask for your guidance in electing the right person, if there is such a person. Personally I hope the rapture comes, this world is too evil.

In Jesus name
Amen

Journal entry August 16, 2011

I love you Lord so much. I know without a doubt if I didn't have you in my life I would not have made it through this long, dark valley of these past few years, these last fifteen months have been so hard.

I miss him so much Lord, I miss knowing he is lying right beside me and the comfort of that feeling. I miss him snuggled next to me when it was cold or when I was scared or stressed. I miss the calm he brought to me in that beautiful deep voice. I miss the banter and playful times I enjoyed watching between him and our son. I so miss that silly giggle of his, it never failed to make me laugh. I miss him Lord. I grieve not for him but for me without him. I know that we will all be together one day, but it is so lonely without him. Besides you, he was the one I could talk to about anything and everything. You are my foundation, he was the rock on that foundation that kept me calm in the storms. He, as well as me, had regrets about our relationship with you, never our family, even when we waded through the teen years and never for taking that chance on love and marriage a second time around after going through so much the first time. I thank you my precious Lord for every single second of life that you gave me with that man. Next to my salvation he was my greatest blessing followed closely by our children and their children.

I am grateful for the money you gave back to us, to relieve some of the financial stress. I pray you guide me as to how to use it wisely. We bought a truck to work with but I truly don't know if the market is going to work out. Lord please see your way to let us go to Mikes for labor day and watch over Casey and keep him safe while he goes to visit Don and Ruth in Charlotte. Let him enjoy that time. I know he misses Jerry so much and he loves Don and I think he helps him feel close to his dad.

Let me find a job or be successful at the market enough to pay the overhead and earn $3500.00 a month to support my family and to maybe help my mom and sister out a little. God I ask your hand on the kids in school. Keep them focused, give them knowledge and wisdom to do well and to be good witnesses to all those that they meet.

Lord I am going to get back to writing my book, my last chapter, I pray it blesses many and blesses us also.

In Jesus name
Amen

We were ecstatic that we would be getting money back from the trustee. Thank God, because when we finally got it, I was at the end of my rope. But what sounds like a lot of money doesn't last long when you are behind on everything, and when you don't have a job. There were still more taxes to be paid, the marker base and vase for his grave, six house payments which took a big chunk of it, payoff the truck, repairs around the house that couldn't wait, and the first check written was to pay the tithes. I wanted to make sure that we paid God first.

I spent money trying to start a business at the new market, which didn't work out, I am shutting it down. My grandaughter and I opened a girls boutique to see if that would work out, I can't say it didn't because I wouldn't go up there enough to see. For some reason and I don't know why, I just got to where I couldn't stand being there. I think because it is too slow, I need to be busy.

(I have since gotten a job with a big retailer, and its as assistant manager, so that is a blessing.)

I am going to end this book here. If you thought it would have a fairy tale happy ending, your wrong, if I did that it would never get finished. Storm clouds are already building on the horizon. We stand a good chance of losing our home which scares my son, he wants to stay here where he was raised, but unless I can get the modification I need there is no way I can afford it alone. But that's ok, we will get an apartment and do what ever we need to do to get by until Casey gets through college and starts his career. Then he can get his own place and I will get something small for me and Kaylain.

Material things are nice and we had a lot of them, a home that we both loved, five vehicles at one time, a camper and a motor home, timeshares, vacations, and travel. But you know what? we would have been happy living in a tent as long as we were together. I don't care that we have lost so much in the way of material things, its him that I want back. I don't know why Gods plan for us is such. But what I do know is that there are always going to be storms to navigate. The thing to remember is stay on the ship and trust Gods word that he will never leave you or forsake you.

The devil tries every day to rob me of my Joy, but, he can't do it. Oh yeah he grabs my happiness all of the time, but never my joy. That joy will carry me right through to that glorious meeting in the sky, and I will never have to worry again. Until then I believe he has more happiness planned for me, I don't know when, who, or how, but I do believe. I believe he has a plan to use me in some way for his purpose, I just have to listen and learn what that is, then I will be going in the right direction.

So when you see storm clouds building in your life, don't be afraid, just batten down the hatches, put your faith in him and be grateful for the anchore that holds.

About the Author

Jeri M. Hart is a fifty-four year old widow living in the foothills of the Smokey Mountains, just outside of Knoxville, Tennessee. She lives with her youngest son, a nineteen-year-old college student, and her fourteen-year-old granddaughter. They lived through a very trying time that has only served to make them stronger in faith and resolve. She and her family have lost so much and yet she thanks God every day for the blessings that remain.

To God be the glory.